THEOLOGY AND
THE *V*ICTORIAN NOVEL

THEOLOGY AND
THE *V*ICTORIAN NOVEL

———◄○►———

J. RUSSELL PERKIN

McGill-Queen's University Press

MONTREAL & KINGSTON • LONDON • ITHACA

© McGill-Queen's University Press 2009

ISBN 978-0-7735-3606-7

Legal deposit fourth quarter 2009
Bibliothèque national du Québec

Printed in Canada on acid-free paper that is 100% ancient forest free
(100% post-consumer recycled), processed chlorine free

This book has been published with the help of a grant from the Canadian Federation
for the Humanities and Social Sciences, through the Aid to Scholarly Publications
Programme, using funds provided by the Social Sciences and Humanities Research
Council of Canada. Funding was also provided by the Faculty of Graduate Studies
and Research, Saint Mary's University, and the Office of the Vice-President Academic
and Research, Saint Mary's University.

McGill-Queen's University Press acknowledges the support of the Canada Council
for the Arts for our publishing program. We also acknowledge the financial support
of the Government of Canada through the Book Publishing Industry Development
Program (BPIDP) for our publishing activities.

Library and Archives Canada Cataloguing in Publication

Perkin, J. Russell (James Russell)
    Theology and the Victorian novel / J. Russell Perkin.

Includes bibliographical references and index.
ISBN 978-0-7735-3606-7

    1. English fiction – 19th century – History and criticism. 2. Christianity and
literature – England – History – 19th century. 3. Christianity in literature. 4. Theology
in literature. I. Title.

PR878.R5P47 2009   823'.8093823   C2009-903056-X

This book was designed and typeset by Pamela Woodland in Minion 11/13.5

To My Parents
James and Dorothy Perkin

CONTENTS

————◄○►————

PREFACE

⸺◄○►⸺

IN AN UNDERGRADUATE COURSE in the 1970s, I became fascinated by Victorian prose, especially by the religious and cultural thought of John Henry Newman and Matthew Arnold, and I have remained so ever since. This interest no doubt owes something to my liberal Protestant upbringing; having a father who was a biblical scholar gave me privileged access to certain aspects of Victorian controversy, and years later, when I set out to write a book on the rhetoric of Victorian fiction, it gradually turned into the one I have written.

I would like to acknowledge numerous individuals and institutions for their contribution to the making of this book. My gratitude to my parents for their role in my education and spiritual development is expressed in the dedication. The book would never have been completed without the support of my wife Deborah Kennedy, who never doubted that I would finish it, even when I did so myself. Her work as a scholar is a constant inspiration to me.

The Social Sciences and Humanities Research Council of Canada provided funding during the initial stages of research. The bulk of the research, including several trips to Toronto and one to England, was funded by a series of research grants from Saint Mary's University. I would like to thank the excellent staff of the Patrick Power Library at Saint Mary's. I am also grateful to the libraries of the University of Toronto, particularly Robarts Library and the Trinity College Library, Dalhousie University's Killam Library, the University of King's College Library in Halifax, the Pusey House Library and Bodleian Library in Oxford, and Dr Williams's Library in Bloomsbury, London.

Wendy Katz, Deborah Kennedy, David Kent, Fred Krieger, James Perkin, and David Shaw read parts or all of this book as it progressed, and they offered valuable advice and encouragement. The anonymous readers for McGill-Queen's University Press made some thoughtful suggestions that helped me during the revision process. I am especially indebted to the late Barbara Pell, who sadly died early in 2009. For many years Barbara was the energetic coordinator of the Christianity and Literature Study Group (CLSG), which meets annually at the Congress of the Humanities and Social Sciences. The colleagues who attend these meetings have been a knowledgeable audience for this work, at once collegial and intellectually rigorous, and the chapters on Thackeray, Trollope, and Pater have their origins in presentations made to CLSG conferences. I am indebted to the large number of students with whom I have studied many of the texts that are discussed in this book. I am especially grateful to the students in two honours seminars on "Crises of Faith and Knowledge in Victorian Literature."

The Anglican Church of Canada is my spiritual home, and thanks to its scholarly and cultural traditions, it is also a congenial intellectual home. Many Anglican clergy are keenly aware of the interplay of past and present in the Christian tradition, and from among them Glen Burgomaster, Dawn Davis, Paul Friesen, David Harris, Fred Krieger, Robert Ross, and Gary Thorne have in various ways given support to the writing of this book. I am happy to record my gratitude to Fr Ross for his most useful gift of his copy of John Keble's *Lectures on Poetry*.

Material from chapter 1 was first published in the *Thackeray Newsletter* and in *Philological Quarterly*. A version of chapter 2 was published in the journal *Studies in the Novel* 40, no. 4 (Winter 2008) and has been reprinted here with permission.

THEOLOGY AND
THE 𝒱ICTORIAN NOVEL

The novel is of all pictures the most comprehensive and the most elastic. It will stretch anywhere – it will take in absolutely anything.

Henry James, "The Future of the Novel"

Well, was truth safe for ever, then? Not so.
Already had begun the silent work
Whereby truth, deadened of its absolute blaze,
Might need love's eye to pierce the o'erstretched doubt.

Robert Browning, "A Death in the Desert"

Men of Letters are a perpetual Priesthood, from age to age, teaching all men that a God is still present in their life; that all "Appearance," whatsoever we see in the world, is but as a vesture for the "Divine Idea of the World," for "that which lies at the bottom of Appearance."

Thomas Carlyle, *On Heroes, Hero-Worship and the Heroic in History*, Lecture 5

INTRODUCTION

THE *V*ICTORIAN BOOK OF LIFE

> In high literature, I doubt that secularization has ever taken place.
> Calling a work of sufficient literary power either religious or secular
> is a political decision, not an aesthetic one.
>
> Harold Bloom, *The Western Canon*

WHAT DO NOVELS HAVE TO DO WITH THEOLOGY? The obvious answer
to this question is, not very much. Of all the literary genres, the novel is
the most this-worldly. Emerging as a picaresque and satirical critique of
the old order, it became an established form during the Enlightenment,
and it is customary to link the rise of the novel with the demise of a religious world view. It is seen as the genre that accompanies an empirical
approach to existence, a bourgeois social order, and the capitalist economic
system. Walter Allen begins his history of the English novel with a description of the genre from William Hazlitt's *Lectures on the English Comic
Writers* that makes this point well: "We find here a close imitation of man
and manners; we see the very web and texture of society as it really exists,
and as we meet it when we come into the world. If poetry has 'something
more divine' in it, this savours more of humanity" (quoted in Allen, *Novel*,
14). Hazlitt uses terms that resonate through the whole tradition of theoretical reflection on the novel, from Henry Fielding to Milan Kundera,
who begins *The Art of the Novel* (1986) with the image of Don Quixote
riding out into a world marked by the disappearance of God, "the single
divine Truth decomposed into myriad relative truths parceled out by
men" (6). For Mikhail Bakhtin as for D.H. Lawrence, the novel provides
a representation of these relative truths. Lawrence writes: "The novel is
the highest example of subtle inter-relatedness that man has discovered.

Everything is true in its own time, place, circumstance, and untrue outside of its own place, time, circumstance" ("Morality," 110). Lawrence's "interrelatedness" resembles Bakhtin's concept of dialogism: "To a greater or lesser extent, every novel is a dialogized system made up of the images of 'languages,' styles and consciousnesses that are concrete and inseparable from language. Language in the novel not only represents, but itself serves as the object of representation. Novelistic discourse is always criticizing itself" (*Dialogic*, 49). In Bakhtin's poetics, the multiplicity of voices that we experience in the novel are contrasted with the monologic voice of official ideologies and systems of thought.

The contemporary novelist Donna Tartt similarly argues that the "rather godless quality of the novel is not an aesthetic or cultural choice, but a necessity grounded in form" ("Writing," 25). She explains that "because of its length, and bulk, the novel cannot sustain the pure tone of the parable or the tale; because of its restless, many-levelled movement, it is ill-equipped to portray the constancy of faith; because its engines are driven by conflict, and struggle, the novel is confounded above all by notions of peace and eternity" (26). Theology, on the other hand, as defined by John Henry Newman in *The Idea of a University* (1873), concerns the revelation of divine truth, the Logos that brings unity to the diversity of subjects taught in a university. In the concluding paragraph of his Third Discourse, Newman writes, "In a word, Religious Truth is not only a portion, but a condition of general knowledge. To blot it out is nothing short, if I may so speak, of unravelling the web of University Teaching. It is, according to the Greek proverb, to take the Spring from out of the year; it is to imitate the preposterous proceeding of those tragedians who represented a drama with the omission of its principal part" (57). Theology, to go back to my opening quotation from Hazlitt, savours of the divine, whereas literature, for Newman, is the voice of the "natural man" (*Idea*, 158). However, Newman's analogy between the university and tragic drama may suggest that literature has a role to play in bridging the gap between the divine and the human.

In spite of the apparently antithetical tasks of fiction and theology, this book will undertake a theological reading of a series of mainly canonical Victorian novels. It will be noted that I have not spent as much time on those novels – traditionally regarded as minor – that deal directly with religious controversy as I have on some carefully selected texts by major writers: Thackeray, Charlotte Brontë, Trollope, Eliot, and Hardy. There are several reasons for this. For one thing, most Victorian religious novels do not offer a particularly profound view of their subject matter and are often in effect fictional pamphlets that argue in favour of positions discussed with greater insight and subtlety in the theologians who formulated those positions. Secondly, there are a number of valuable studies that survey Victorian religious fiction, or at least aspects of it such as the novel of faith and doubt, the novel and the Oxford Movement, or the historical novel of the early church.[1] My underlying assumption in this book is that if religion was as central to the life of Victorian England as we generally assume that it was, then it should have a significant impact on the Victorian novel in general, and not just on those novels in which religious issues are the primary theme. Another assumption I make is that great works of literature offer profound insight into issues of fundamental human concern; this view of literature is currently unfashionable and is identified by some with neoconservative ideology. An argument against such an identification might begin by considering the cases of Wayne Booth, Harold Bloom, and Martha Nussbaum, each of whom brings something more than suspicion to literary hermeneutics.[2] None of these is a neoconservative, nor do they agree with one another. If literature does give us insight into the human condition, then it should not surprise us if the Victorian novel has something to say about even so unnovelistic a subject as theology. After all, Dostoevsky, Bakhtin's great example of the polyphonic or dialogical novelist, is a writer whose works are often accorded prophetic and spiritual insight.[3] Similarly, James Wood has argued against the tendency to separate Lawrence the writer from Lawrence the preacher, arguing that "Lawrence is one of the century's greatest religious writers" (*Essays*, 116). I am interested in exploring the spiritual significance of Victorian novels, not merely for their historical interest, though that is part of my concern, but also for their relevance to the twenty-first century. Theology and literary criticism have moved closer together in the last few decades, and I hope that my critical account of a selection of nineteenth-century novels will contribute to the dialogue between these two disciplines.

Owen Chadwick begins his history of the Victorian church with the declaration, "Victorian England was religious" (*Victorian* 1:1). Nevertheless, in the early nineteenth century the position of the established Church of England was far less secure than it was at the end of Victoria's reign, by which time a series of adjustments and reforms had eased the political pressure that was brought to bear on the church in the period of constitutional change during and following the years 1829–32. During that period, according to Chadwick, the key question was "whether representative government was compatible with an established church" (1:6). Thus Victorian religion must be studied with reference to its role in the public sphere, as well as its role in shaping family life and individual consciousness. In her classic study *Novels of the Eighteen-Forties* (1954), Kathleen Tillotson credits the religious novels of the period with reinforcing, if not initiating, "the growing tendency to introspection in the novel" (131), but she also notes that "the most 'thorny' of the 'topics of the day' in the eighteen-forties were the controversies in religion" (126).

To take a specific example, John Henry Newman's conversion to Roman Catholicism was not just an individual pilgrimage – the concern, as he put it, of "two and two only absolute and luminously self-evident beings" (*Apologia*, 18) – but a nineteenth-century media event in which the public took a keen interest. At Oxford University, during the course of the Oxford Movement, there were bitter disputes over the *Tracts for the Times* (1833–41), the appointment of the liberal R.D. Hampden as Regius professor of divinity, E.B. Pusey's doctrine of the eucharist, and the granting of an honorary degree to a Unitarian American ambassador.[4] In Lewes there was a riot in opposition to an Anglican sisterhood,[5] and in London and elsewhere there were riots and legal prosecutions over the growth of Anglo-Catholic ritualism. To those who took offence, the pope's restoration of a Roman Catholic diocesan hierarchy in England (1850) was seen as an act of aggression – the "Papal Aggression" – by a foreign power. The publication of *Essays and Reviews* in 1860 eventually led to the prosecution of two of the seven essayists in an ecclesiastical court for heresy.[6]

Religion played a prominent role in the lives of the novelists I consider in this book. William Thackeray struggled all his life with the burden of his mother's strong evangelical convictions; George Eliot's intellectual career was defined by her repudiation of her own early evangelical faith. Charlotte Brontë was an evangelical clergyman's daughter; Trollope's father laboured over an ecclesiastical encyclopedia, to the neglect of his domestic responsibilities. For Charlotte Mary Yonge, the central intellectual and spiritual experience in her life was probably John Keble's confirmation classes. Mary Ward's father converted to Roman Catholicism twice; her famous uncle Matthew Arnold was one of the nineteenth century's most influential popular religious writers. Both Thomas Hardy and Walter Pater considered taking holy orders, were influenced by liberal theology, and ended up in complex but characteristically Victorian positions, Hardy as a sceptic who loved the church in which he could not believe, Pater as a practising Christian who believed that philosophical scepticism applied to arguments against as much to arguments in favour of religious belief.

There has been something of a turn towards religious topics in literary and cultural studies in the new millennium, so that the argument I have just made about Victorian religion is likely to be more readily accepted today than it would have been even a decade ago. Two signs of the times have been Stanley Fish's much-cited and oft-discussed article in the *Chronicle of Higher Education* (7 January 2005), and a special issue of the journal *English Language Notes* devoted to the topic *Literary History and the Religious Turn* (2006). There are a variety of reasons for this development. In many ways trends in literary theory in the 1980s prepared the way, trends that were deplored by such secular-minded critics as Edward Said and Jonathan Culler.[7] The end of the twentieth century naturally led to a higher profile for the apocalyptic strains of Christianity associated with millennial prophecy, and in the United States Christian evangelicals were seen to be increasingly influential on public policy. The confident secularism that prevailed in the humanities was at a loss to explain events such as the siege at Waco, Texas in 1993. (I recall an incident at the Modern Language Association convention in December 1993, when Walter Benn Michaels referred to the fact that "we no longer believe in ghosts." Then he recalled a poll in a recent newsmagazine that revealed that the majority of Americans believe in supernatural beings. He gestured to encompass those present in the room and rephrased his remark, "*We* do not believe in ghosts.") The terrorist attacks of 11 September 2001 on the World Trade Center in New York and on the Pentagon underscored the fact that religion remains a dominant factor in global politics, a factor one ignores at one's own peril. In the first decade of the new millennium, a number of films with religious or at least spiritual content have been very popular: the *Lord of the Rings* trilogy (2001–03), Mel Gibson's *The Passion of the Christ* (2004), and the adaptations of C.S. Lewis's *The Lion, the Witch, and the Wardrobe* (2005) and *Prince*

Caspian (2008). The phenomenal popularity of Dan Brown's novel *The Da Vinci Code* (2003) was at least in part due to its story of the "secret truth" of Christianity. Not surprisingly, this return to prominence of religion has provoked a reaction, with the appearance of books of a militantly secular nature that seek to continue the tradition of the Enlightenment. Some prominent examples are Richard Dawkins's *The God Delusion* (2006), Daniel Dennett's *Breaking the Spell* (2006), and Christopher Hitchens's *God Is Not Great* (2007).

Religion has often been considered in combination with gender and sexuality in recent literary scholarship, much of which breaks new and interesting ground – for example, Hogan and Bradstock's *Women of Faith in Victorian Culture* (1998), Bradstock's *Masculinity and Spirituality in Victorian Culture* (2000), and Hanson's substantial book *Decadence and Catholicism* (1977), which addresses the issue of homosexuality. In 2003 the journal *Victorian Literature and Culture* devoted a special issue to *Victorian Religion*. My only reservation about much recent and excellent commentary on Victorian religion is that it often seems grounded primarily in the concerns of the present, so that it reads the Victorian texts very selectively, looking for those elements that prefigure the concerns of postmodernity. I would not deny that the study of the past inevitably is shaped by the concerns of the present; in fact, I agree that one of the reasons why we study the past is to understand ourselves better. But we also study the past to gain new perspectives, and to escape from the confines of our own ideological paradigms, and I am concerned that literary and cultural studies do not always sufficiently attend to the otherness of Victorian culture. Thus, I seek first of all to engage as far as possible with Victorian religious experience and literature on their own terms.[8] I hope that the contemporary resonances that emerge do so all the more powerfully because I have consciously tried to detach myself from the context in which I am writing.[9]

A knowledge of Victorian theology and theological controversy can illuminate the Victorian novel in a variety of ways. These will be treated fully in the chapters on individual novelists, but I shall touch on them here. As I have just noted, religion in Victorian England was a matter for heated public controversy. If matters of church ritual or of the theology of baptism were the stuff of public debate, then they are part of the cultural framework of Victorian fiction. To read George Eliot or Charlotte Brontë attentively, we need some idea of the differences between Anglicans and

Methodists, as well as an understanding of the affinities between evangelical Anglicans and Methodists. Trollope and Hardy, to name but two novelists out of many, assume considerable knowledge of the differences between Tractarian and evangelical Anglicans. The "Papal Aggression" lies behind the portrayal of Roman Catholics by novelists such as Brontë and Thackeray. The treatment of erotic love is sometimes – most explicitly in the fiction of Charles Kingsley but implicitly in many places – a rejection of the Roman and Anglo-Catholic emphasis on celibacy. This aspect of Victorian fiction is but one strand in the dense network of "small timely particulars" that Richard Altick suggests create "the effect of contemporaneity" in Victorian fiction (*Presence*, 2).[10] But references of this kind can be explicated in footnotes and undergraduate contextual guides such as Altick's own invaluable *Victorian People and Ideas* (1973). I suggest that theology informs Victorian fiction in more profound and complex ways, beyond these topical allusions – although of course the allusions often indicate the presence of a larger theme.

A second way in which theology makes an impact on the Victorian novel is the most obvious: among its many other uses, the Victorians employed the novel as a means of conducting religious controversy. There is a distinct Victorian subgenre of religious fiction that has been well recognized by scholars. It can be further broken down into categories such as the evangelical novel, the novel of the Oxford Movement, the Roman Catholic novel, and the novel of religious crisis or doubt.[11] Another category, employed by writers of all religious persuasions, is the historical novel of the early church, which has been authoritatively studied by Royal W. Rhodes, and which produced a delayed minor masterpiece in the twentieth century, Evelyn Waugh's *Helena* (1950). Many of these novels were written by clergymen; many others were written by devout women. For the most part, they are more interesting as episodes in the careers of their authors, and documents in the religious history of the period, than for any specifically literary merit. Rhodes notes that these novels constitute "an array of highly significant and articulate documents for the study of Church history" (*Lion and Cross*, 2).

In 1977 Garland reprinted 121 Victorian "Novels of Faith and Doubt" in an expensive series, but very few of these works are in print today: for the most part they were bypassed during recent efforts to enlarge the canon of Victorian fiction. As the beginning of the new millennium has distanced us from the latest Victorians by a full century, critics are more concerned with the sensation novel and with issues of gender and sexuality than with religious novels. At the time of writing, John Henry Newman's *Loss and Gain* (1848) is no longer in print, and even Pater's *Marius the Epicurean* (1885), which transcends the genre and is of considerable interest to students of modernism and those interested in gender and sexuality in the late nineteenth century, is not available from a major publisher. Some of the controversial novels, like those of the Reverend William Gresley and the Reverend Francis Paget, are certainly now of purely antiquarian interest; for they are, as Wolff notes, "in effect fictionalized tracts, short campaign documents with one or other Tractarian purpose in view and only the crudest attempts at characterization" (*Gains*, 117). Others cannot be so described. Charles Kingsley's *Hypatia* (1853), for example, is a very readable and interesting if in many ways bizarre novel. Charlotte Mary Yonge cannot simply be pigeonholed as a novelist of the Oxford Movement. George Eliot's *Adam Bede* (1859) can hardly be considered a religious novel, yet it sets out Eliot's conception of a "religion of humanity" in the guise of Christianity so subtly that few of its first readers realized what was happening. I will refer to a number of these religious novels in the course of my argument, but this is not a study of Victorian religious fiction as a distinct subgenre. I will examine Charlotte Brontë's *Shirley* (1849) as a novel of religious controversy to foreground what I consider a neglected aspect of the text. Mary Ward's *Robert Elsmere* (1888) is certainly the most celebrated Victorian novel of doubt, and yet, as Henry James recognized in Charlotte Yonge's work as well, more is going on in it than mere theological polemic.[12]

A third, rather different aspect of the relationship between theology and the Victorian novel is the way that, for some readers, novels took on the role of religious texts. These readers could not believe in the truth of the biblical narratives, which they often regarded as unedifying, and they sought an alternative spiritual standard. For them, novels were not merely entertainment, or even insightful representations of human character and society; instead fiction filled the need for an authoritative text, and novels became secular scriptures. Of course, this exalted view of literary texts did not just apply to the novel. Writers such as Carlyle and Ruskin spoke for many Victorians with the authority of prophets, while Wordsworth provides the clearest example of the way that writers were seen as moral and spiritual teachers. In "The Study of Poetry" (1880), Matthew Arnold famously quoted words that he had first written in the introduction to a popular collection of English poetry: "More and more mankind will discover that we have to turn to poetry to interpret life for us, to console us, to sustain us. Without poetry, our science will appear incomplete; and most of what now passes with us for religion and philosophy will be replaced by poetry" (*Complete Prose* 9:161–2). Distressing as this might have been to some religious teachers and philosophers, Arnold was hardly saying anything new in this work that was aimed, as R.H. Super notes, at "a middle-class public not sophisticated in the reading of poetry" (in Arnold, *Complete Prose* 9:379n).

From the early letters of George Eliot we can see the process by which a representative Victorian intellectual who began by reading evangelical religious works first expressed some suspicion of works of fiction, then lost her faith as a result of an encounter with biblical criticism and found inspiration in secular literature, notably Wordsworth and the works of other Romantic writers. In 1839 Eliot admired Wordsworth greatly but wished that she could find in him "an indication of less satisfaction in terrene objects, a more frequent upturning of the soul's eye" (*Letters*, 1:34). Ten years later she wrote to her friend Sara Hennell a fervent tribute to the influence of Rousseau and George Sand. While she preserved her independence by noting that the writers who have "most profoundly influenced me ... are not in the least oracles to me," she uses religious language to describe this influence: "Rousseau's genius has sent that electric thrill through my intellectual and moral frame which has awakened me to new perceptions, which has made man and nature a fresh world of thought and feeling to me – and this not by teaching me any new belief. It is simply that the rushing mighty wind of his inspiration has so quickened my faculties that I have been able to shape more definitely for myself ideas which had previously dwelt as dim 'ahnungen' in my soul" (1:277). As for George Sand, Eliot claimed that she had reason "for bowing before her in eternal gratitude to that 'great power of God' manifested in her" (1:277–8).

For a testimonial to a writer who is regarded without reservation as an oracle, we can cite F.W.H. Myers's tribute to Wordsworth as a religious teacher in his 1899 study of the poet in the English Men of Letters series. According to Myers, Wordsworth has added "the contemplation of Nature" to the four kinds of mystical enthusiasm identified by Plato (*Wordsworth*, 128). Wordsworth's achievement "was of a kind which most of the moral leaders of the race have in some way or other performed. It was that he turned a theology back again into a religion" (130). Like Christ, Wordsworth gave the unity of "one memorable personality" to ideas that may have been uttered as individual maxims by others before:

> To compare small things with great – or rather, to compare great things with things vastly greater – the essential spirit of the *Lines near Tintern Abbey* was for practical purposes as new to mankind as the essential spirit of the *Sermon on the Mount* … Therefore it is that Wordsworth is venerated; because to so many men – indifferent, it may be, to literary or poetical effects, as such – he has shown by the subtle intensity of his own emotion how the contemplation of Nature can be made a revealing agency, like Love or Prayer, – an opening, if indeed there be any opening, into the transcendent world. (131)

As we shall see, this exalted view of poetry was shared by the conservative Tractarian John Keble, and it is a key element in Victorian poetics. In the aesthetics of the modernists, art itself becomes the transcendent world, rather than the gateway to it, and in that sense James Joyce is the heir to a Victorian religious view of art, which should be no surprise when one considers that he and Gerard Manley Hopkins drew on similar Catholic sources in their theorizing of their literary practices.

The genre of the novel was viewed with deep suspicion at the beginning of the nineteenth century by both utilitarians and evangelicals. As the form regained intellectual seriousness in the 1840s after a decline in the previous decade, it began to be taken more seriously by critics and readers. As Walter Houghton notes, "Every writer had his congregation of devoted or would-be devoted disciples who read his work in much the same spirit they had once read the Bible" (*Victorian*, 101). He adds somewhat condescendingly that "even the novelists, notably George Eliot, had their followers" (102), something John Holloway acknowledges by devoting chapters to both Eliot and Thomas Hardy in *The Victorian Sage* (1953). We will see Thackeray referring to himself ironically as a preacher in *Vanity Fair* (1848); Trollope uses the same analogy in his *Autobiography* (1883).[13] The increasing influence of the novel was the subject of W.R. Greg's article in *The National Review*, "False Morality of Lady Novelists" (1859). He expresses concerns about the genre's impact on impressionable readers similar to those that Samuel Johnson had articulated a century earlier in his *Rambler* No. 4 (1750), with the difference that Greg explicitly uses religious analogies: "We incline to think that a far larger number of persons receive the bias of their course and the complexion of their character from reading novels than from hearing sermons ... Numbers who *might* no doubt have acquired their estimates of the relative gravity or excellence of favourite faults or difficult virtues from authorised Bibles or accredited moralists, have in reality learned them – often, alas, blended with a fearful degree of error – from fictitious histories" (146–7).

In her own life George Eliot enacted the process by which the novel rose to respectability. Initially cut off from society due to her unconventional relationship with George Henry Lewes, she came to be admired by Queen Victoria and received distinguished visitors at her weekly salon.[14] Eliot's novels are humanistic myths that consciously rework biblical narratives, and like other writers who had an Evangelical upbringing her work is full of biblical allusions. For all its apparent realism, *Adam Bede*, as I show in chapter 5, is an extensive example of the novel as midrash.[15] Stephen Prickett has argued that the rise of the novel in the eighteenth century changed the way that the Bible was read: "the Bible – and in particular the Old Testament – ceased to be read as though it spoke with a single omniscient dogmatic voice, and began instead to be read as dialogue, with a plurality of competing voices. At the same time, what had been universally accepted as an essentially polysemous narrative, with many threads of meaning, was narrowed into a single thread of story, which was almost invariably interpreted as being 'historical'" (*Origins*, 108). In Eliot's fiction the process is reversed; works of secular fiction signal, by their reworking of scriptural material and their theological significance, that they can and should be read with the same attention as Scripture itself. Some readers accepted the invitation, which may well have been a significant impetus for the discipline of literary criticism as it evolved in the early twentieth century. By 1874 the novel had become serious enough for Edward King, professor of Moral and Pastoral Theology at Oxford University, to advise students preparing for the priesthood to read "good novels," since by so doing they would "travel into the circumstances, and conditions, and situations of life" (in Chadwick, *Spirit*, 303). In the twentieth century, for D.H. Lawrence at least, "the Bible is a great confused novel," while "the novel is the one bright book of life" ("Why the Novel Matters," 105).

For some Christian thinkers, poetry was important even if it did not replace religion. In a well-known passage in the *Apologia* (1864), Newman links the Oxford Movement to Romanticism (93–4). In his lectures as the Oxford Professor of Poetry (1832–41), Keble explains at length how poetry can serve as the "handmaid" (*Lectures* 2:484) of theology. For Keble, God is revealed in the Book of Nature as well as in the Bible, and poetry serves to explicate the connections between the visible world and the invisible. This understanding of nature is set out in Keble's poem for "Septuagesima Sunday" in *The Christian Year* (1827), with its epigraph from Romans 1:20: "The invisible things of Him from the creation of the world are clearly seen, being understood by the things that are made." The poem concludes:

> Two worlds are ours: 'tis only Sin
> Forbids us to descry
> The mystic heaven and earth within,
> Plain as the sea and sky.
>
> Thou who has given me eyes to see
> And love this sight so fair,
> Give me a heart to find out Thee,
> And read Thee every where. (43, lines 41–8)

Keble's thought, as Stephen Prickett has demonstrated, fundamentally depends on Wordsworthian romanticism (*Romanticism*, 91–119). Other Victorian poets, such as Tennyson, lacked Keble's firm belief – grounded in his reading of the Church Fathers and explained in his Tract 89, *On the Mysticism Attributed to the Early Fathers of the Church* – in an elaborate system of correspondences between the divine order and the realm of nature. Nevertheless, they followed Wordsworth in gesturing towards some sort of spiritual order or presence underlying or beyond the material world. This is found in the symbolism of Tennyson's *Idylls of the King* (1859–85), but there it is located in a remote and mythological past; it is less confidently expressed but still present in the image of the veil in his *In Memoriam* (1850), "which filters both God and nature through a screen of analogy" (Shaw, *Veil*, 3). Generally speaking, the Victorian novel remained close to its secular origins. However, Charlotte Yonge, as a disciple of John Keble, incorporates Romantic sacramentalism into her fiction, as I will discuss in chapter 3. And a number of novelists are interested in the way that theological concepts are linked to human psychology, to the operations of desire and repression for example. We can see this in George Eliot and in Thomas Hardy. W. David Shaw includes works of fiction along with poetry in his study *Victorians and Mystery* (1990), where he explores the way that Victorian literature manifests the crises of representation created by the impact of developmental thought on modes of faith and knowing. Shaw demonstrates how Victorian novelists struggle with the unsayable, and I will consider some of the theological implications of this struggle in the chapters that follow. I will pay particular attention to the way sexual and romantic love are connected to divine love and to ideas of cosmic order.

Even novelists who were not particularly interested in theology or spirituality often reward attention to these matters, because of the pressure placed on their language by the religious culture they inhabited and the texts that influenced them. By taking Vanity Fair as his central image, derived as it is from Bunyan and ultimately from the Bible, Thackeray draws intertextually on the entire Christian tradition to give resonance to his satire. Similarly, his use of biblical allusions and references to authors such as Milton and his foregrounding of theologically charged words such as "world" bring the latent theological significance of the book to the surface. Thus, the novel, however secular, can be read within a frame of reference that transcends secularity. If literature is to serve as a Jacob's ladder, however, I recognize that the novel is probably the bottom rung. Accordingly, I will conclude this introductory survey of the ways that novels have theological significance by returning to the realm of the social.

Theology and the novel can be related in a manner that emphasizes the mimetic aspect of the literary text rather than the sacramental. The novel is able to represent what it feels like to believe or to doubt, and to identify some of the social and psychological factors involved in faith and loss of faith. To take a twentieth-century example, David Lodge's 1980 novel *How Far Can You Go?* is an extremely convincing account of the lives of a group of middle-class English Roman Catholics from the 1950s to the 1980s. Lodge shows how a variety of social developments and personal events affect the way that his characters understand their faith, and how the changes brought about by the Second Vatican Council are produced by social pressure and at the same time lead to new ways of understanding the faith. In the nineteenth century, poets such as Matthew Arnold and Arthur Hugh Clough anatomized religious doubt, but so did novelists from J.A. Froude to Samuel Butler. In Geraldine Jews-bury's *Zoe* (1845) and Froude's *Nemesis of Faith* (1849), doubt is rendered through melodramatic romance, which serves to establish a link between erotic love and religious doubt, a topic explored again late in the century in Thomas Hardy's *Jude the Obscure* (1895). In a more realistic register, Elizabeth Gaskell in *North and South* (1855) shows the impact of a cler-gyman's change of belief on his family, while in *Middlemarch* (1871–72) George Eliot's portrayal of Dorothea's loss of faith in Christianity is the more effective for the way she does not draw attention to it. Like numerous other heroines in Eliot's fiction, and like many Victorian intellectuals, Dorothea tries to reconstruct a religious outlook apart from the doctrine and institution of the Church, to find a way of living "an epic life" amidst "the conditions of an imperfect social state" in which she found herself ("Prelude," 3; "Finale," 821). Trollope's *The Bertrams* (1859) is an insightful account of the process by which personal circumstances and psychological factors shape matters of faith and doubt, showing that changes in "religious opinions" do not always take place because of rational argument and intellectual dispute, let alone spiritual illumination or abandonment. Mary Ward's psychological insight in *Robert Elsmere* has not received sufficient recognition, since it coexists with her extended authorial com-mentary about the hero's loss of faith. Robert's marriage to Catherine is among other things a means of bolstering his own rather fragile faith, and Ward acutely analyzes the strain put on the marriage by Robert's crisis of faith.

Thomas Hardy is especially insightful in his analysis of the interaction of social ambition, sexual desire, and religious feeling, most notably in *Jude the Obscure*; in the minor work *Two on a Tower* (1882) he gives a memorable picture of the mixture of erotic desire and religious fervour in the character Viviette Constantine. Finally, in a very different register and setting, Walter Pater dramatizes in *Marius the Epicurean* the dynamics of assent that Newman analyzed in his *Grammar of Assent* (1870). While works such as Newman's *Grammar* and his *Apologia* are concerned with the epistemological and theological questions raised by conversion and loss of faith, it is the novel that shows us the way that these changes work themselves out in the texture of everyday living, in domestic relationships and the business of "living in the world." For this reason alone, Professor Edward King gave his theology students good advice when he told them to read novels.

◄O►

The Victorians were obsessed with the idea that they lived in an "age of transition,"[16] a feeling best captured in Matthew Arnold's memorable formulation in his 1855 poem "Stanzas from the Grand Chartreuse":

> Wandering between two worlds, one dead,
> The other powerless to be born,
> With nowhere yet to rest my head,
> Like these, on earth I wait forlorn.
>   (*Poems*, 288–9, lines 85–8)

The Victorian period can be seen as both an age of doubt and an age of faith, depending where one places the emphasis. Two of the most influential studies of nineteenth-century poetry have traced the story of secularization, as even their titles reveal: M.H. Abrams's *Natural Supernaturalism* (1971) and J. Hillis Miller's *The Disappearance of God* (1963). The former concentrates on the way that religious concepts and concerns are displaced into poetry and aesthetic theory, while the latter tells the story of how Victorian literature records the process of God's gradual disappearance from the human world to a realm in which He is so inaccessible that He might as well not exist. Responding specifically to Abrams, Stephen Prickett argues, in the context of an analysis of Wordsworth's *Prelude*, "It needs to be said (*pace* Abrams) that this is, given its historical context, not so much the language of secularization, but of religious revival" (Prickett, *Words*, 104).[17]

One can equally respond to Miller by saying that God was understood *differently* by the end of the nineteenth century, rather than being experienced simply as an absence. My concluding chapter indicates how, in *Marius the Epicurean*, the "sceptic" Walter Pater wrote a book that can be considered a religious classic for a postmodern age. In the preface to *The Disappearance of God*, Miller links the desacralization of the world with the processes of industrialization and urbanization: "The city is the literal representation of the progressive humanization of the world. And where is there room for God in the city? Though it is impossible to tell whether man has excluded God by building the great cities, or whether the cities have been built because God has disappeared, in any case the two go together. Life in the city is the way in which many men have experienced most directly what it means to live without God in the world" (5). Miller ignores the etymologies of the words "pagan" and "heathen," and the fact that Christianity is "a big-city religion with a strongly urban basis in its organization and symbolism" (Frye, *Myth*, 299). After all, St Paul wrote epistles to the Ephesians, Corinthians, and Romans. Christian images of evil cities (Babel, Sodom, Nineveh, Babylon, and Rome) are opposed by the image of the heavenly city or city of God. A radically incarnational theology, which broke free of Romantic pastoralism, could find God in human relationships in a big city as much as in the solitude of the Lake District. Just as many Victorian religious reformers sought to adapt the Church of England to an increasingly urbanized world, so Victorian literature took as one of its tasks the exploration of the consequences of urbanization and the redefinition of religious experience. In her last novel, *Daniel Deronda* (1874–76), George Eliot left behind her beloved Midlands countryside for the cosmopolitan world of major European cities, while turning to Judaism as her image of spiritual vitality. Pater's Marius comes to his new religious view of the world as the eventual result of moving to the capital of the empire.

In this book I concentrate on the relationship between the novels I have selected and two significant Victorian religious movements, the Anglo-Catholic revival stemming from the Oxford Movement and the liberal theology that received its impetus from biblical criticism, and that is often associated with that somewhat loosely defined group known as the Broad Church.[18] I will not discuss evangelicalism in as much detail, for several reasons. Elisabeth Jay has already written an impressive study of evangelicalism and the nineteenth-century novel, *The Religion of the Heart* (1979). Furthermore, although evangelicalism was one of the main components of the Victorian ethos, its historical moment occurred before the period began. Many Victorian novelists are reacting against elements of evangelicalism; Thackeray, Charlotte Brontë, and George Eliot all had evangelical upbringings. In the life and work of each of them, we can see, in varying degrees, the impact of liberalism as they modify their views. Given the revival of evangelical Christianity in the late twentieth century, its history in the Victorian period is of considerably more than antiquarian interest.

The connection between the Oxford Movement and literature was close from the beginning.[19] We have seen how Newman linked the Tractarian revival to Romanticism when he looked back on its origins in the *Apologia*. Of the Tractarian leaders, John Keble, John Henry Newman, and Isaac Williams were poets.[20] Newman also wrote novels (after his conversion to Roman Catholicism), as did numerous other supporters of the Oxford Movement, including Elizabeth Missing Sewell, Felicia Skene, and Charlotte Mary Yonge.[21] This literary affinity arises from the Tractarians' theology of the Church. Whereas it had been understood by many Anglicans as a branch of the state that interpreted the Bible in a Protestant manner, the Tractarians taught that the Church of England was the same mystical body that had existed since the days of the apostles, and that by apostolic succession the true teaching of Christ had been passed on through the centuries. This Catholic and mystical notion of the Church had a romantic appeal, implied by Newman's comment on Keble: "He did that for the Church of England which none but a poet could do: he made it poetical" (Newman, "John Keble," 442).[22] Speaking after his conversion, Newman suggests that the whole idea of the Catholic nature of the Church of England was a product of Keble's personality: "His happy magic made the Anglican Church seem what Catholicism was and is. The established system found to its surprise that it had been all its life talking not prose, but poetry" (444). Keble's *Lectures on Poetry* imply that there is a continuity between poetry and the Church, because poetry is itself sacramental in nature. He defines the poetic as that which gives "an indirect expression to the feelings of an eager and overflowing heart" (*Lectures* 2:465). Discussing Virgil, he writes, "what more conceivable than that all poetry may have been providentially bestowed on man as the first elements, the prelude, so to speak, of genuine piety? since, for one thing, ancient records as a rule bear out the conclusion that there has seldom been a revival of religion unless a high and noble order of poets has first led the way" (2:473). It is interesting to note that in the peroration of the whole series of forty lectures, Keble himself uses the image of magic:

For, once let that magic wand, as the phrase goes, touch any region of Nature, forthwith all that before seemed secular and profane is illumined with a new and celestial light: men come to realize that the various images and similes of things, and all other poetic charms, are not merely the play of a keen and clever mind, nor to be put down as empty fancies: but rather they guide us by gentle hints and no uncertain signs, to the very utterances of Nature, or we may more truly say, of the Author of Nature. And thus it has come to pass, that great and pre-eminent poets have almost been ranked as the representatives of religion, and their sphere has been treated with religious reverence.

In short, Poetry lends Religion her wealth of symbols and similes: Religion restores these again to Poetry, clothed with so splendid a radiance that they appear to be no longer merely symbols, but to partake (I might almost say) of the nature of sacraments. (2:481)

Although it is stated in a very different way, we can find the same conception of the poetic nature of the Church and the same close connection between literature and religion in some of the writings of the liberal school of theology. Indeed, they had much in common, as both were the products of an academic culture, deeply learned in the classics, and there were many personal ties, which led to some bitter fallings-out, as between Thomas Arnold and the Tractarians. It is easy to forget that Matthew Arnold was John Keble's godson; both J.A. Froude and F.D. Maurice had initially been attracted to Tractarianism, while Charles Kingsley was sympathetic to some of the beliefs and practices of the Oxford Movement (Chapman, *Faith*, 96–7). Froude was also, of course, the younger brother of Hurrell Froude (1803–36), the flamboyant figure who had a significant influence on John Henry Newman.[23] Looking back on the early days of the movement in chapter 2 of the *Apologia*, Newman sees the issue very clearly in his own mind: "My battle was with liberalism; by liberalism I mean the anti-dogmatic principle and its developments" (54). The opposition between liberalism and Tractarianism structures his narrative. To many observers at the beginning of the twenty-first century, the issue does not look so clear-cut; it is ironic that the introduction to a recent anthology of Anglican spiritual writing, edited by three scholarly bishops, suggests that by claiming the right "to redefine Anglican identity from within … the Tractarians had been 'liberals' without realizing it" (Rowell et al., eds., *Redeeming*, xxx).[24]

The liberal, or "Broad Church," party was less-clearly defined in the mid-Victorian period than either the High or Low Church party. Its existence was proclaimed in an influential article in the *Edinburgh Review* entitled "Church Parties," by W.J. Conybeare (himself the author of a Broad Church novel entitled *Perversion; or, The Causes and Consequences of Infidelity*, 1856). For Conybeare, the party had always existed in the Church of England: "It is called by different names; Moderate, Catholic, or Broad Church, by its friends; Latitudinarian or Indifferent by its enemies. Its distinctive character is the desire of comprehension. Its watchwords are Charity and Toleration" (330). Lying behind the Broad Church was the influence of Samuel Taylor Coleridge, who mediated German critical thought and biblical criticism to a group of liberal Anglican clergy.[25] Coleridge's approach to the Bible anticipated the approach taken by the contributors to *Essays and Reviews* in 1860. When Newman outlined the Romantic antecedents of the Oxford Movement in the *Apologia*, he praised Coleridge for having prepared the ground for the cause of "Catholic truth" by instilling "a higher philosophy into inquiring minds, than they had hitherto been accustomed to accept." Of course, this praise came with a stern proviso: Coleridge "indulged a liberty of speculation, which no Christian can tolerate, and advocated conclusions which were often heathen rather than Christian" (94). In *Confessions of an Inquiring Spirit* (1840), Coleridge distilled the effect of his reading in German criticism in the following statement about the interpretation of the Bible: "I take up this work with the purpose to read it for the first time as I should read any other work, – as far at least as I can or dare. For I neither can, nor dare, throw off a strong and awful prepossession in its favour – certain as I am that a large part of the light and life, in and by which I see, love, and embrace the truths and the strengths co-organised into a living body of faith and knowledge ... has been directly, or indirectly derived to me from this sacred volume, – and unable to determine what I do not owe to its influence" (25).[26]

The effect of biblical criticism and scientific discovery (Lyell in geology, Darwin in biology) was to create a conflict between the Bible and human reason. The Broad Church theologians were the first to realize that the only intellectually credible resolution to this impasse was that the Bible must yield to the fields of history and science when there was a conflict over questions of knowledge. They recognized that this was the only way to save the authority of the Bible in matters of faith. The effect was – and this is what caused Protestants who claimed the infallibility of the scripture so much grief – that the authority of the Bible was dethroned, in that it was subject to the judgments of human reason to a far greater extent than had previously been the case.

An important precursor of the Broad Church proper was Thomas Arnold, who drew on Coleridge and German biblical criticism to produce his own account of biblical hermeneutics in his 1844 "Essay on the Right Interpretation and Understanding of the Scriptures." Arnold in turn influenced such notable Broad Church figures as A.P. Stanley, Benjamin Jowett, and Frederick Temple, along with his son Matthew, who stands on the boundary between the Broad Church and Victorian agnosticism.[27] (Matthew Arnold's religious thought will be discussed in more detail in chapter 4.) Thomas Arnold's theory of interpretation made much of the doctrine of accommodation, by which he meant that God's revelation is accommodated to the social and cultural conditions of its receivers. In the "Essay," he assumes that revelation is progressive, as the human race proceeds from its infancy towards perfection (387). We can distinguish between the truth of revelation and the historical record of that revelation, which may be imperfect and marked by error (415). There must be a balance between reason and faith in order "that intellectual wisdom, which exercises over this world more than imperial dominion, may not be denied her lawful tribute. It is within her province to judge of all questions of science, of history, and of criticism, according to her own general laws, nor may her decisions on these matters be disputed by an appeal to the higher power of spiritual wisdom, who leaves such points wholly to her lower jurisdiction" (423–4).

The impact of biblical criticism on English literature was considerable, as it stimulated the Romantic rethinking of religion that is the subject of Prickett's *Romanticism and Religion* (1976). By taking away the security of the absolute authority of an infallible scripture, biblical criticism paved the way for the novel of doubt, and for the disappearance of God experienced by some Victorian poets and intellectuals. In the fiction of George Eliot we can see the influence of biblical criticism more overtly, as she explores the sources of religious feeling in human situations and comments in her authorial voice from the perspective of someone thoroughly versed in all the most advanced religious thought of her time. In a poem like Robert Browning's "A Death in the Desert" (1864) we see a writer grappling with the hermeneutic questions that biblical criticism has raised. Elinor Shaffer's book *"Kubla Khan" and "The Fall of Jerusalem"* (1975) explores these questions in detail, with extended discussions of Coleridge, George Eliot, and Robert Browning. In chapters 1 and 4 I will show how Thackeray and Trollope too are aware of hermeneutic issues, and how that awareness affects their treatment of religion.

Matthew Arnold is a key figure in mediating between the liberal theological school and the sphere of literary criticism. He was not only a critic but the author of several theological works that popularized liberal thought and developed it in a literary direction, anticipating developments in the twentieth century. As A.O.J. Cockshut has suggested, Arnold is quite close to the ideas of Catholic Modernism (*Unbelievers*, 72). For

Arnold as for Keble, though in a different way, the Church is a poetic entity. Similarly the Bible for Arnold is a literary text, albeit one with special authority in ethical matters; in addition, the liturgy of the Church has a poetic appeal. Arnold had a Modernist vision of the future of the Church, which diverges from the Tractarian position in its rejection of dogma but is close in other ways to the tradition of Catholic spirituality. In the preface to *Last Essays on Church and Religion* (1877), Arnold wrote that the forms of Christian worship "will survive as poetry," and that Christianity will remain as "the indispensable background" to human culture and knowledge (*Complete Prose* 8:162). I will consider liberalism and Modernism in more detail in my final chapter, while looking at the relationship between Arnold's theology and the fiction of his niece Mary Augusta Ward and that of her friend Walter Pater.

Victorian novelists were preoccupied above all other subjects with romantic love. Trollope writes in his *Autobiography*: "It is admitted that a novel can hardly be made interesting or successful without love. Some few might be named, but even in those the attempt breaks down, and the softness of love is found to be necessary to complete the story" (224). In looking at Victorian novels from a theological point of view, one becomes aware of the recurrent connection between human and divine love. This is sometimes presented in negative terms, as with the novel of doubt, in which religious questioning and sexual temptation are intimately linked. In works where the connection is positively presented, an incarnational theology allows human love to be seen as a form of divine love. In Carlyle's *Sartor Resartus* (1833–34), written at the beginning of the Victorian period, Professor Teufelsdröckh sets out on his spiritual pilgrimage after the failure of his youthful love affair. Shortly after the Victorian period ended, D.H. Lawrence wrote novels in which erotic love and marriage become spiritual quests in themselves. In between these positions, novelists such as Trollope, Hardy, and George Eliot explore the spiritual dimensions of human love and the erotic sources of religious faith and doubt. Among clerical novelists, one finds writers as diverse in their theological views as Kingsley and Newman both presenting erotic love as the prelude to spiritual love and by extension suggesting that religious feelings are sexual in origin.[28] The treatment of the spiritual implications of erotic love will be a recurring theme in the analyses of Victorian novels that follow.

◄○►

To conclude the introduction, I will give a brief account of the critical and theological work to which this study is indebted and then comment on my choice of novels for detailed analysis. I have found inspiration in the recent flourishing of literary approaches in biblical and religious studies and in the development of the interdisciplinary study of literature and theology. Some of this crossing of disciplinary boundaries resembles the fusion (and perhaps occasionally confusion) of religion and literature that we find throughout the nineteenth century, examples of which I have discussed in the previous section of this introduction. Coleridge shocked Newman and others by suggesting that the Bible should be studied as far as possible like any other work. A generation later, Baden Powell, Savilian Professor of Geometry at Oxford, wrote in his contribution to *Essays and Reviews* that "it is generally admitted that many points of important religious instruction, even conveyed under the form of fictions (as in the instances of doctrines inculcated through parables) are more congenial to the spirit of faith than any relations of historical events could be" (*Essays*, 252). *Essays and Reviews* thus severed the connection between "the truth of Christianity" and "the exact truth of a detailed record of events" (Chadwick, *Victorian Church* 2:77).

In the twentieth century there were two closely connected developments in the relationship between the study of literature and the study of religion (using that broad term to incorporate, among other things, biblical studies and theology). The first of these is that the Bible became the object of literary study, as critics such as Northrop Frye, Robert Alter, Frank Kermode, Mieke Bal, and Harold Bloom applied the techniques of secular literary criticism to the Jewish and Christian scriptures.[29] Partly under the influence of these critics, and partly under the influence of developments in literary and cultural theory from feminism to postmodernism, biblical studies has started to incorporate a literary approach. Hans Frei's book *The Eclipse of Biblical Narrative* (1974) gave impetus to this trend towards studying the Bible as narrative literature, rather than attempting through more and more complex methodologies to determine the core of fact that lies beneath the layers of multiple sources and redactions.

Secondly, theologians began to draw on the insights of literature and literary criticism to a far greater extent than before. Again this convergence has a prehistory. I have already discussed the way that John Keble allowed a sacramental dimension to poetry. Since the Reformation, in the Anglican tradition in particular, there has been a pronounced overlap between literature and spirituality that is especially prominent in writers such as George Herbert, Samuel Johnson, Samuel Taylor Coleridge, Christina Rossetti, and T.S. Eliot.[30] While the connection is less apparent in the novel than in poetry, the importance of narrative in contemporary theology, and the literary approaches to the Bible I have just mentioned, have created considerable theological interest in literature and in film. The theological uses of literature might also be the result of the kind of attention that has been paid to literary texts since Arnold's declaration in "The Study of Poetry" that poetry will replace religion. Valentine Cunningham quotes Freud's observation that the dream text should be treated "wie einen heiligen Text" (like a sacred text) and comments: "Anyone reading *Don Quixote* or *Macbeth* or the *Chanson de Roland* as the Bible has been read would be reckoned, Borges properly believes, quite mad. But this is precisely what has happened and is happening" (*Reading Gaol*, 388, 389). Secular literature is now scrutinized with the kind of hermeneutical rigour and attention that was once reserved for the Bible alone.

In his book *Freedom and Limit: A Dialogue between Literature and Christian Doctrine* (1991), the theologian Paul S. Fiddes considers writers from William Blake to Iris Murdoch and William Golding. He writes that

> Holy scripture ... is itself a piece of literature containing narrative, poetry and drama with all the openness to multiple meaning that these have. The character of scripture should, indeed, lead us to realise that the primary forms of talk about God are metaphor and story, and that they invite an assent of faith which is like the imaginative assent we give to these forms in literature. After all, only a kind of speech which resists being trapped in a single, fixed meaning can begin to express the mystery of the Kingdom of God which we are invited to enter rather than analyse. (12)[31]

Fiddes thus emphasizes the literariness and the dialogical quality of the Bible and finds a value for the theologian in reading fiction that goes far beyond that perceived by Edward King in the nineteenth century. From a literary perspective, Stephen Prickett has suggested that the separation of biblical and literary studies has impoverished both theology and secular criticism (*Origins*, xii–xiii). In his own work he has done a great deal to overcome this separation, as have David Jasper, T.R. Wright, and others exploring the topic of literature and theology.[32] In recent years the convergence of literature and theology has had an eminent practitioner in Rowan Williams, archbishop of Canterbury since 2003, a poet as well as a scholar, and the author of books on literature and culture.[33]

It could be that one of the conditions encouraging the convergence of literature and theology has been the development of postmodern theology. My own approach has been influenced by the radical orthodoxy movement, which seeks "in the face of the secular demise of truth ... to reconfigure theological truth." Radical orthodoxy "visits sites in which secularism has invested heavily – aesthetics, politics, sex, the body, personhood, visibility, space – and resituates them from a Christian standpoint; that is, in terms of the Trinity, Christology, the Church, and the Eucharist" (Milbank et al., eds., "Introduction," 1).[34] Unlike the liberal theology of modernity, which sought to reconcile Christianity with a scientific positivist world view by demythologizing the Scriptures and seeking the core of historical truth, radical orthodoxy upholds the traditional creedal affirmations and focuses on the narrative element of Scripture, linking it to other, secular, forms of narrative. The assumption is that if divine revelation was made in the human world, then it must be explored in terms of the categories of that world. In my concluding chapter, I will indicate some of the affinities between Walter Pater's *Marius the Epicurean* and postmodern theology.

T.S. Eliot was prominent among those who censured Matthew Arnold, I.A. Richards, and others for thinking that poetry could do the work of religion. Eliot's response was that "nothing in this world or the next is a substitute for anything else; and if you find that you must do without something, such as religious faith or philosophic belief, then you must just do without it" (*Use of Poetry*, 113). Recently James Wood has applied a similar logic in objecting to some of the critical and theological developments I have been outlining above. Wood argues that

> it was not just science but perhaps the novel itself which helped to kill Jesus's divinity, when it gave us a new sense of the real, a new sense of how the real disposes itself in a narrative – and then in turn a new scepticism toward the real as we encounter it in narrative. Ultimately, this "break" was good neither for religion nor perhaps for the novel, although it was perhaps a beneficial moment in our progress away

from superstition. For Christianity, instead of disappearing, merely surrendered its truth-claims and turned itself into a comforting poetry on the one hand or an empty moralism on the other. Truth slipped away. (*Broken Estate*, xvi)

Wood's analysis depends upon a simplistic notion of religious truth, in which Christianity can only be true if it can be validated by scientific rationalism; since in his judgment it cannot, it ought to acknowledge reality and disappear. My theological readings of a series of Victorian novels will show that the question should not be posed as such a clear pair of alternatives.

In defining the scope of this book, I chose to focus, for reasons already mentioned, on the impact of Tractarianism and liberal theology on the Victorian novel. I then realized that the novelists I selected all had a Church of England upbringing, and that I was therefore writing about *Anglican* theology and the Victorian novel. The writers I found most rewarding were for the most part the major canonical figures, although Charlotte Yonge and Mary Ward are exceptions to that rule. My omission of Charles Dickens may trouble some readers and should be briefly explained. Dickens was not as interested in theological issues as the writers I discuss in detail. Although it would be productive to analyze the religious dimension of his fiction, it would require a very different approach from the one I have taken to my chosen authors.[35] I therefore decided to leave Dickens out in order to retain a consistency of focus. My selection of novelists and my approach is certainly shaped by my own presuppositions and sympathies. I hope that the narrative that emerges has an interest and an explanatory power that make up for any lack of comprehensiveness.

Charlotte Yonge exemplifies a religious orthodoxy that all of the other novelists question in some way or other, and I considered placing my chapter on her fiction first. However, a chronological order proved to be more workable. Victorian religious history did not unfold in a consistent narrative towards the goal of a Christianity finally purged of illusion. Religious history in general does not follow such neat patterns, or the radical theology of the likes of the Cambridge theologian Don Cupitt and the American bishop John Spong in the latter part of the twentieth century would not have been accompanied by the revival in other quarters of a conservative charismatic form of evangelicalism, instanced by the remarkable spread of the Alpha course, and by the proliferation of such movements as the Promise Keepers and Focus on the Family. Proceeding chronologically, I begin with *Vanity Fair*, a sceptical and ironic text, and one that is often seen as postmodern in its subversion of attempts to interpret it. But *Vanity Fair* is a satire whose moral norms draw on the Bible and Christian tradition, and by examining its intertextual aspects in the context of a biographical investigation of Thackeray's religious views, a theological reading of the novel becomes a possibility.

Thackeray was hailed as a moral regenerator by Charlotte Brontë and deeply admired by George Eliot. Brontë was a loyal churchwoman, yet she believed that the Church of England needed drastic reform. Her opposition to the theological and ecclesiastical aims of the Oxford Movement is expressed in her novel *Shirley*, which hints at the outline of a feminist theology; for it conducts its religious speculation in the context of a narrative about gender politics and industrial relations. By looking at *Shirley* within the horizon of literature contemporary with it, including the various novels of religious controversy, we can recover a dimension of meaning that would have been part of the cultural frame of reference of any educated Victorian reader.

Following my discussion of Brontë, I turn to the most accomplished novelist of the Oxford Movement, Charlotte Mary Yonge, to examine the way that she incorporates a Romantic view of nature into her Tractarian fiction. *The Heir of Redclyffe* (1853) was her most popular work with the Victorian reading public, and I argue that if read as a "theological romance" – a term that I have adapted from the Enlightenment genre of the philosophical romance – it becomes a more substantial work than it is generally held to be. Too often Yonge's conservative political views and particularly her understanding of the proper role for women have obscured the mythic force of her major work.

Anthony Trollope is best known for his Barchester chronicles, which deal exhaustively with the Church, but largely with its institutional politics and with the clergy in their social role. Trollope was well aware of the liberal trends at work in the church that culminated in *Essays and Reviews* in 1860, and in *The Bertrams*, a novel that is not very well known and that Trollope himself denigrated, he examines some of the personal, psychological factors that shape the religious opinions of an individual. George Eliot does this as well but much more besides; in her early works she reworks biblical narratives to show the human truths that, following

Feuerbach, she sees as their essence. In her great novels *Middlemarch* and *Daniel Deronda*, she tries to create alternative mythic visions out of the lives of ordinary people of her own century, though in the latter work she complicates this by implying a kind of truth in Judaism that she could no longer find in Christianity. I will concentrate on her first full-length novel, *Adam Bede*, and conclude the chapter with a brief discussion of *Daniel Deronda*.

A theological reading of Thomas Hardy may seem perverse, as *Jude the Obscure* is a memorably bleak attack on the inadequacies of Christianity as a way to live one's life in the late nineteenth century. The novel is dominated by a conflict between the flesh and the spirit, the flesh winning out in every case. Yet Hardy's knowledge of the church and of theology means that his critique is made as it were from the inside; his satire shows the way that Christianity is tainted by hypocrisy, and so in some cases it affirms a kind of residual essence of Christianity. The intensity of Hardy's vision ensures that his work is of theological interest.

In my last chapter I violate chronology slightly in the interests of narrative coherence. I reverse the order of Mary Ward's *Robert Elsmere* and Walter Pater's *Marius the Epicurean* in order to highlight the contrast between Ward's liberalism and what I see as Pater's postmodernism. Ward's story of a demythologized alternative to Christianity (which sounds like Unitarianism even though she repeatedly tells us it is not) dramatizes the liberal position. Christianity must be adapted to the *Zeitgeist* and its creeds purged of outmoded mythological thinking. In Pater, however, my study finds its appropriate terminus, in that he anticipates the position of radical orthodoxy a hundred years later. A philosophical sceptic, he nevertheless holds that the kind of faith that creates a church is the acknowledgment of the possibility of something beyond the material. He expresses this in a narrative work that blends literary genres and exists on the borderline of the *Bildungsroman* and the fictionalized spiritual autobiography. The theologians who wrote *Lux Mundi* (1889) had begun to express Anglo-Catholic beliefs in the idiom of a changed time; Pater, as a prescient literary artist, anticipated many of the themes of postmodern theology, writing what Nathan Scott called one of "the few great religious classics of the modern period" ("Imperative," 115). For Pater, literature does not so much take the place of religion as provide a point of entry for the spiritual; the aesthetic and the religious are distinct, but they overlap.

In reading each of these novels, I will consider how the novelists represent the sources of religious feeling, especially in connection with human love, how they use the Bible, what their attitude to sacramental theology is, and how they deal with religious doubt. I hope to highlight aspects of the novels that are not generally well recognized and to suggest how sophisticated was the Victorian novel's engagement with the theological issues of the day. Additionally, I hope that my commentary will obliquely contribute something to the understanding of the relationship between literature and spirituality in our own time.

ONE

THE IMPLIED THEOLOGY OF
VANITY FAIR

What right have you to say that I am without God because I can't
believe that God ordered Abraham to kill Isaac or that he ordered
the bears to eat the little children who laughed at Elisha for being
bald. You don't believe it yourself.

William Makepeace Thackeray, to his Mother.

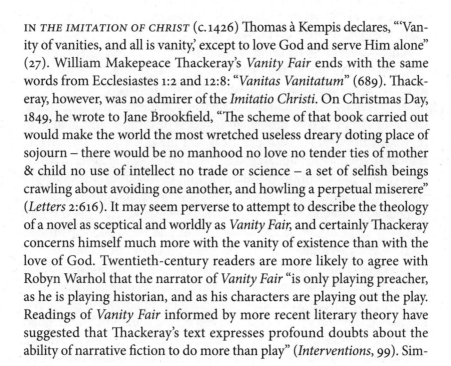

IN *THE IMITATION OF CHRIST* (c.1426) Thomas à Kempis declares, "'Vanity of vanities, and all is vanity,' except to love God and serve Him alone"
(27). William Makepeace Thackeray's *Vanity Fair* ends with the same
words from Ecclesiastes 1:2 and 12:8: "*Vanitas Vanitatum*" (689). Thackeray, however, was no admirer of the *Imitatio Christi*. On Christmas Day,
1849, he wrote to Jane Brookfield, "The scheme of that book carried out
would make the world the most wretched useless dreary doting place of
sojourn – there would be no manhood no love no tender ties of mother
& child no use of intellect no trade or science – a set of selfish beings
crawling about avoiding one another, and howling a perpetual miserere"
(*Letters* 2:616). It may seem perverse to attempt to describe the theology
of a novel as sceptical and worldly as *Vanity Fair*, and certainly Thackeray
concerns himself much more with the vanity of existence than with the
love of God. Twentieth-century readers are more likely to agree with
Robyn Warhol that the narrator of *Vanity Fair* "is only playing preacher,
as he is playing historian, and as his characters are playing out the play.
Readings of *Vanity Fair* informed by more recent literary theory have
suggested that Thackeray's text expresses profound doubts about the
ability of narrative fiction to do more than play" (*Interventions*, 99). Sim-

ilarly, Barry Qualls does not treat *Vanity Fair* at length in his study of secular pilgrims in Victorian fiction, arguing that Thackeray does not provide a narrative of natural supernaturalism but rather a parodic treatment of the secular world.[1] I agree with Qualls's overall distinction between Thackeray on the one hand and Eliot, Brontë, and Dickens, on the other. However, Thackeray's novel hints at a realm of existence beyond that of the world of vanity, and it is from those hints that the implied theology of the novel can be constructed. This implied theology is in some ways closer to an Augustinian orthodoxy than it is to the Broad Church position with which William Makepeace Thackeray the historical individual can be identified.[2]

Thackeray's religious beliefs can be inferred from his letters and journalism, though the evidence must be handled carefully since it is somewhat ambiguous. It is certain that he went through phases of scepticism, which have been documented by his biographer.[3] He struggled throughout his life with the powerful influence of his Evangelical mother, trying to distance himself from aspects of her creed while trying to show her that he did believe in what he considered to be the essential truth of Christianity. "My dearest Mammy," he begins one letter, "I must write you a line, and kiss my dearest old Mother, though we differ ever so much about the Old Testament" (*Letters* 3:168).

A quick survey of Thackeray's strongly expressed religious opinions may help to place him on the Victorian ecclesiastical map. He particularly disliked the Evangelical creed in which he was raised, and he rejected its belief in the historical accuracy of the Old Testament narratives. As his Christmas letter to Jane Brookfield suggests, he disliked any attempt to revive medieval devotional practices. On the other hand, he greatly respected Thomas Arnold and admired Stanley's *Life of Arnold*, which he reviewed favourably in the *Morning Chronicle* and recommended to anyone who wanted to know "how great, and good, and noble" a clergyman could be (*Snobs*, 218n6, 51). He was well aware, from his youthful visit to Weimar, of German biblical criticism, and he no doubt distressed his mother by writing: "The doctrine here [in Germany] is not near so strict as in England – many of the dogmas by w^h. we hold are here disregarded as allegories or parables – or I fear by most people as fictions altogether" (*Letters* 1:140). Thackeray thought that the authors of *Essays and Reviews*, reviled by some as the "*Septem contra Christum*," were "good men" (Ray, *Thackeray* 2:367). He admired Francis Newman and Clough, "thinking men, who I daresay will begin to speak out before many years are over, and protest against Gothic Xtianity" (2:121). I think that S.S. Prawer sums up Thackeray's religious views fairly when he writes, "No-one who scans Thackeray's letters and diaries can long remain in doubt that he retained Christian beliefs throughout his life which enabled him to remain, without difficulty, a member of the Church of England" (*Israel*, 12–13).

The opinions that I have quoted tend to put Thackeray in the Broad Church camp, as does his emphasis on the ethical dimension of Christianity. The essence of his faith seems to have been a belief in the importance of "doing your duty." Duty by Thackeray's lights was clearly set out, largely identified with the idea of being a gentleman, and sanctioned by the divine example of Jesus Christ. He expressed his reverence for Christ with a reticence akin to the reserve practised by the Tractarians. Thus, he wrote to his mother: "Why do I love the Saviour? (I love and adore the Blessed Character so much that I don't like to speak of it, and know myself to be such a rascal that I don't dare) – Because He is all Goodness Truth Purity – I dislike the Old Testament because it is the very contrary: because it contains no Gentleness no Humility no forgiveness" (*Letters* 2:206). A similar statement occurs when he writes to thank Robert Bell for his review of *Vanity Fair*: "You have all of you taken my misanthropy to task – I wish I could myself: but take the world by a certain standard [*drawing of a large cross*] (you know what I mean) and who dares talk of having any virtue at all?"[4]

Thackeray rejected the notion of eternal punishment as barbaric, and in spite of his frequently expressed intolerance for those of other races and nationalities, he regarded tolerance as an ideal.[5] In interpreting the Bible, Thackeray tended to demythologize, and his disputes with his mother over biblical interpretation suggest, as Prawer asserts, that his "revulsion against the Old Testament is bound up with attempts to free himself from the influence of his mother's overpowering personality" (*Israel*, 341). The conflicts with his mother were particularly acute when they disagreed over the religious upbringing of Thackeray's two daughters, and his views are perhaps most clearly stated in the letters he wrote to the girls on this topic during the times when they lived with their grandmother. He wrote to Anne Thackeray:

To my mind Scripture only means a writing and Bible means a Book. It contains Divine Truths: and the history of a Divine Character: but imperfect but not containing a thousandth part of Him – and it would be an untruth before God were I to hide my feelings from my dearest children: as it would be a sin, if having other opinions and believing literally in the Mosaic writings, in the 6 days cosmogony, in the serpent and the apple and consequent damnation of the human race, I should hide them; and not try to make those I loved best adopt such opinions of such immense importance to them. (*Letters* 3:95–6)

Thackeray here echoes Coleridge's words in the *Confessions of an Inquiring Spirit*; eight years after Thackeray's letter, Benjamin Jowett, Regius Professor of Greek at Oxford, scandalized the university and the Church of England by his contribution to *Essays and Reviews*, in which he summarized his understanding of biblical hermeneutics as follows: "*Interpret the Scripture like any other book.* There are many respects in which Scripture is unlike any other book; these will appear in the results of such an interpretation. The first step is to know the meaning, and this can only be done in the same careful and impartial way that we ascertain the meaning of Sophocles or of Plato" (*Essays*, 504; Jowett's emphasis). Thackeray's treatment of Jesus Christ as the embodiment of all human perfection is in accord with the image of Jesus emphasized in liberal Protestantism, an image that was summed up in *Literature and Dogma* (1873), in one of Matthew Arnold's more unfortunate phrases (translating St Paul's *epieikeia*), as the "sweet reasonableness" of Jesus (see for example M. Arnold, *Complete Prose* 6:219, 405, 406).

The passages just quoted help to provide a context for another letter, a famous one that Thackeray wrote to his mother on 2 July 1847, on the appearance of the seventh monthly number of *Vanity Fair*. He claimed that he was not concerned "to make a perfect character or anything like it," a point his novel clearly signals to the reader in the subtitle of the volume edition, "A Novel Without a Hero." "What I want," he continues in his letter, "is to make a set of people living without God in the world[6] (only that is a cant phrase) greedy pompous mean perfectly self-satisfied for the most part and at ease about their superior virtue" (*Letters* 2:309). This statement has often been repeated by critics, for it is Thackeray's clearest statement of intention concerning his novel; what is not generally quoted, however, is the conclusion to the paragraph in which the statement occurs, which, strikingly enough, is a prayer: "Save me, save me too O my God and Father, cleanse my heart and teach me my duty" (2:309). This should cause interpreters of the novel to take more seriously than they usually do the reference to "living in the world without God."

A knowledge of Thackeray's religious opinions should alert the reader of *Vanity Fair* to interpretive possibilities that would otherwise be overlooked. It is also worth noting that some of his Victorian readers regarded Thackeray as a serious moralist who could be read in the context of Christian belief. Among those who admired him thus was Charlotte Brontë, who clearly viewed Thackeray as a latter-day prophet. In the preface to *Jane Eyre* she wrote, "There is a man in our own days whose words are not framed to tickle delicate ears: who, to my thinking, comes before the great ones of society, much as the son of Imlah came before the throned Kings of Judah and Israel; and who speaks truth as deep, with a power as prophet-like and as vital – a mien as dauntless and as daring … I regard him as the first social regenerator of the day" (xxix–xxx).[7] It takes some historical imagination for us to be able to see Thackeray as a "social regenerator"; I hope to make this task easier by opening up a neglected perspective on Thackeray's masterpiece.

There has not been much discussion of religion in *Vanity Fair*, beyond the obvious recognition of the significance of the title. The dominant view among critics is that the novel has a religious dimension, but that it is not particularly important. A typical view is that of A.E. Dyson, who says that "religious judgments are inescapably present, though not directly expressed," and that Thackeray "has nothing of Bunyan's clear-cut doctrine to depend upon" ("*Vanity Fair*," 14). Barbara Hardy is more sceptical, suggesting that religion sits very lightly on Thackeray and that his novels are characterized by an absence of "embodied religious feeling" (*Exposure*, 12). I suggest that Thackeray's understanding of Christianity, although not dogmatic, was more clearly formulated than Dyson's comment suggests, and that the reserve that Hardy identifies does not necessarily indicate that Thackeray took Christianity lightly.

In examining the religious dimension of *Vanity Fair*, I am well aware not only that the novel is the most worldly of literary genres but that Thackeray's novel is a particularly good example of a polyphonic or dialogic novel. However, I will argue that Christian belief is one of the numerous languages of *Vanity Fair*, and that the pervasive metaphor of the title is one of several means by which Thackeray inserts Christianity into the dialogical world of the book. Before looking at his use of Ecclesiastes and Bunyan, I will elaborate on the notion of dialogism in *Vanity Fair*. In a pioneering discussion of dialogical form in the Victorian multiplot novel, Peter K. Garrett analyzes the instability of Thackeray's narrative voice. Garrett's discussion of what Dyson calls "one of the world's most devious novels" ("*Vanity Fair*," 12) comes to the conclusion that, because of "the doubtful authority of the narrator as moral commentator ... every comment or interpretation which the narrator introduces can exert only conditional authority. His formulations raise but cannot resolve the novel's issues; they must be tested against the implications of the narrative as a whole" (Garrett, *Multiplot Novel*, 107–9).

Bakhtin's poetics of the novel provide another valuable dimension for an analysis of *Vanity Fair*, in addition to the points that Garrett makes. For Bakhtin, the conflicting voices in a novel, or "languages" as he calls them, represent competing world views, "each characterized by its own objects, meanings and values," grounded in specific social circumstances and embodied in particular stylistic features in the text (*Dialogic*, 291–2). Garrett's analysis can be extended by defining some of the voices in *Vanity Fair*. Thackeray's narrator is far from stable, and he embodies a number of different and sometimes incompatible attitudes. At different points in the novel his voice approximates to the voices of various characters, whether the satirical tone and suspiciousness about people's motives that characterize Rebecca Sharp, or the voice of the bourgeois gentleman, like William Dobbin. One particularly distinct voice that Thackeray employs is that of the disillusioned cynical moralist who, in the manner of La Rochefoucauld, sees every human action as the result of self-interest. Matilda Crawley and Lord Steyne are two examples and the narrator, on occasion, a third. Thackeray thus links this sceptical attitude to a class whose ascendancy is coming to an end, while at the same time giving it a great deal of persuasive force in the novel (it is in fact closely related to the postmodern reading of *Vanity Fair*). If, as is generally accepted, *Vanity Fair* redefines gentlemanliness in middle-class terms, it also embodies considerable resistance to such a redefinition.

An example of the cynical voice occurs during the narrator's introduction of Rawdon Crawley. He quotes Mr Pitt Crawley alluding to Rawdon's contempt not only for death but for "what follows after death." The narrator then adds, in a manner that prevents the reader from identifying with Pitt Crawley's censure, "He was always thinking of his brother's soul or of the souls of those who differed with him in opinion – it is a sort of comfort which many of the serious give themselves" (Thackeray, *Vanity Fair*, 98). Here virtue, or at least the appearance of it, is reduced to self-interest, as Thackeray astutely identifies one of the temptations of religious faith.

A second voice of Thackeray's narrator is more sentimental, indulging in the kind of ironically tinged nostalgia, of which Thackeray is a master, that colours, for example, *The Roundabout Papers* (1863). Here the social position can be characterized as more middle class, for the references tend to be to bourgeois pleasures and experiences. This voice can thus be identified with the narrator as a character on the same social level as William Dobbin who shares some of Dobbin's experiences. When employing the sentimental voice, the narrator often includes himself in the behaviour he observes, and his tone tends to be the understanding irony of mature years, rather than the bitter cynicism of the more aristocratic voice. An example occurs in chapter 6, "Vauxhall," where after disingenuously suggesting that he doesn't understand the language of the fashionable world, the narrator says ingratiatingly that "we must if you please preserve our middle course modestly amidst those scenes and personages with which we are most familiar" (52). The narrator twice refers to his own experience of visiting Vauxhall. Like Dobbin, he was not socially accomplished enough to avoid being on his own, and he remembers being alone at Vauxhall as "one of the most dismal sports ever entered into by a bachelor" (56). Like Joseph Sedley, he also knows from personal experience the dreadful after-effects of drinking too much Vauxhall punch (58–9).

The voices I have just described may be termed worldly cynicism and worldly sentimentalism; for the perspective of religious belief we must consider the intertexts of Ecclesiastes and John Bunyan's *Pilgrim's Progress* (1678), which are the sources of Thackeray's title metaphor. The book of Ecclesiastes is an example of wisdom literature, but instead of the conservative advice that characterizes much of the wisdom tradition, it presents a more disillusioned, sceptical view of the world. The writer, who identifies himself as Qoheleth,[8] investigates a range of possible attitudes to life and comes to the conclusion that each of them has as its root vanity or emptiness. For Qoheleth, the repetitive cycles of nature and the fact of human mortality produce the same conclusion to each of his investigations: "This also is vanity and vexation of spirit." The only advice he can offer is that one should enjoy life as long as one is able to. There is no point to striving for virtue, zealously observing God's ordinances, nor is there any need for radical repentance; for "all things come alike to all: there is one event to the righteous, and to the wicked; to the good and to the clean, and to the unclean; to him that sacrificeth, and to him that sacrificeth not; as is the good, so is the sinner; and he that sweareth, as he that feareth an oath" (Ecclesiastes 9:2). The appeal of this perspective to a disillusioned Evangelical like Thackeray is obvious, and in fact it has affinities to the attitudes he embraced as a student under the influence of Edward FitzGerald (see Ray, *Thackeray* 1:131-2). Just as Qoheleth returns repeatedly to his refrain that all is vanity, so Thackeray's narrator constantly reiterates the title of the novel, referring to both the social world of the diegesis and the social world he shares with the narratee as "this Vanity Fair of ours" (213). As in Ecclesiastes, "vanity" becomes the negative principle which underlies all human activities, all different world views.

In a passage in Ecclesiastes (1:12-2:26) that one commentator has referred to as the "royal fiction" or "royal experiment" (Crenshaw, "Ecclesiastes," 271, 273), Qoheleth surveys the world from the perspective of King Solomon, and he comes to the same conclusion he reaches elsewhere, that "all is vanity and vexation of spirit" (1:14). Similarly, in *Vanity Fair* Becky is admitted to the society of the "best" people, but the narrator cautions: "Ah, my beloved readers and brethren, do not envy poor Becky prematurely – glory like this is said to be fugitive. It is currently reported that even in the very inmost circles, they are no happier than the poor wanderers outside the zone; and Becky, who penetrated into the very centre of fashion, and saw the great George IV face to face, has owned since that there too was Vanity" (503). The view that vanity is all-pervasive obviously has something in common with the cynical voice that I earlier attributed to both Miss Matilda Crawley and to the narrator. But Matilda Crawley is terrified of death, like a number of Thackeray's characters, whereas the narrator continually alludes to the common end of all humanity. Miss Crawley is thus exposed as a fair-weather cynic, while the narrator's awareness of mortality is one of the principal reasons for his disillusionment, as it is for Qoheleth. For example, the narrator describes a lady's companion as a memento mori, "as jolly a reminder as that of the Death's-head which figured in the repasts of Egyptian *bon-vivants*, a strange sardonic memorial of Vanity Fair" (376).

The references to mortality in *Vanity Fair* reinforce the vanity theme I have just identified and, more specifically, serve to undermine social pretensions by drawing attention to the common end of all humanity,

rich and poor, gentle and common. Death and madness overshadow high
society throughout the novel, from the moment when Becky Sharp first
enters Great Gaunt Street, with its hatchments and closed shutters, "in
which gloomy locality death seems to reign perpetual" (67). Miss Crawley,
the witty lady of fashion, becomes a hysterical invalid, and the narrator
underlines the moral of her demise with an allusion to the celebrated
poetic account of decline and death in the last chapter of Ecclesiastes:
"The last scene of her dismal Vanity Fair comedy was fast ap-proaching;
the tawdry lamps were going out one by one; and the dark curtain was
almost ready to descend" (257). The famous meditation on the arch in
the staircase at the beginning of chapter 61 re-enacts the same biblical
passage, brilliantly employing imagery of bourgeois Victorian family life
in order to reinforce the point that mourning doesn't last very long, and
that those "who love the survivors the least" are those who are most passionately mourned (604). Such passages, as they accumulate, begin to
take on a prophetic dimension, emphasizing the emptiness of social status
in the face of death and implying the need for more durable and genuine
virtues than the values of Vanity Fair.

The narrator's sentimental voice also figures in the references to "vanity,"
for they do not all refer to mortality. Some of them take a more tolerant
view of vanity, implying that it is merely ordinary human frailty, not
without its lovable or humorous side. These passages counter the prophetic
voice in the novel and remind us that Thackeray was a humorist as well
as a satirist and moralist. A good example is the opening to chapter 36,
"How to Live Well on Nothing a-Year," with its references to the entertainment habits of the "Jenkinses in the Park," which begins: "I suppose
there is no man in this Vanity Fair of ours so little observant as not to
think sometimes about the worldly affairs of his acquaintances, or so
extremely charitable as not to wonder how his neighbour Jones, or his
neighbour Smith, can make both ends meet at the end of the year" (361).
The narrator details the kind of subterfuges the Jenkinses employ, with
an amused detachment that comes from being someone who does not
himself have to employ such measures. While he suggests that his "I" is
here intended to personify the censoriousness of the world, "the Mrs
Grundy of each respected reader's private circle" (362), it is clear that the
passage is more of an expression of curiosity and interest in the ways of
the world than of genuine moral disapproval, for he then implicates himself in what goes on: "Many a glass of wine have we all of us drunk, I

have very little doubt, hob-and-nobbing with the hospitable giver, and wondering how the deuce he paid for it" (362). Clearly this narrator is not too proud to dine with the Jenkinses; in fact, wondering how the meal was paid for only seems to add to the interest of the experience. Thus the recurring theme of *vanitas* is used with varying degrees of moral intensity throughout the novel, contributing to the dialogical quality that emerges as one analyzes it.

According to Northrop Frye, the Hebrew word *hebel*, whose core meaning is fog or mist, and which the Vulgate renders as *vanitas*, is a concept like "the *shunyata* or 'void' of Buddhist thought" (*Great Code*, 123).[9] Peter Garrett suggests something similar when he implies that *Vanity Fair* is a representation of the postmodern condition: "The final stress on common vanity may be seen as the conclusion of the novel's moral argument, but it can also be seen as a return to the basis of its logic. Its elaborate, restless play on patterns of difference and similarity, exaggerating oppositions in order to collapse them, never allowing the reader a single, stable perspective or standard, this method too rests on *vanitas*, or emptiness, the emptiness which underlies the production of meaning from sheer difference" (*Multiplot Novel*, 127). This is a compelling statement, and it is supported by W. David Shaw's subtle analysis of *Vanity Fair* in *Victorians and Mystery*. For Shaw, Thackeray's text is characterized by double ironies that result in the collapse of moral norms, so that "moral language, like the moral masks of the performers, is empty of content" (146). It is certainly true that the moral language employed in the text and the world view that Thackeray characterizes as "Vanity Fair" are incommensurate. It is also true that the narrator expresses a variety of diverse positions through the course of the novel. It is up to the reader, however, to decide whether the result of the incommensurability is that the various positions cancel each other out. My own contention, in spite of the eloquent voices I have just quoted, is that the ironies of *Vanity Fair* do not necessarily amount to postmodern scepticism. In order to pursue this argument further, it is necessary to consider another of *Vanity Fair's* intertexts.

Thackeray's title owes some of its resonance to the fact that it is a double allusion. If the concept of *vanitas* functions in Ecclesiastes to show the nothingness of any attempt to order existence and can thus be assimilated to a poststructuralist idea of *différance*, Vanity-Fair in Bunyan's *Pilgrim's Progress* has a more specific function in a Christian allegory. Like Thomas à Kempis, Bunyan uses *vanitas* to mean life without God. Such a reading of Ecclesiastes was encouraged during the Reformation when Reformers rendered the name Qoheleth incorrectly as *Prediger*, "the Preacher" (Crenshaw, "Ecclesiastes," 271). "The Preacher" is the subtitle of Ecclesiastes in the King James Bible, as well as the translation of "Qoheleth."

It is interesting to note that the cover of Thackeray's original installment represents a preacher, albeit one wearing ass's ears like his auditors. In an ambiguous passage the narrator refers to both this illustration and the title:

> My kind reader will please to remember that these histories in their gaudy yellow covers, have "Vanity Fair" for a title and that Vanity Fair is a very vain, wicked, foolish place, full of all sorts of humbugs and falsenesses and pretentions. And while the moralist who is holding forth on the cover, (an accurate portrait of your humble servant) professes to wear neither gown nor bands, but only the very same long-eared livery, in which his congregation is arrayed: yet, look you, one is bound to speak the truth as far as one knows it, whether one mounts a cap and bells or a shovel-hat, and a deal of disagreeable matter must come out in the course of such an undertaking. (83)

When we remember the meaning that Bunyan gave to Vanity-Fair, then the theological voice in Thackeray's novel will begin to make itself heard. It is partly qualified by Thackeray's tone, as in the passage above, with its hint of parodic allusion to Sunday-school discourse in the phrase "a very vain, wicked, foolish place," and its reference to the "long-eared livery." The Christianity of the implied author is also concealed by the fact that the novel restricts itself to the world of Vanity Fair, so that to a large extent the theology that one finds in the novel is a negative theology, hinted at through the discourse of one who declares himself bound to "speak the truth as far as one knows it." This statement could refer either to the limitations of the speaker or to the unknowability of the truth.

While Thackeray's approach to theology is largely negative, some positive content is implied by his allusions to *Pilgrim's Progress* and to the Bible.[10] For Bunyan, Vanity-Fair is the symbol of a godless world, a world, moreover, of competitive capitalism in which everything is up for sale:

> Therefore at this Fair are all such merchandise sold, as houses, lands, trades, places, honours, preferments, titles, countries, kingdoms, lusts,

pleasures, and delights of all sorts, as whores, bawds, wives, husbands, children, masters, servants, lives, blood, bodies, souls, silver, gold, pearls, precious stones, and what not.

And moreover, at this Fair there is at all times to be seen jugglings, cheats, games, plays, fools, apes, knaves, and rogues, and that of all sorts.

Here are to be seen too, and that for nothing, thefts, murders, adulteries, false-swearers, and that of a blood-red colour. (*Pigrim's Progress*, 125)

There are many parallels between this passage and Thackeray's novel: *Vanity Fair* has thefts, false-swearers, adulteries (at least hinted at), and possibly a murder. We see the sale of property and honours; we see the commercialization of all human relationships in what George Osborne, speaking more than usually perceptively, characterizes as a "ready-money society" (*Vanity Fair*, 204), and the imagery of the novel often echoes Bunyan's fairground references to jugglings and games.

Thackeray's novel, however, only has one city, the world he constantly refers to as Vanity Fair, whereas in Bunyan's allegory "Vanity" is only a town on the way to the Celestial City, which is the goal the pilgrims have in sight from the beginning. Thackeray takes a small part of Bunyan's original conception and expands it to a vast extent; for he is writing a satirical novel, not an allegorical dream-vision.[11] As Robyn Warhol aptly remarks, "Of all the canonic English novels of the realist period, *Vanity Fair* is the one that makes the least pretense of presenting a slice of life: as 'Before the Curtain' makes clear, the novel is only a slice of a fair" (*Interventions*, 85). Thus Walter Allen is simply making a basic error of genre when he denigrates Thackeray as a novelist by saying that "no novelist of genius has given us an analysis of man in society based on so trivial a view of life" (*Novel*, 176). It is precisely because it is a satirical novel that *Vanity Fair* is not a moral allegory; the Celestial City is not directly represented, and the satire is firmly anchored in the quotidian realities of the time and place of its setting.

But this does not mean that *Vanity Fair* is without a theological dimension. It alludes to the possibility of the existence of what Augustine called the city of God, although the nature of that city is left undefined. The implied theology of the novel is to that extent a liberal theology. Thackeray's understanding of Christianity in many ways resembles that of

Matthew Arnold a generation later. Like Arnold, Thackeray focuses on "conduct," which, Arnold reiterates throughout *Literature and Dogma*, is three-quarters of human life (see for example M. Arnold, *Complete Prose* 6:173). Responding to an article in the *Guardian* on the meaning of Christmas, Arnold wrote in the preface to the Popular Edition of *Literature and Dogma* (1883), "How strange that on me should devolve the office of instructing the *Guardian* that 'the fundamental truth' for Christians is not the incarnation but the imitation of Christ! In insisting on 'the miracle of the Incarnation,' the *Guardian* insists on just that side of Christianity which is perishing. Christianity is immortal; it has eternal truth, inexhaustible value, a boundless future. But our popular religion at present conceives the birth, ministry, and death of Christ, as altogether steeped in prodigy, brimful of miracle; – *and miracles do not happen*" (6:146; Arnold's emphasis). Like Arnold, Thackeray uses religious language to facilitate ethical judgments, but there is no sense in *Vanity Fair* of a God who acts in history. In fact, Thackeray's representation of the narrator as a stage manager or a puppet-master could be seen as a parody of a Calvinist deity. Thackeray does not use the analogy between God and the author of a novel to make serious theological points, as Catholic novelists of the twentieth century such as Muriel Spark or David Lodge have done; instead, these passages treat omniscience and authority in a comic manner that emphasizes the limitations of knowledge. They are also countered by other passages in which the narrator is a fallible character whose knowledge of what has happened is imperfect. Thus, like many liberals who do not entirely reject Christianity, Thackeray takes advantage of the traditional implications of Bunyan's metaphor without committing himself to the theology it implies, in order to make a moral critique of his society.

Another of the means by which *Vanity Fair* implies a theology is in the theological overtones of language which also has a secular signification. If it were not for the pervasive use of the title metaphor and the references to Ecclesiastes and Bunyan, these nuances of language would be less striking, but in the structure that Thackeray has created, they resonate significantly.

We have seen that in the letter to his mother of 2 July 1847, Thackeray refers to characters living without God in the "world." This particularly resonant word occurs frequently in *Vanity Fair*, and, like almost everything else in the novel, it is not a simple term.[12] In Christian theology, *world* (translating the Greek *kosmos*) can refer simply to all of creation, to heaven and earth. Hence one of the best-known verses of Christian scripture, John 3:16, declares that "God so loved the world, that he gave his only begotten Son, that whosoever believeth in him should not perish, but have eternal life." But at the same time, and especially in John's gospel, being a Christian is opposed to being "of the world," an opposition that has been emphasized recurrently throughout the Christian tradition. Jesus Christ declares, "My kingdom is not of this world" (John 18:36), and throughout John's gospel he is figured as the light that comes into the world to save sinners.

"World" can mean the adult affairs of human society, so that a young person coming of age is said to make his or her way in the world, which is the basic subject matter of the *Bildungsroman*.[13] "World" more specifically can refer to "high or fashionable society," according to the *Oxford English Dictionary*. In a culture steeped in biblical language, there is often in both of these uses at least a hint of the religious contrast between "this world" and what the Nicene Creed calls the "world to come." Miss Crawley is a "worthy woman of the world" (*Vanity Fair*, 140), or alternatively, "a godless woman of the world" (97); a "man of the world" is someone knowledgeable about and accepting of the social conventions of a given society, and the expression becomes even more morally ambiguous when applied to a woman, since she is expected to be more attuned to a higher realm.[14] Immediately following the reference to Miss Crawley as a "worthy woman of the world" we are told that "Mr Crawley sent over a choice parcel of tracts, to prepare her for the change from Vanity Fair and Park Lane for another world" (140).

When Becky and Amelia leave the finishing school at the beginning of the novel, the narrator echoes Milton: "The world is before the two young ladies" (9). This observation, not without irony given the limited expectations implied by the schooling at Miss Pinkerton's Academy, obviously refers primarily to the social world, and to the experiences, especially of love, that await them. The Miltonic echo, and the ambiguity of the word "world," might also suggest that they are beginning a kind of parodic pilgrim's progress. Similarly, when Becky goes from London to Queen's Crawley, she "was accommodated with a back seat inside the carriage, which may be said to be carrying her into the wide world" (72). Victorian readers, schooled in *Pilgrim's Progress*, were sensitive to echoes of that book in the literature of their own time. For example, in her review of *Vanity Fair* for the *Quarterly Review*, which was better known for its comments on *Jane Eyre*, Elizabeth Rigby noted that Becky Sharp is a pilgrim, but unfortunately a pilgrim "travelling the wrong way" ("Review," 81).

By the time we get to the end of the novel, Thackeray's ambiguous use of the word "world" has associated it with a context of Christian moral and theological discourse. Thus, when the narrator, wearing his preacher's robes, asks pointedly, "Which of us is happy in this world?" (689), he could be reflecting on the vanity of the world from the point of view of the sceptical moralist of Ecclesiastes, as the Latin quotation "*Vanitas vanitatum*" preceding the question might imply; or he could be hinting at a Christian alternative to the world. If "this world" means everything that exists, the first sense I mentioned above, then its vanity can be seen simply as the endless cycles of change and repetition that characterize the world, and the novel's world view can be seen as akin to the bleak view of life that is found in Ecclesiastes. The "progress" of Bunyan's title is a journey, a narrative of repentance and salvation, whereas a fair is a static location where the same "jugglings, cheats, games, plays, fools, apes, knaves, and rogues, and that of all sorts" have been witnessed for centuries (Bunyan, *Pilgrim's Progress*, 125). On the other hand, *Vanity Fair* read as a Christian moral satire would condemn life without God by implying the existence of a realm other than the world ("that which is not world," in T.S. Eliot's phrase from "Burnt Norton"), the love of God that Thomas à Kempis opposed to vanity. The dialogical nature of the novel form means that sources such as Bunyan may be carnivalized, and Ecclesiastes is at least as readily identified with sceptical disillusion and resignation as with Christian teaching; however, true dialogue works both ways, and Thackeray's use of terms such as "world" and "vanity," combined with the resonance of some of his biblical allusions, generates for the reader the possibility of a sphere completely separate from Vanity Fair. His greatest novel is woven out of many voices, one of which is clearly Christian. *Vanity Fair* is suspended between these two alternatives, holding them in dialogue, just as in specific passages the narrator presents the reader with different possibilities without choosing between them.

At several points in *Vanity Fair* the narrator draws attention to a gap in the text, something that is not narrated, leaving the reader to speculate about what is left unsaid.[15] These passages allow him to gesture beyond the limitations of the satirical world that circumscribes the novel, without actually departing from its generic norms by directly representing a world of grace. Such discourse operates as a kind of negative theology, invoking an absent God, or at least a God who is only seen by indirection. As W. David Shaw shows in *The Lucid Veil*, this negative approach is a common theme in Victorian theology, and it can be found in the self-consciously orthodox Tractarians, in their doctrine of reserve, as much as in more sceptically minded and intellectually daring theologians.

One example of such a passage in *Vanity Fair* occurs after Amelia returns from her wedding-journey to Brighton. The narrator describes her visit to her mother and her old room and asks: "Have we a right to repeat or to overhear her prayers? These, brother, are secrets, and out of the domain of Vanity Fair, in which our story lies" (262). This realm that is "out of the domain of Vanity Fair" is a possible location for the implied norms of the satire, and the prayers suggest that that realm has a religious dimension. Prayer is more directly represented when Lady Jane prays for "that poor wayworn sinner" (533), her brother-in-law Rawdon. Lady Jane is the most unequivocally good character in the novel, and her influence produces the moral transformation of Rawdon, the most positive change that takes place in any character in *Vanity Fair*. Her virtue is several times opposed to Becky's vice: "Lady Jane's sweetness and kindness had inspired Rebecca with such a contempt for her ladyship as the little woman found no small difficulty in concealing. That sort of goodness and simplicity which Lady Jane possessed, annoyed our friend Becky, and it was impossible for her at times not to show, or to let the other divine her scorn" (454). There might well be a hint of irony implicit in the phrase "that sort of goodness and simplicity," but equally the phrase "our friend Becky" implies that the reader is more likely to resemble Becky than Lady Jane. The unreasonable scorn Becky feels for Lady Jane's goodness is a recurrent feature of representations of virtue in literature, and here one finds a hint of something that is central to Dostoevsky's vision, for example in the destructive energy of Peter Verkhovensky in *The Devils*. Similarly, Philip Morville, with the best of intentions, unreasonably persecutes his cousin Guy in Charlotte Yonge's *Heir of Redclyffe* (1853).

The boundaries of the world of *Vanity Fair* are again acknowledged in the following passage: "Well, well – a carriage and three thousand a-year is not the summit of the reward nor the end of God's judgment of men. If quacks prosper as often as they go to the wall – if zanies succeed and knaves arrive at fortune, and, *vice versâ*, sharing ill luck and prosperity for all the world like the ablest and most honest amongst us – I say, brother, the gifts and pleasures of Vanity Fair cannot be held of any great account, and that it is probable … but we are wandering out of the domain of the story" (385). The reference to "God's judgment" and the imagery of reversal links this passage to the parable of Dives and Lazarus, which will be discussed shortly. The boundaries of "the domain of the story" are useful to Thackeray in that he does not have to proffer any specific alternative to the rising and falling movement that governs the world of Vanity Fair; at the same time he is able to imply that there *is* such an alternative by relying on the traditional Christian remedies that for many of his readers would have come readily to mind.

One of the most extended passages of self-conscious narration in *Vanity Fair* occurs at the conclusion to chapter 8. It is significant that it comes immediately after the long letter in which Becky takes over the role of narrator, introducing the reader to Queen's Crawley in a manner that reveals a lively satirical energy akin to that of the primary narrator. The narrator is at pains to distance himself from Becky's irreverent mockery of the Crawley family, and he claims the right to abuse villainy "in the strongest terms which politeness admits of" (593), calling to mind the chaplain who "never mentions Hell to Ears polite" in Alexander Pope's "Of the Use of Riches" (*Poems*, line 150). If he did not abuse villains, the narrator concludes,

> you might fancy it was I who was sneering at the practice of devotion, which Miss Sharp finds so ridiculous; that it was I who laughed good-humouredly at the reeling old Silenus of a baronet – whereas the laughter comes from one who has no reverence except for prosperity and no eye for anything beyond success. Such people there are *living and flourishing in the world* – Faithless, Hopeless, Charityless – let us have at them, dear friends, with might and main. Some there are, and very successful too; mere quacks and fools: and it was to combat and expose such as those no doubt, that Laughter was made." (84; my emphasis)

Here the phrase "living in the world" takes on the religious overtones I have already discussed as a result of being identified with the absence of the three Christian virtues. The passage implies a severe judgment on Becky, certainly a harsher one than many readers would see as one of the "implications of the narrative as a whole" (Garrett, *Multiplot Novel*,

109). Thackeray here has his cake and eats it too: he has used the convenient mask of Becky's letter to provide a mocking portrait of the entire Crawley household, but now he stands back and makes moral distinctions that Becky is unable or unwilling to make. Yet on another level the novel's satire potentially extends to all of humanity; for it is orthodox Christian theology to claim that no human being has sufficient virtue to be justified on his or her own merits.

Finally, before I take this particular passage too seriously, it is important to note, as Peter L. Shillingsburg has shown, that at the end of chapter 8 the narrator cannot be regarded as speaking in a "trustworthy" voice, because it is in two ways double-voiced discourse. First, the narrator mimics the stage manager of Drury Lane greeting the audience: "I warn 'my kyind friends'"; in the next paragraph he represents himself as a black slave, echoing a famous abolitionist slogan with the words "Am I not a friend and brother?" (84).[16] This ventriloquism does not negate the point I am making about the effect of the religious references, but it certainly qualifies it, ensuring that any conclusion is drawn by the reader and not the narrator.

Earlier I quoted an example of what I called the cynical voice in the novel, suggesting that eternal values are often alluded to for the worldly comfort of the religious person. But there is another voice to be considered in *Vanity Fair*, that of the moralist as Christian preacher, "having at" those living without faith, hope, and charity "with might and main." This voice has often caused problems for readers. In his introduction to the Penguin edition of *Vanity Fair*, J.I.M. Stewart quotes the following address from the narrator to the reader: "Picture to yourself, oh fair young reader, a worldly, selfish, graceless, thankless, religionless old woman, writhing in pain and fear, and without her wig. Picture her to yourself, and ere you be old, learn to love and pray!" (*Vanity Fair*, 141–2). Stewart's comment is "What, it is asked, could be said for such stuff?" (22). One thing that can be said is that the passage is a brief example of the preacher's voice, reflecting on the vanity of Miss Crawley's worldly values and drawing a moral conclusion. Such a passage would undoubtedly seem heavy-handed were it offered unequivocally as the moral of the entire work, or even as the last word on Matilda Crawley; as a voice within the work, however, expressing the possibility of a set of values that exists outside of Vanity Fair, it seems to me to have its place. The narrator here, in the manner of a preacher, addresses the reader directly and demands that the reader re-evaluate her (or his) moral priorities. By having the statement addressed to a "fair young reader," Thackeray again introduces an element of parody, momentarily and – in the context of the entire novel – absurdly moving his narrative discourse into the world of Mrs Sherwood and the Evangelical novel. But under this guise, wearing "the very same long-eared livery" as his reader, the preacher has for a moment mounted his tub.

I alluded earlier to another significant aspect of the religious subtext of *Vanity Fair* – Thackeray's use of the parable of Dives and Lazarus (Luke 16:19–31). This parable, found only in Luke's gospel, is unusual in that it includes a named character and depicts life beyond the grave; biblical scholars have seen parallels with the literature of the Cynics in its critique of wealth and its use of reversal, as well as in the common satirical device of testimony from beyond the grave (Hock, "Lazarus," 267). In the parable, Lazarus is a poor beggar who spends his time at the gate of a rich man's house (the Vulgate's *dives*, "rich man," led to the popular creation of the proper name of the rich man). When the two men die, Lazarus is carried by angels to the bosom of Abraham. Dives sees him from the torments of hell and asks for mercy; he asks also that his brothers be warned of the fate in store for them. Abraham tells him that they have the prophets, to whom they should listen, and "if they hear not Moses and the prophets, neither will they be persuaded, though one rose from the dead" (Luke 16:31).

The parable of Dives and Lazarus was a favourite biblical point of reference for Thackeray, probably because it is one of the more "novelistic" parables, with analogues in classical literature. As R.D. McMaster points out, Thackeray was fond of alluding to "the everyday and anecdotal, one might say secular and novelistic, episodes of the Bible" (*Allusion*, 5). There are a number of allusions to the parable in his correspondence. Its relevance to *Vanity Fair* is obvious. It points to the vanity of riches, and the reversal of fortune of the two men finds parallels in the worldly reversals of a number of Thackeray's characters. The representation of death and the testimony of the dead ties in with the novel's fondness for meditations on mortality. The parable is an important means of hinting at another realm, where a moral judgment will take place that will reverse the standards of Vanity Fair.

In the course of an extended meditation on the subject of an auction of the goods of the late "Lord Dives," there is an allusion to Dives and

Lazarus that combines the vanity theme with the reference to the parable: "O Dives, who would ever have thought, as we sat round the broad table sparkling with plate and spotless linen, to have seen such a dish at the head of it as that roaring auctioneer?" (*Vanity Fair*, 171). Here the judgment after death is a secular one, namely; that the heir of the wealthy lord is rapidly dissipating his fortune and that his carefully accumulated property is being sold off. The use of the name Dives adds a hint of divine judgment, and the whole scene exemplifies the vanity of human activity. Compare the following passage from Ecclesiastes: "Then I looked on all the works that my hands had wrought, and on the labour that I had laboured to do: and, behold, all was vanity and vexation of spirit, and there was no profit under the sun" (Ecclesiastes 2:11).

In another passage Thackeray contrasts two imagined deathbed speeches, creating a fable that has echoes of the story of the Pharisee and the tax collector (Luke 18:9–14) and perhaps also that of the rich man and the poor widow (Luke 21:1–4). Thackeray's rich and self-satisfied man boasts, among other things, of having lent his college friend Jack Lazarus fifty pounds. The poor man owns up to his sins and asks for forgiveness from the "Divine Mercy." The passage intimates the existence of judgment beyond death and brings in one of the narrator's more explicitly Christian statements: "Which of these two speeches, think you, would be the best oration for your own funeral? old Sedley made the last; and in that humble frame of mind, and holding by the hand of his daughter, life and disappointment and vanity sank away from under him" (607). The parabolic formula "which of these" emphasizes the degree to which Thackeray is imitating the narrative devices of the gospels. The narrator's parable implies that not everything is vanity, but after that it is silent. We do not follow Mr Sedley into the world where vanity no longer exists (a world represented in *Pilgrim's Progress* and the parable of Dives and Lazarus); instead, the passage is followed immediately by a judgment in a very different register. Old Osborne tells George, "Look at your poor grandfather, Sedley, and his failure. And yet he was a better man than I was, this day twenty years – a better man I should say, by ten thousand pound" (607). Readers who react negatively to the account of old Sedley's death, perhaps finding it sentimental or false, not only are forced to consider as the other alternative the complacent speech of the well-to-do man but will find themselves brought up short by the crass calculation of the senior Osborne, whose attitude results from the exclusion of any possibility of sentimentality from one's calculation of value.

One dominant strain of Victorian religious teaching was that everyone should do their duty in the station to which God had called them, which of course easily blended into the view that God had ordained the social hierarchy and the differences in wealth and status that it rested on. This attitude is summed up in the third verse (generally excluded from versions of the hymn that are still in use) of Mrs Cecil Frances Alexander's hymn "All Things Bright and Beautiful":

> The rich man in his castle
> The poor man at his gate
> God made them, high or lowly
> And ordered their estate. (Bradley, *Hymns*, 30)

It is therefore not surprising that the parable of Dives and Lazarus should have an especial appeal to the Victorians. It is strikingly double-edged. A conservative interpretation would see it as legitimizing the social order by projecting divine judgment on the sinful rich into the afterlife and regarding the judgment on Dives as the result of his lack of charity; a more radical interpretation would take the judgment as an existential imperative and the parable as a comment on the evils of riches. Thackeray's allusions to the parable of Lazarus and Dives serve to cast a critical shadow over the novel's preoccupation with the world of the upper bourgeoisie, and they add to the references to mortality in the novel the suggestion that at death human beings are judged by a set of values outside those of Vanity Fair. The book of Ecclesiastes specifically suggests that the life of a rich man is one of vanity; this is the significance of the "royal experiment." Thus, to answer one of the questions readers of *Vanity Fair* like to debate, Becky would not have been good with five thousand pounds a year (see page 422). She refuses to face the possibility that there might be values other than those of Vanity Fair, just as, the narrator's revealing analogy tells us, Sir Pitt Crawley's children do not like to confront the memento mori that his body provides them with: "It may, perhaps, have struck her that to have been honest and humble, to have done her duty, and to have marched straightforward on her way, would have brought her as near happiness as that path by which she was striving to attain it. But, – just as the children at Queen's Crawley went round the room, where the body of their father lay; – if ever Becky had these thoughts, she was accustomed to walk round them, and not look in" (423).

—<o>—

Thus far my main argument has been that *Vanity Fair* includes a Christian perspective that is evident in a series of allusions, in religiously inflected diction, and in a number of double-voiced passages. The consistent ironies of the novel and the lack of positive content in its theology are compatible with the doctrinal fuzziness of the Broad Church position, particularly with the extremely influential liberal restatement of Christianity to be found in Matthew Arnold's *Literature and Dogma*, a work whose varied reception suggests that it straddles the divide between orthodoxy and apostasy. Once again, however, Thackeray's greatest novel resists definition. Certainly no one would term it a "Broad Church novel"; in fact, through its invocation of some dominant motifs from the tradition of western Christianity, *Vanity Fair* exposes some of the weaknesses and difficulties inherent in the Broad Church position. In particular, Thackeray's novel resists the temptation to identify the secular ideal of gentlemanliness with the demands of the Christian gospel.[17] It was this identification, or confusion as one might more accurately term it, that led John Henry Newman to make his provocative statement that "a lousy, lying beggar-woman" might be in a state of grace whereas a "good wise honest humble conscientious man earnestly trying to fulfil his duty," to quote Thackeray's paraphrase of Newman's lecture (*Letters* 2:676) might not have the same prospect of heaven if his conduct was the result of natural virtue. Thackeray's reaction to this statement was predictably one of outrage, but his own novel raises some of the same doubts about the worth of the gentlemanly ideal.

In the introduction to his life of Thackeray, Gordon Ray argues that Thackeray's achievement as a Victorian moralist was to redefine "the gentlemanly ideal to fit a middle-class rather than an aristocratic context" (*Thackeray* 1:13). This is a useful starting point for an examination of Thackeray's fiction, but a careful reading of *Vanity Fair* soon reveals that the gentlemanly ideal is seriously flawed, and that one possible alternative is the ideal common to Thomas à Kempis and John Henry Newman. Almost everywhere in Thackeray's novel, we see human goodness and gentlemanliness as weak and foolish and vulnerable to selfishness and deceit. William Dobbin's chivalrous conduct is the result of a false idealization of his friend George, and an equally blinkered veneration of Amelia. He attributes to her qualities that she does not really possess, just as he thinks that a fashion plate with "an impossible doll's face simpering over it" resembles her (435). And as John Sutherland points out, after marrying Amelia Dobbin devotes his life to doing nothing in particular, except working on "a book which he is unlikely to finish, and which few will want to read" ("Introduction," xxix). Lady Jane is far more actively a good character, and her rescue of Rawdon is the most spontaneously charitable moment in the novel. The gentlemanly ideal simply does not amount to much, on the evidence *Vanity Fair* provides. It may well be that on a conscious level Thackeray regarded the Christian and the gentlemanly codes as congruous, whereas his novel, by representing the inadequacy of the latter and the vanity of all human endeavour, suggests that the alternative of a Christian life is "difficult, exacting, and contrary at many points to natural instincts" (Cockshut, *Anglican Attitudes*, 64).

Similarly, the novel makes clear, at the level of plot and frequently in the narrator's discourse, that human beings are all foolish and flawed; hence the subtitle, "A Novel without a Hero." The narrator as preacher, as Thackeray both depicts and describes him, wears "the very same long-eared livery, in which his congregation is arrayed" (*Vanity Fair*, 83). This does not mean that there are no relative standards, by which Dobbin, for example, is superior to George and Becky, but it does mean that any human being is tainted with what Christian theology calls original sin. As Thackeray wrote to Bell, "take the world by a certain standard [*drawing of a large cross*] (you know what I mean) and who dares talk of having any virtue at all?" (Harden, ed., *Letters* 1:228). Reticence and the decorum of the literary form he is working in prevent him from mentioning the divine alternative by name, but it is certainly implied in *Vanity Fair* by the title and the allusions I have discussed. In this respect the use of allusion rather than direct definition or content is another double-edged aspect of *Vanity Fair*. It is generally read as further evidence of Thackeray's scepticism, but it is worth pointing out that the perfect man, the Rousseauistic Jesus of nineteenth-century liberalism, was often a projection of the culture's ideal of itself. This meant that Jesus sometimes resembled a public-school gentleman; in more sinister versions, the Jewishness of Jesus was denied, as the perfect man was defined through ethnocentric and sometimes racist assumptions.[18] Thackeray's hint that the workings of God are greater than human comprehension means that his novel does not fall into the sentimental mire of Victorian liberalism at its worst, which is perhaps another way of saying that ironists tend to be conservatives.

As a final approach to Thackeray's theological aporia in *Vanity Fair*, I want to return to the novel's preoccupation with the vanity of human life, and its insistent reference to human mortality. The frequent reiteration of these themes points in two different directions, that are perhaps but two sides of the same coin. They may be taken as evidence of the need for divine grace, or they may be seen as the reason for a sceptical attitude to life. The latter alternative is the one most critics of the novel have chosen to emphasize, but the evidence for the former is there too. I think Joseph Baker's Augustinian interpretation of *Vanity Fair* still provides a valuable perspective, however neglected and unpopular, and however inadequately it is documented from Thackeray's text. Baker does at least imply that he is aware of the dialogic nature of the novel, for he refers to Thackeray's prose as "ambivalent, or multivalent" ("Celestial City," 95).

Vanity Fair neither rejects nor affirms Christianity. At times Thackeray's narrator might seem to be offering a sentimental moral to his story, but such sentimentality is always countered by what I have called the cynical voice, so that the reader is not given any final resting place. One of the best images for the novel as a whole is the opening to chapter 61, "In Which Two Lights Are Put Out." Human life is presented in all its aspects, young and old, male and female, servant and master. The passage is finely observed and richly textured, but at the same time the whole pageant of human activity on the staircase of the house takes place under the sign of the "little arch" (*Vanity Fair*, 603) which both provides light to the stair and facilitates the easy removal of coffins from the house: "what a memento of Life, Death, and Vanity it is – that arch and stair" (604). With *Vanity Fair*, as with the book of Ecclesiastes, we can either regard vanity as the corrosive concept that undoes any human attempt to order existence and exposes the void that lies beneath all appearances, or we can view vanity as the condition of living in Vanity Fair, in a world without God, who provides the ordering principle beyond "the domain of Vanity Fair, in which our story lies" (262). It is up to the reader to decide whether the remedy recommended by Thomas à Kempis is applicable; the narrator remains almost ostentatiously noncommittal on the matter.

TWO

CHARLOTTE BRONTË'S *SHIRLEY* AS A NOVEL OF RELIGIOUS CONTROVERSY

We are now, as members of the Church of England placed under peculiar trials, outwardly, from the numerous, and inveterate enemies of both the church and state, and we may have enemies within.

Patrick Brontë to Mrs J.C. Franks, 6 July 1835

AT THE BEGINNING OF THE TWENTY-FIRST CENTURY religious identity has emerged as a significant category of cultural analysis. Scholars of the Brontës have thus begun to consider the relationship between the religious beliefs of the members of that most theologically literate family and the novels they wrote.[1] Charlotte Brontë's anti-Catholicism in *Villette* (1853) has been scrutinized, likewise the religious aspects of *Jane Eyre* (1847).[2] While *Shirley* (1849) is less well known, one can learn a great deal about Charlotte Brontë's religious views, as well as gain significant insights into *Shirley* itself, by seeing it in relation to the internal politics and theological controversies of the Anglican church during the 1840s. Chief among these were Newman's conversion to Rome in 1845, which ended the first phase of the Oxford Movement, and the restoration of the Roman Catholic diocesan hierarchy in England, the so-called "Papal Aggression," in 1850.

In what follows I consider *Shirley* solely as an example of the novel of religious controversy, although it can also be considered from other generic perspectives, for example as an industrial novel, or a novel about the "woman question." The religious novel was a flexible category that subsumed many other types of fiction, and Brontë's admixture of issues of religion, work, social class, and gender has many resonances for our own time. *Shirley* has always presented problems to interpreters; Tim Dolin refers to its "compound form – part regional novel, part industrial novel" ("Fictional Territory," 198). In adding another element to the compound my aim is to situate *Shirley* more precisely in the literature of the 1840s, and to show the significant relationship it bears to the body of religious novels that remain neglected by most recent scholars of Victorian literature, even as the canon is being expanded by recently edited works of sensation fiction and novels of interest to postcolonial critics.[3] Susan M. Griffin rightly points out in her study *Anti-Catholicism and Nineteenth-Century Fiction* (2004) that "nineteenth-century religious fiction remains under-read" (26).

I was first prompted to approach *Shirley* in this way by a sentence in Kathleen Tillotson's classic study *Novels of the Eighteen-Forties*: "The most 'thorny' of the 'topics of the day' in the eighteen-forties were the controversies in religion, and these are occasionally reflected in most novels of the time, not excepting the historical ones and those concerned with the recent past: the novels of Ainsworth, as later of Kingsley and Reade, have their propagandist slant, while Mrs Bute Crawley in *Vanity Fair*, Eliza Reed in *Jane Eyre*, the curates in *Shirley*, though all ostensibly pre-1820, gain in definition from their authors' awareness of contemporary circumstances" (126). The importance of these controversies receded from attention during the latter part of the twentieth century, when criticism of the Brontës was dominated by issues of gender and class and by psychological and historical approaches. John Maynard helped to right this imbalance in his essay on "The Brontës and Religion" (2002) with the reminder that "no subject occupied the Victorians ... as much – in the privacy of their meditations and in the public outpouring of their endless works, sermons, tracts, confessions, spiritual autobiographies, interpretations and re-interpretations of every aspect of the Bible and the Church fathers – as religion" (192). Maynard nevertheless seems to regard Victorian religion as a foreign country from which contemporary scholars, with their "essential ignorance of Victorian religion" (193), are barred. Like many other critics he seems interested only in those aspects of religion in the Brontës that are challenging to or subversive of orthodoxy. Yet Charlotte's letters show her to be a loyal member of the Church of England, with strong latitudinarian tendencies, as I will demonstrate in due course.

I am less pessimistic than Maynard about the possibility of attaining some understanding of Victorian religion. My theoretical approach is to locate *Shirley* within the "horizon of expectations," to use Hans Robert Jauss's term, of the reader of the 1840s.[4] To do this one needs to reconstruct the terms of religious debate of the time. This means taking seriously theological issues that seem abstruse and even irrelevant in the spiritual climate of today, when ideas of religious authority, conformity, or orthodoxy are anathema, and when, even among practising Christians, there is widespread ignorance about Christian doctrine and the Bible. Heather Glen is correct in observing of twenty-first-century readers that "all too often, any invocation of the Bible signifies unquestioning belief" ("Introduction," 9). Today's critics of Victorian fiction are sometimes guilty of seeing the Victorian church as a monolithic structure, not realizing that some of the most bitter intellectual and institutional controversies of the century raged under its roof. To ignore Victorian Christianity is to risk serious misunderstanding of Victorian fiction, while to study Victorian Christianity is to become aware of how complex and diverse a phenomenon it really was.

Readers of *Shirley* have long wrestled with the problem of the unity of the novel. Among the first of these critics was George Henry Lewes, who found no "artistic fusion" to link the disparate parts (Unsigned Review, 164). Like several other Victorian reviewers, Lewes found in the presence of the three curates a particularly egregious example of apparently irrelevant material. Among modern critics, Jacob Korg began his analysis – written in the late 1950s and still well worth reading – by noting that the novel is about so many things that "it is a wilderness in which the forest constantly disappears among the trees" ("Problem," 125). As an example of the particular "irrelevancies" that must be accounted for, Korg too cited the scenes devoted to the curates (126). In the 1990s Gisela Argyle employed Jauss to read *Shirley* as an amalgam of "novelistic sub-genres" in an interpretation that focused on its place in the sequence of Brontë novels ("Gender," 742).

Shirley is not alone among the novels of the 1840s in presenting readers with a problem of unity. Charles Kingsley's *Alton Locke* (1850) and *Yeast* (serialized in 1848, published as a volume in 1851) are notorious examples; another less well known example is William Sewell's *Hawkstone* (1845). In the epilogue to *Yeast*, Charles Kingsley anticipates the likely objections of his readers, suggesting that they "will probably complain of the fragmentary and unconnected form of the book." However, he adds, "Let them first be sure that that is not an integral feature of the subject itself, and therefore the very form the book should take" (336). A society changing as rapidly as England was in the 1840s offered unique difficulties for a novelist who sought to depict it comprehensively. A further reason that some of these novels, including *Shirley*, have confused their readers is that their analysis of social and political problems is often couched in religious terms, and they sometimes propose spiritual solutions to those problems. Thus, I will begin with a generic definition of the Victorian religious novel. Drawing on feminist readings of Brontë's novel and on Victorian cultural history and church history, I argue that *Shirley* can be read as a critique of the High Church ideology informing various novels of religious controversy. Insofar as it conforms to the genre, *Shirley* could be classified as a Broad Church novel. Its uniqueness consists in the fact that it examines the religious controversies of the 1840s from the perspective of a woman who, while loyal to the Church of England, harbours the questioning spirit so characteristic of the novel of doubt, a genre that also figures in my consideration of *Shirley*.

If we take the novel, as commonly defined, to be the literary form that provides a representation of characters in society, the "novel with a purpose" tends more towards either the anatomy or the confession, which in Northrop Frye's generic model of fiction are both more concerned with ideas than the novel proper (see *Criticism*, 303–14).[5] My own understanding of the properties of the novel of religious controversy is based in part on the work of the few literary historians who have studied it, and in part on my own inductive survey of a corpus of religious fiction mainly from the 1840s, with a few texts from the 1850s. This sample comprises eighteen novels, some reasonably well known and others very obscure. It is certainly not exhaustive, but I have taken some pains to make it representative.[6]

Religious fiction does not, of course, begin in the 1840s. Leaving aside the world of medieval religious romance, religious tales, often aimed at the literate poor, and edifying fiction for children flourished in the late eighteenth and early nineteenth centuries. Some of the most popular writers in these genres were Hannah More, Mary Martha Sherwood, and Legh Richmond.[7] The novel of religious controversy, however, adds a polemical purpose to the edifying intent of such works. It seeks to assert the claim of a particular party within the Church, and to refute the claims of another. As Margaret Maison notes, "it was the Oxford Movement which really launched the religious novel on a large scale" (*Eustace*, 3). Tractarian novelists, beginning with William Gresley and Francis Paget, and proceeding to the more talented Elizabeth·Missing Sewell and Charlotte Mary Yonge, used fiction to advance the aims of the Oxford Movement. Since these novelists saw a revitalized church as the key to dealing with a whole array of social problems, the Oxford Movement novelists have something in common with other writers concerned with the condition of England, such as Carlyle, Kingsley, or Charlotte Brontë. Other novelists soon took up the challenge, writing anti-Tractarian novels. At the same time, the "novel of doubt," beginning with Geraldine Jewsbury's *Zoe* (1845) and the more infamous *Nemesis of Faith* by J.A. Froude (1849), dramatized the loss of faith in orthodox Christianity and the quest for a new structure of belief. Such fiction owes a considerable debt to Romanticism, and the influence of George Sand is important.

The problematic curates at the beginning of *Shirley* who have puzzled many readers do have one clear literary function, even if it does not develop in the expected direction as the novel proceeds. As I have already noted, *Shirley* was published at the end of a decade of religious controversy that saw, among other things, the conclusion of the *Tracts for the Times*, Newman's conversion, Kingsley's Christian Socialist solution to the problems of the nation, and an outpouring of religious fiction.[8] By opening *Shirley* with the curates, Brontë led her readers to expect a religious novel, although their awareness that the author had also written *Jane Eyre*, as the title page announced, may have resulted in some confusion. The ironic manner with which Brontë's narrator treats practices and beliefs dear to the Oxford Movement makes it clear from the beginning that the novel is not a work of Tractarian fiction. The opening remarks on the "unromantic" nature of the narrator's fare have often figured in discussions of literary realism, but the precise metaphor Brontë uses is worth further consideration: "It is not positively affirmed that you shall not have a taste of the exciting, perhaps towards the middle and close of the meal, but it is resolved that the first dish set upon the table shall be one that a Catholic – ay, even an Anglo-Catholic – might eat on Good Friday in Passion Week: it shall be cold lentiles and vinegar without oil; it shall be unleavened bread with bitter herbs and no roast lamb" (*Shirley*, 7–8). The biblical references to the Passion are appropriate in a novel whose main characters all endure more or less serious illnesses or injuries, while the reference to the Passover meal typologically links England with Israel. Furthermore, the subtle criticism of Anglo-Catholics[9] suggests that *Shirley* will be critical of the Oxford Movement. This suggestion is reinforced by the overtly satirical tone of the next paragraph, in which the narrator identifies the date of the action as 1811–12:

> The present successors of the apostles, disciples of Dr Pusey and tools of the Propaganda, were at that time being hatched under cradle-blankets, or undergoing regeneration by nursery-baptism in wash-hand-basins. You could not have guessed by looking at any one of them that the Italian-ironed double frills of its net cap surrounded the brows of a preordained, specially sanctified successor of St Paul, St Peter, or St John; nor could you have foreseen in the folds of its long night-gown the white surplice in which it was hereafter cruelly to exercise the souls of its parishioners, and strangely to nonplus its old-fashioned vicar by flourishing aloft in a pulpit the shirt-like raiment which had never before waved higher than the reading-desk. (8)

Brontë told Mrs Gaskell in 1854 that Arthur Bell Nicholls, curate of her father, the Reverend Patrick Brontë (and her own future husband), "groaned a little" when he read the remark about "nursery-baptism" (Smith, ed., *Letters* 3:252).

In her useful study *The Brontës and Religion* (1999), Marianne Thor-mählen emphasizes what she considers the good-natured humour of the opening of *Shirley* and asserts that "the satirical edge is not directed against the parties in the ongoing Church controversy so much as against controversy itself" (195). However, aspects of *Shirley* that Thormählen does not discuss suggest that the novel engages in a more sustained way with Victorian ecclesiastical issues. Brontë clearly has her preferences when it comes to church parties and ecclesiastical conflict. A satirical tone is common in Victorian religious novels, suggesting their affinity to the genre Frye calls the anatomy. In *Loss and Gain*, for example, Newman describes a procession of people representing different Victorian religious beliefs calling one after another on his hero Charles Reding to dissuade him from converting to Roman Catholicism (Part 3, chapters 7–8). In *Hawkstone*, William Sewell creates in the villainous character Pearce a grotesquely evil Roman Catholic, who at the end of the novel is eaten alive by rats. Sewell claims in the preface that his novel invents nothing that does not have a counterpart in historical reality and further defends his satirical tone: "Falsehood and error at times can only be exposed by putting them strongly and directly in contrast with truth, and then the ridiculous necessarily and unavoidably follows" (*Hawkstone*, vii). Before writing *Shirley*, Charlotte Brontë had already contributed Mr Brocklehurst and his family as exemplars of Evangelicalism in *Jane Eyre*, while *Villette* contains much anti-Catholic satire, some of which, though not all, is the product of Lucy Snowe's paranoid consciousness. There is also the passage from the preface to *Jane Eyre*, quoted in the previous chapter, in which Brontë defends her work by invoking the example of Thackeray, the power of whose sarcastic words and satirical voice make him "the first social regenerator of the day" (xxx).

If the state of the English church were to be extrapolated from the behaviour of the three curates in the first chapter, the need for church reform would be very clear. They are socially condescending, although, or rather because, as Brontë is at pains to show, their own claims to gentility are shaky. Instead of visiting the poor they visit one another and engage in mean-spirited raillery. While the Oxford Movement had insisted, for theological reasons, on the dignity due to the clergy and the independence of the church from state control, Brontë implies that its tenets allowed self-important and unreflective young men to assert themselves unduly. The old-fashioned High Churchman Mr Helstone rebukes them by comparing them to Primitive Methodists: "Oh! settling the Dissenters – were you? Was Malone settling the Dissenters? It sounded to me much more like settling his co-apostles. You were quarrelling together; making almost as much noise – you three alone – as Moses Barraclough, the preaching tailor, and all his hearers, are making in the methodist chapel down yonder, where they are in the thick of a revival" (*Shirley*, 16–17).

This satire reflects Charlotte Brontë's own ecclesiastical views, as far as they can be documented from her letters. The underlying theme of her religious views is a dislike of extremes and of polemical religious parties. While living in Brussels, probably in July 1842, Brontë wrote to her friend Ellen Nussey, "I consider Methodism, Quakerism & the extremes of high & low Churchism foolish but Roman Catholicism beats them all" (Smith, ed., *Letters* 1:289–90). She had a low opinion of the three curates who lived in the vicinity of Haworth, and who obviously were the basis of the curates in *Shirley* (see Smith, ed., *Letters* 1:399 and 1:400n6). Brontë had a particular antipathy to the Anglo-Catholic doctrine of the priest-hood. According to Marion J. Phillips, she "embraced the priesthood of all believers and was receptive to forms of it which even excluded any kind of institution. She held advanced latitudinarian sympathies" ("Priest-hood," 153).[10] In fact, Brontë applied the word "latitudinarian" to herself on several occasions (see Smith, ed., *Letters* 3:152, 252). For Thormählen the term "Broad Church," which she associates with an indifference towards matters of doctrine, does not adequately describe Charlotte Brontë's religious views (*Brontës*, 42). Admittedly the term is somewhat vague, but Thormählen notes that Charlotte admired Thomas Arnold and that the Brontë sisters' approach to religion resembled that of F.D. Maurice (40, 47); both Arnold and Maurice are generally associated with the Broad Church position.[11]

While Brontë clearly thought for herself in religious matters, she nevertheless thought of herself as a loyal churchwoman. Referring to a favourable notice of *Jane Eyre*, she wrote in December 1847 to W.S. Williams of Smith, Elder: "The notice in 'the Church of England Journal' gratified me much, and chiefly because it *was* the *Church* of *England* Journal – Whatever such critics as He of the Mirror may say, I love the Church of England. Her Ministers, indeed I do not regard as infallible personages, I have seen too much of them for that – but to the Establish-ment, with all her faults – the profane Athanasian Creed *e*xcluded – I am sincerely attached" (Smith, ed., *Letters* 1:581). The Athanasian Creed was something of a touchstone in debates about doctrinal authority through-out the Victorian period.[12] Its controversial status, and Brontë's declaration that it was "profane," resulted from clauses condemning to eternal damna-tion those who do not keep the Catholic faith "whole and undefiled." It gradually fell into disuse in the Anglican church, unlike the other two historical creeds. In his "Note on Liberalism" appended to the *Apologia*, Newman's first example of liberal thinking is the idea that "no religious tenet is important, unless reason shows it to be so. Therefore, e.g., the doctrine of the Athanasian Creed is not to be insisted on, unless it tends to convert the soul" (260). In chapter 11 of *Shirley*, Mr Helstone catechises Shirley, mockingly suggesting that she may be a "Jacobin – for anything I know, a little free-thinker, in good earnest" (221). She recites the Apostle's Creed to him "like a child" but changes the subject when the Athanasian Creed is brought up. When Helstone urges, "You believe it all – don't you?" Shirley says only that she "can't remember it quite all" (222), antic-ipating her later doctrinal questioning.

An anti-Tractarian novel must have a hero who exemplifies the true apostolic Christianity, in contrast to the misguided exemplars of Catholic revivalism. In Brontë's novel this part is played by Cyril Hall. Unlike the three curates, he is an admirable clergyman, and he serves as a reminder of the need to temper industrialism with charity; for his treatment of the workman William Farren and his family is carefully contrasted with Robert Moore's initial lack of sympathy. However, Brontë does not altogether follow the typical pattern of the religious novel. Hall neither marries one of the young unattached women in the novel, nor guides them into an appropriately pious and Christian way of life, as the heroine's uncle does in Elizabeth Sewell's *Margaret Percival* (1847).

While Cyril Hall is contrasted with the curates, he himself has some affinities with the hero of a Tractarian novel. His piety, simple way of life, and association with single women are characteristics of the exemplary clerical characters of Elizabeth Sewell and Charlotte Yonge. Hall is happy with the celibate life he leads with his sister and does not discourage Caroline Helstone from living a similar life. The issue of celibacy is central to fiction of religious controversy. Charles Kingsley is famous for his attacks on the Catholic ideal of celibacy, both in his fiction and in the controversy with John Henry Newman that spurred Newman to write the *Apologia*.[13] Newman, on the other hand, satirizes the comfortable and unspiritual life of married Anglican clergy in *Loss and Gain*, making it of the reasons for his hero's conversion to Rome. To take one more example, Charles Maurice Davies's *Philip Paternoster: A Tractarian Love Story, By an Ex-Puseyite* (1858) is the satirical and sometimes very funny story of a fervent young Tractarian who eventually renounces his creed for a more sober Broad Church position, at which point he is rewarded with a charming young wife. In *Shirley*, Cyril Hall – whose parish is appropriately called Nunnely – asserts the value of the single life when he praises the unattractive spinster Miss Ainley for living closer to God than Caroline or Shirley:

> "Young ladies, when your mirror or men's tongues flatter you, remember that, in the sight of her Maker, Mary Anne Ainley – a woman whom neither glass nor lips have ever panegyrized – is fairer and better than either of you. She is indeed," he added, after a pause – "she is, indeed. You young things – wrapt up in yourselves and in earthly hopes – scarcely live as Christ lived: perhaps you cannot do it yet, while existence is so sweet and earth so smiling to you; it would be too much to

expect: she, with meek heart and due reverence, treads close in her
Redeemer's steps." (320)

Hall's strongly expressed views are undermined by Caroline's attempt
to live a life like Miss Ainley's, which nearly kills her. The novel makes
it clear that her romantic and erotic yearnings cannot be satisfied by
Christian faith alone. Mr Hall is a kindly man, but he is unable to help
Caroline with her deepest needs; nor is his kindness to an individual
workman adequate as a solution to the fundamental social and economic
problems created by industrial capitalism. Hall's inadequacy is partly
suggested by means of Brontë's attention to gender roles. His charity is
domestic and therefore feminized; he is always associated with his sister
and Miss Ainley, while the more energetic and assertive Mr Helstone
takes part in the defence of mill owners' property against the Luddites.
During the Whitsuntide celebrations, Mr Hall and his female admirers
are treated ironically, with another of Brontë's characteristic swipes at
Roman Catholicism: "The four ladies stood round their favourite pastor:
they also had an idea that they looked on the face of an earthly angel:
Cyril Hall was their pope, infallible to them as Dr Thomas Boultby to
his admirers" (336). Later that day, Caroline and Shirley watch a "war-
council" of mill owners (352) in which the combative Helstone and Malone take part. Like Caroline and Shirley, Mr Hall is excluded from the
council.

Caroline's longing results in part from a lack of nurturing care from
her uncle, who treats her with a mixture of condescension and neglect.
The narrator comments that although a clergyman, Helstone would have
been better suited to the military life (44), and he prefers women who
are frivolous and flirtatious – "he could not abide sense in women" (130).
Caroline is an intelligent woman in an atmosphere that allows her talents
no expression. As a woman, she cannot take the initiative in expressing
the love she feels for Moore, and she feels the burden of what George
Eliot described as "the gentlewoman's oppressive liberty" (*Middlemarch*,
272). This life of constrained freedom, of tedious purposelessness, is
punctuated by disappointments that Caroline is expected to be able to
disregard with equanimity. In one particularly powerful image, alluding
to a change in Robert Moore's demeanour that Caroline must pretend
not to notice, the narrator adapts a saying of Christ: "If a son shall ask
bread of any of you that is a father, will he give him a stone? Or if he ask

a fish, will he for a fish give him a serpent? Or if he shall ask an egg, will he offer him a scorpion?" (Luke 11:11–12). When it comes to a daughter, rather than a son, it is clear that parents, or God, or both, are not so generous:

> A lover masculine so disappointed can speak and urge explanation; a lover feminine can say nothing … You held out your hand for an egg, and fate put into it a scorpion. Show no consternation: close your fingers firmly upon the gift; let it sting through your palm. Never mind: in time, after your hand and arm have swelled and quivered long with torture, the squeezed scorpion will die, and you will have learned the great lesson how to endure without a sob. For the whole remnant of your life, if you survive the test – some, it is said, die under it – you will be stronger, wiser, less sensitive. (117–18)

However, the narrator disingenuously assures us, this passage was an irrelevant digression, "not germane to Caroline Helstone's feelings" (119). The narrator is thus split between an empathetic voice, speaking in what could be read as free indirect discourse, setting out in bleak terms the situation Caroline finds herself in, and a more detached voice that accepts all the constraints of Victorian womanhood and blames Caroline for any suffering that she endures. While Brontë strives for the impression of authoritative masculine objectivity that characterizes Thackeray's omniscient narrators, she subverts the voice thus created by identifying with Caroline's plight.[14]

A similar ambivalence can be seen in the novel's political sympathies, a point made by Albany Fonblanque, whose review of *Shirley* Charlotte Brontë valued. Fonblanque noted that the novel seems to acquiesce in the political changes that are taking place in England; at the same time, however, "there is a hankering, not to be suppressed, after the fleshpots of England – a strong sympathy with Toryism and High Church. The writer sees that these are things of the past, but cannot help regretting them" (Review, 129). Brontë's treatment of Cyril Hall provides a clear example of what Fonblanque is talking about. On the one hand, he is an exemplary clergyman whose treatment of the poor is held up for our admiration; on the other hand, Brontë does not generalize from Hall and endorse the politics of nostalgia of the Young England movement and the extreme Tractarian novel. Unlike Charles Kingsley with his

Christian socialism, Brontë offers no prescription for the condition of England. Linking old maids with "the houseless and unemployed poor," Caroline Helstone reflects "that to such grievances as society cannot readily cure, it usually forbids utterance, on pain of its scorn" (Shirley, 441). Shirley does give utterance to such grievances, but it shares society's inability to recommend a cure.

At the end of the passage containing the scorpion allusion, Caroline asks herself, sitting alone after dinner, "How am I to get through this day?" (120). This question, applied to all days and all women, is part of Brontë's treatment of what Victorians called the woman question. Those who posed such a question (if a man it would typically arise after a loss of faith) were usually exhorted to do the duty that lay nearest them. This is the solution that Carlyle offered in Sartor Resartus; to some extent it was also recommended by George Eliot in Middlemarch and Daniel Deronda, though in a heavily qualified manner. For a single middle-class woman, doing one's duty normally involved some sort of charitable work or other form of self-giving, and in some cases it found expression in the life of a religious community. In his book Parochial Work (1850), Edward Monro refers to women "who want a work to employ wasted energies, to give them a recognised place in social and active life, and to find objects on which to bestow strong sympathies and yearnings, which otherwise would have no special channel for exhaustion" (cited in Heeney, Movement, 19–20).[15] Parochial philanthropic work was recommended, and the church made good use of the energy of unfulfilled women. Religious novels of all parties were fond of contrasting the lives of pious women, visiting the sick and poor and supporting the work of the Church, with those dominated by social pleasures and the love of material possessions – a juxtaposition that was fundamental to the fiction of Charlotte Yonge. More sceptically, Shirley questions the extent to which a life of religious service can fulfil the aspirations of a young woman.

Apart from the affinities she draws between Cyril Hall and Tractarian heroes, Brontë employs another technique dear to the Tractarian novelist when Shirley and Caroline discuss Nunwood, a wood in the heart of which lie "the ruins of a nunnery" (Shirley, 238). Tractarians often moralized about such ruins and sometimes combined their moralizing with the recommendation that religious orders be revived. In the preface to his novel Ayton Priory, or the Restored Monastery (1843), J.M. Neale, the distinguished translator of liturgical texts, wrote: "There is perhaps

hardly any subject which has recently occupied a larger share of Churchmen, than the possibility and expediency of a revival of the Monastick
System ...The following tale is intended, as well to set forth the advantages,
and all but necessity, of the re-introduction of monasteries, as to suggest
certain practical details connected with their establishment and subsequent working" (iii). Neale would himself play a prominent role in the
revival of sisterhoods.

The Romantic movement, with its interest in things medieval, can be
credited with some of the inspiration for the restoration of religious communities in England. In 1829 Robert Southey made an explicit and influential plea for religious orders.[16] Among many literary treatments of
the subject, Thomas Carlyle's *Past and Present* (1843) contrasted the meaningful and organized life of a medieval religious community with the
social fragmentation of life in Victorian England. Against this background,
the first Anglican religious community since the Reformation, the sisterhood of the Holy Cross, was founded in London in 1845. Such communities were extremely controversial, in part because they were similar
to Roman Catholic institutions, in part because they allowed women to
leave home and act independently.[17] The climax of opposition was the
Lewes Riot of 1857, which resulted from the death one Sister Amy, a member of the East Grinstead community founded by J.M. Neale.[18] Accusations
were made that the deceased was the victim of a plot to gain her money.
As A.M. Allchin notes, the riot demonstrated "the panic fears and suspi-
cions which existed just beneath the surface of the public mind. Any
rumour, however unlikely, was enough to awaken powerful and unpredictable feelings, and to jeopardize the life and work of these small and
unknown societies" (*Rebellion*, 98).

Victorian anxieties about and fascination with nuns are amply evident
in visual art and literature. In *Jane Eyre*, St John Rivers presents Jane with
a copy of Sir Walter Scott's *Marmion* (1808), a poem in which a nun is
buried alive, while the ghostly apparition of a nun features prominently
in *Villette*. Appealing to powerful anti-Roman Catholic sentiment in England, the Gothic tradition frequently linked members of religious orders
with sexual intrigue and violence. Susan P. Casteras has documented the
manner in which early Victorian artists portrayed nuns, reinforcing a
mixture of attitudes, "partly sensational, partly sentimental" ("Vows,"
157).[19]

In *Shirley*, Brontë treats the idea of a dedicated religious life for a woman with scepticism. It is significant that Caroline's mother has taken the name "Mrs Pryor," linking her role as Shirley's governess to a life of religious supervision. Mrs Pryor's touchstones are submission to authorities and deference to betters (425); while she is in some ways an admirable character, she is guilty of the weakness and cowardice that allowed her to reject her daughter years earlier. It is clear that Brontë felt revulsion for the life of a nun; it was unnatural, as her treatment of the "old maids" in the novel implies. After all, nuns voluntarily embraced a life closely resembling that which Charlotte Brontë endured, against her own strongest aspirations and desires, for too long, a life of isolation, submission, and celibacy. Two of the "old maids" in *Shirley*, Miss Ainley and Miss Hall, are treated more sympathetically than Mrs Pryor, but Caroline's attempts to emulate them do not satisfy her: "Does virtue lie in abnegation of self? I do not believe it. Undue humility makes tyranny; weak concession creates selfishness. The Romish religion especially teaches renunciation of self, submission to others, and nowhere are found so many grasping tyrants as in the ranks of the Romish priesthood" (194).

In her study *Independent Women: Work and Communities for Single Women 1850–1920* (1985), Martha Vicinus notes that "if the prostitute symbolized the extremes of unbridled passion and evil in woman, the spinster had thrust upon her absolute purity and goodness. She was supposed to remain virginal and utterly self-sacrificing for all who needed her. Single women transformed this passive role into one of active spirituality and passionate social service" (5). The assumption of the spiritual superiority of single women found its fullest expression in the Tractarian revival of sisterhoods, but Vicinus shows that it was shared by virtually all Christian denominations in Victorian England.[20] In *Shirley*, Brontë questions the spiritual value of female renunciation. Caroline's religious endeavours bring her little joy, and the conclusion of the chapter "Old Maids" represents her mental state through imagery of death and winter. The imagery of nature in *Shirley* is generally more powerful than that drawn from Christian devotion, and the following passage suggests that Caroline may have been doomed to an early death from lack of love: "An elegy over the past still rung constantly in her ear; a funereal inward cry haunted and harassed her: the heaviness of a broken spirit, and of pining and palsying faculties, settled slow on her buoyant youth. Winter seemed conquering her spring: the mind's soil and its treasures were freezing gradually to barren stagnation" (206).

Later in the novel, Caroline explicitly rejects the Tractarian model of female life. Thinking again of Miss Ainley, she compares the spinster's little cottage to a nun's cell and thereby to a grave; Miss Ainley, she concludes, "says, often, she has no fear of death – no dread of the grave: no more, doubtless, had St Simeon Stylites, lifted up terrible on his wild column in the wilderness: no more has the Hindoo votary stretched on his couch of iron spikes. Both these having violated nature, their natural likings and antipathies are reversed: they grow altogether morbid … God surely did not create us, and cause us to live, with the sole end of wishing always to die" (441). This passage, like Charles Kingsley's attacks on celibate religious life or Tennyson's poem "St Simeon Stylites," stresses again that such lives are "unnatural" and implies that Christian life should be lived in accordance with nature, a conclusion that would surprise many of the Church's teachers through the ages. The word "unnatural," however, has a specific resonance in the context of anti-Catholic discourse, as Diana Peschier notes (*Discourses*, 71). Protestant polemic held that convents were unnatural because they provided a context in which women could reject marriage and live in community, under the supervision of celibate men, a situation that gave rise to much prurient imagining.

Novels of religious controversy seek to prove the truth of a particular understanding of Christianity at the expense of others. Fraternizing with dissenters leads characters into trouble in the novels of William Sewell and Charlotte Mary Yonge, while Roman Catholics are treated harshly by many Anglican novelists. Newman castigates liberals, evangelicals, and Anglo-Catholics in *Loss and Gain*, while Ann Howard and Charles Davies emphasize the dangers of the Oxford Movement. In *Shirley*, Brontë parodies these controversies. Her curates "settle the dissenters" by having a noisy dinner-party, while in the mock-heroic climax of the novel (coming on the afternoon before the attack on Moore's mill) conflict arises between the Anglican and dissenting Sunday schools as they march for superiority in a country lane.[21] Kate Lawson suggests that *Shirley* "may be considered, on one level, as [Brontë's] examination of the relationship of Dissent to orthodoxy" ("Voice," 729). Brontë does not question the Church of England's superiority to nonconformity; instead, there is another, more subversive, form of dissent in the novel, a "feminist dissent which undermines the conservative orthodoxy of the narrative's surface endorsement of the established church" (730). Similarly, Sally Greene, focusing on Brontë's use of romantic hermeneutics, finds in *Shirley* a utopian and feminist mode of biblical interpretation. I agree with these arguments, with the additional suggestion that the feminist hermeneutics identified by Lawson and Greene may be linked to *Shirley*'s affinities with the novel of doubt, which frequently opposed the spiritual influence of nature to the institutional church.

It is important to ask of any religious novel what its true source of revelation or authority is. In *Shirley* the curates and Mr Helstone serve a church that seems largely an arm of the state, not, as the Oxford Movement presented it, as something mysterious and poetic. Supernatural visions are vouchsafed to Michael Hartley, the Antinomian weaver who is variously described as a "violent Jacobin and leveller" (20) and a "mad Calvinist and Jacobin" (266), and who stands at the opposite social pole to the defenders of the Establishment. Mystical insight is thus seen as a form of insanity. The authority of the Bible is equally problematic. When Caroline and Shirley debate with Joe Scott about the authority of the biblical injunctions concerning the place of women in 1 Timothy 2, we see Brontë's awareness of the issues involved in biblical criticism. Scott asks for Caroline's reading "o' them words o' St Paul's." She replies:

> "Hem! I – I account for them in this way: he wrote that chapter for a particular congregation of Christians, under peculiar circumstances; and besides, I dare say, if I could read the original Greek, I should find that many of the words have been wrongly translated, perhaps misapprehended altogether. It would be possible, I doubt not, with a little ingenuity, to give the passage quite a contrary turn; to make it say, 'Let the woman speak out whenever she sees fit to make an objection;' – 'it is permitted to a woman to teach and to exercise authority as much as may be. Man, meantime, cannot do better than hold his peace,' and so on." (371)

Brontë's use of parody extends beyond the doctrines of the Oxford Movement to the sacred text of Scripture when she names the disreputable leaders of the workers Noah and Moses. Clearly the Bible is not a reliable guide for a young woman's life, at least not as it is interpreted by men.

Shirley can be analyzed in terms of a conflict, a dialogue at any rate, between Christian belief and Romantic sensibility; Christianity leads Caroline to a bleak sense of the absence of God, or to the absence of

God's grace, prefigured earlier in the novel when she recites Cowper's poem "The Castaway" to Shirley. After the battle at Hollow's-mill, the narrator comments:

> Caroline was a Christian; therefore in trouble she framed many a prayer after the Christian creed; preferred it with deep earnestness; begged for patience, strength, relief. This world, however, we all know, is the scene of trial and probation; and, for any favourable result her petitions had yet wrought, it seemed to her that they were unheard and unaccepted. She believed, sometimes, that God had turned his face from her. At moments she was a Calvinist, and sinking into the gulf of religious despair, she saw darkening over her the doom of reprobation. (394)

The narrator shortly after this offers the consolation that God will never desert those who cling to Him, but Caroline is redeemed by human love, not Christian faith. Her life is saved by the revelation of her mother's identity and her mother's care; at the end of the novel she fulfills her romantic aspiration and marries Robert Moore.

The only real source of *religious* feeling presented directly in *Shirley* is Nature. The opening of the second chapter describes at length the natural phenomena to which Peter Malone is oblivious as he walks along the road to Moore's mill. Unlike Brontë's more sympathetic characters, Malone cannot read the Book of Nature, that Wordsworthian construct described by John Keble in explicitly Christian terms as:

> a book, who runs may read,
>   Which heavenly truth imparts,
> And all the lore its scholars need,
>   Pure eyes and Christian hearts.[22]

Midway through *Shirley* there is a key passage in which Caroline and Shirley are communing with nature, shortly after the victorious "battle" with the dissenters. Everybody else is in church, listening to the clergy defend the Establishment and oppose schism. Shirley observes that "Nature is now at her evening prayers" (358), and she persuades Caroline to remain outside the church and join her in this heterodox Romantic version of vespers. Instead of listening to the local clergy, Shirley preaches her own heretical sermon about Eve, boldly rewriting the scriptural account using the language of the Romantic imagination.[23] To Shirley, Eve is the mother of Titans, the source of the boldness that led Prometheus to challenge Omnipotence. Eve is a "heaven-born" woman (360), the ultimate source not just of Prometheus but of the Messiah as well, so that in Shirley's account Eve and Mary are fused into one in what Caroline refers to as "a hash of Scripture and mythology" (360). Reminded that this no more resembles Milton's Eve than it does the biblical figure, Shirley says to Caroline, "Milton was great; but was he good? ... Milton tried to see the first woman; but, Cary, he saw her not" (359). Shirley's visionary Eve is described in terms of the landscape from which she seems to emerge and is finally identified with Nature herself. Shirley tells Caroline that she will not go into the church: "I will stay out here with my mother Eve, in these days called Nature. I love her – undying, mighty being! Heaven may have faded from her brow when she fell in paradise; but all that is glorious on earth shines there still. She is taking me to her bosom, and showing me her heart" (361). To Caroline, however, the word "mother" suggests not the visionary mother of the human race or the Mother of God, "not the mighty and mystical parent of Shirley's visions, but a gentle human form – the form she ascribed to her own mother" (361–2). That is, for Caroline, domestic love is the product of nature's influence in a manner that might be described as Wordsworthian in contrast to the Shelleyan or Blakean mode of Shirley's visions. We see this again when Caroline recovers from her serious illness through the combined influences of her mother's love and a healthy turn in the weather: "Caroline's youth could now be of some avail to her, and so could her mother's nurture: both – crowned by God's blessing, sent in the pure west wind blowing soft as fresh through the ever-open chamber lattice – rekindled her long-languishing energies" (500).

In her challenge to the Tory and High Church view that the truth is to be found in submission, resignation, and obedience to the teaching of the Church, Brontë follows novelists like George Sand as well as the Romantic poets.[24] She separates Nature's message from the teaching of the Church, particularly that concerning gender roles, and also imaginatively reinterprets Scripture to support her views. Margaret Kirkham has helpfully elucidated the connections between *Shirley* and Romantic feminism, and the novel's rewriting of the "myth of Corinne." The same points can be made with reference to Brontë's treatment of religion. While

Brontë partly supports the Church in her portrayal of Cyril Hall, *Shirley* also has affinities, as noted earlier, with the novel of doubt. In both Jewsbury's *Zoe* (which interestingly is the name of Shirley's horse) and the fiction of J.A. Froude, Nature is a comforter and source of religious inspiration when the hero loses his faith in the doctrines taught by the Church. In the more extreme moments of despair endured by Caroline, Brontë's novel resembles that novel of religious questioning most shocking to the Victorians, George Sand's *Lélia* (1833).

Brontë is not usually read in terms of the Victorian narrative of spiritual crisis, but Ruth Y. Jenkins persuasively argues that this is because the received models of such narratives have neglected the female perspective. Jenkins suggests that as a result, "scholars have misconstrued the full scope of Victorian spirituality" (*Myths*, 19). If we read *Shirley* as a religious novel, Caroline's story emerges as an embedded narrative of spiritual crisis. Brontë critiques the conservative politics of the High Church novel and the sacerdotal claims of Tractarians and Roman Catholics alike. Reading Caroline's story as a spiritual biography, we can see that the Church fails her when Nature and human affection do not. In relation to both the class conflicts of the day and the issues facing a middle-class young woman, the Church of England is seen as inadequate, though Brontë does not abandon her faith in it as an institution.

The Tractarian novel advanced solutions to both the national political questions and to the "woman question." Class conflict was to be dealt with by a restored church, that would distribute charitable relief, counsel submission to workers, and impress on employers a sense of their moral obligations. The gender issue was addressed by providing a channel for the aspirations and ideals of intelligent and idealistic young women. In *Shirley*, Charlotte Brontë shows that the politics of class conflict are controlled by economic forces beyond the control of a revived feudalism. Similarly, the aspirations of her young heroines are better expressed in the language of Romantic poetry than in the language of the Church. Among Caroline's most fervent moments are her recitations of André Chénier's "La Jeune captive" and William Cowper's "The Castaway."

Shirley cannot be seen as an attack on the Church root and branch; the portrayal of Cyril Hall alone prevents such a reading. The chapter entitled "Whitsuntide" precedes the mock-epic confrontation of the Anglican and dissenting parades, and it concludes with the following piece of narratorial commentary: "It was a joyous scene, and a scene to do good: it was a day of happiness for rich and poor; the work, first, of God, and then of the clergy. Let England's priests have their due: they are a faulty set in some respects, being only of common flesh and blood, like us all; but the land would be badly off without them: Britain would miss her church, if that church fell. God save it! God also reform it!" (337–8). As I have already suggested, Cyril Hall is neither a suitable marital partner for Caroline nor a spiritual director who can resolve her troubled soul. She finds resolution only when she marries the man she wants; but the ending of *Shirley* is not optimistic. Caroline reforms Robert Moore to the extent that he now has more concern for his workers, but she is only able to do this because the peace, with its resultant prosperity, allows him the luxury of humanity. Professions for women are beyond the vision of the novel, even though it adumbrates the need for them; still further beyond the vision of the novel is the notion of professions for women in the Church, something that did not arrive in the Church of England until the 1990s. The Church, as the narrator acknowledges, is in need of reform; but unlike the typical Tractarian novel, *Shirley* makes no suggestion that the solution to the problems of industrial England lies in a reformed and regenerated church. Perhaps the utopian views that can be intuited at points in the novel were so utopian that Brontë herself was hardly able to contemplate them; after all, the kind of "broad-church feminism" that the novel hints at remained untenable for nearly a hundred and fifty years after *Shirley* was published.

Finally, in terms of locating a spiritual presence in nature, especially for Caroline and Shirley, the conclusion is again pessimistic.[25] The very prosperity that ensures a truce in the struggle between worker and mill owner replaces the picturesque scenery of the Hollow with an industrial landscape. In the final paragraphs, which are a kind of epilogue, the narrator becomes a character visiting the scene of the story that has just been told, "and there I saw the manufacturer's day-dreams embodied in substantial stone and brick and ashes – the cinder-black highway, the cottages, and the cottage-gardens; there I saw a mighty mill, and a chimney, ambitious as the tower of Babel" (739). Perhaps Brontë's suggestion is that patriarchal authority has passed – as Thomas Carlyle might have wished – from church to industry.[26] She makes no comment on this transition, beyond the implications of further discord in her biblical allusion, which in turn implies the continuing relevance of the metanarrative of the Christian church in this landscape.

THREE

"GLEAMS FROM A BRIGHTER WORLD": CHARLOTTE MARY YONGE'S TRACTARIAN POETICS

Reserve, reverent reserve, was ever a characteristic of the teaching of the school of divines of which the "Christian Year" was the first utterance. Charlotte Mary Yonge,
Musings over the "Christian Year"

————◀◯▶————

FROM THE TIME SHE BECAME A FAMOUS NOVELIST with the publication of *The Heir of Redclyffe* (1853), Charlotte Mary Yonge provoked strong and widely divergent responses among her readers. She spent her long literary career, which largely coincided with the reign of Queen Victoria, promulgating the ideals and values of the Oxford Movement in a vast number of novels, children's stories, articles, pamphlets, and expository books.[1] Unlike many of the other religious novelists of the nineteenth century, Yonge appealed to a broad spectrum of the reading public, and her best books were taken seriously by readers such as Charles Kingsley, Alfred Tennyson, and George Eliot.[2] Her historical importance is generally recognized, but her critical standing early in the twenty-first century is far from clear. She does not receive a great deal of critical attention, few of her works are in print, and they do not often appear on undergraduate reading lists.[3] She has attracted some attention from feminist scholars and historians of domestic and religious fiction, though given her status as one of the best-known Victorian women of letters, it is surprising that she has not attracted more. It could be that the sheer volume of her output is daunting, especially for those who find themselves ideologically at odds with much of what it has to say. Yonge's social, political, and religious values are not congenial to the postmodern era, and she remains provocative. One could say of her entire oeuvre what Lionel Trilling famously said of Jane Austen's *Mansfield Park*: "There is scarcely one of our modern pieties that it does not offend" ("Jane Austen," 115).

Whatever one thinks of Yonge, it cannot be denied that her work has greater literary value than most Victorian novels of religious controversy. Her novels are solidly crafted, and, as Walter Allen has observed, they display considerable skill in creating characters (*English Novel*, 199). The reception of Yonge's fiction, as I will show, poses an interesting example of the interaction of ideological and literary judgments.

There are a number of reasons why I focus on *The Heir of Redclyffe* in this chapter. The popularity of the book established Yonge as an important Victorian literary figure; and while her most devoted admirers often prefer her lengthy family chronicles, notably *The Daisy Chain*, the simpler outline and strong romantic elements in *The Heir* give it a kind of mythical quality that makes it stand out from her other works. It combines romance and domestic realism, at the same time making fascinating use of Keble's Tractarian teaching. In effect, Yonge reconfigures medieval chivalry for the Victorian domestic world, a task that Tennyson undertook in verse in the *Idylls of the King*, and that the Pre-Raphaelites realized in the visual arts.

When *The Heir of Redclyffe* appeared in 1853, the twenty-nine-year-old Charlotte Yonge had published a number of works, but, in Kathleen Tillotson's words, *The Heir* "was a new departure for her, both in kind and in popular response. With it, she stepped beyond her little public of Sunday-school teachers, to Mr Mudie's subscribers – to share the season's success with *Villette* and [Elizabeth Gaskell's] *Ruth*" ("*The Heir*," 49). Elizabeth Wordsworth, later a friend of Charlotte Yonge's, noted that "*The Heir of Redclyffe* won instant popularity, not only with girls in the schoolroom, but with grown men, scholars, artists, and men of the world" (quoted in Cruse, *Victorians*, 50). Those who were hostile to the Oxford Movement were as negative in their responses as other readers were positive. Wilkie Collins, writing in Charles Dickens's weekly *Household Words* in 1858, mocks the response of a female reader:

A young and charming lady, previously an excellent customer at the circulating libraries, read this fatal domestic novel on its first appearance some years ago, and has read nothing else ever since. As soon as she gets to the end of the book, this interesting and unfortunate creature turns back to the first page, and begins it again … Her course of proceeding, when she comes to the pathetic passages, has never yet varied on any single occasion. She reads for five minutes, and goes up-stairs to fetch a dry pocket handkerchief; comes down again, and reads for another five minutes; goes up-stairs again, and fetches another dry pocket handkerchief. ("Doctor," 622)[4]

The ideological basis of this objection becomes clear when Collins writes, "Throughout the book, up to the scene of his last illness, Sir Guy is the same lifeless personification of the Pusey-stricken writer's fancies on religion and morals, literature and art" (624). It is interesting to note that, early on in *The Heir of Redclyffe*, the two Edmonstone sisters are contrasted by means of their reactions to the death of Paul Dombey in Dickens's *Dombey and Son* (1848); Amy is found weeping in the greenhouse, while Laura – although she didn't laugh as Oscar Wilde did at the death of Little Nell – remains "stony hearted," not knowing whether Paul lived or died (30).

Henry James was a perhaps surprising admirer of Charlotte Yonge, praising her biography of Bishop John Coleridge Patteson, and in spite of his somewhat disparaging view of the genre, he commends her ability to write the type of edifying literature suitable for family reading: "It would be unjust to deny that these semi-developed novels are often very charming. Occasionally, like the 'Heir of Redclyffe,' they almost legitimate themselves by the force of genius. But this only when a first-rate mind takes the matter in hand" (*Essays*, 826). Richard Holt Hutton, on the other hand, raised questions about the relationship between fiction and dogma that go to the heart of any attempt to deal critically with fiction that has a particular religious or political purpose. Hutton was a great admirer of George Eliot, regarding her as the novelist who best exemplified his own poetics of fiction.[5] He discussed a number of Yonge's works in an essay for *The National Review* in 1861. While he regarded what he called "Ethical Fiction" as superior to the realism of Thackeray and Trollope ("the brilliant daguerreotypes of superficial life alternating with heathen passion"), Hutton said of Charlotte Yonge that "the free play of her moral idealism is only permitted within the limits marked out by certain dogmatic rules" ("Ethical," 211, 214). Thus she had an excessive respect for "the hierarchical order of society" in which she had been brought up

(216), and "no Catholic of the middle ages could ignore more loftily than she the existence of any true moral life external to the Church" (217). Hutton implied that Yonge was unwilling to test the limits of dogmatic social and moral teachings, and that she confused orthodox Christian faith with adherence to certain values of her own time and class. The author's condemnation of the secret engagement between Philip and Laura was, he wrote, "extravagant beyond measure" (215). There is a grey area where Christian truth shades into social conventions, and Hutton's emphasis on the speculative faculty and the "free play" of moral idealism suggests that in his view it was the ethical novelist's task to explore this grey area.

A few years earlier, writing about three of Yonge's works for the *Prospective Review*, Hutton praised her ability to create male characters ("The Author," 462–3) and contrasted *The Heir of Redclyffe* with *Heartsease; or, The Brother's Life* (1854), which had just been published. Hutton found *Heartsease* "decidedly inferior in *interest*" to *The Heir* thanks to its deficient narrative element (463). This comparison hints at the quality that makes *The Heir* so successful, the way that it embodies its religious theme in a compelling romance structure, blending the archetypal shape of the gospel story with a Gothic melodrama. Sometimes this is concealed beneath a surface of domestic realism, while at other times, as in the narration of Guy's heroic sea rescue, the work reads as pure romance. As Northrop Frye repeatedly emphasized, the Christian scriptures as a whole have the structure of romance; in view of Yonge's overtly Tractarian objectives, *The Heir* may be read as a theological romance,[6] a term I have coined by analogy with the Enlightenment genre of the "philosophical romance."

Yonge's popularity declined in the latter part of her life. She was still read, but mainly in Anglican girls' schools, if anecdotal evidence is to be believed.[7] By the twentieth century she was regarded as a minor writer, historically noteworthy but with a very limited appeal. Walter Allen's 1954 history of the English novel gives a judicious mid-century summary that probably represents the consensus of those critics who did not have strong feelings one way or another about her religious views: "Every age has its novelist who sets down a portrait of the age as it would like to see itself. Miss Yonge, with her High Anglican piety, did this for the Victorians, depicting idealized family life in numerous novels. Books like *The Daisy Chain*, *The Heir of Redclyffe*, and *Heartsease* remain interesting as revelations of the mid-century's notion of itself" (*English Novel*, 199).

The impetus of the Oxford Movement persisted well into the twentieth

century, and there was a parallel and related Roman Catholic revival referred to by John Henry Newman as "The Second Spring" in a famous
sermon of that title.[8] The Catholic revival had a considerable literary influence during the first half of the twentieth century and attracted many
converts in the literary world, T.S. Eliot and Evelyn Waugh being two of
the best known. As a result Charlotte Yonge's work found new readers
and apologists. Georgina Battiscombe (1943) and Margaret Mare and
Alice Percival (1947) produced biographical and critical studies that while
useful, are more labours of love than examples of scholarly and critical
rigour. The Anglo-Catholic church historian Owen Chadwick, in his classic history *The Victorian Church*, is speaking from within the tradition
of positive Christian response to Yonge when he writes that "*The Heir of
Redclyffe* ... did as much for the moral idealism of the educated classes
as any book of the reign ... As one of the true creative novelists of the
nineteenth century, with two or three of her books ranking among the
best Christian novels of any age, she was in one respect a channel for the
most powerful influence which shy and reserved John Keble exercised
upon the Victorian churches" (2:215). While Chadwick's comment leaves
unanswered the question what a Christian novel really is, he praises Yonge
as highly as any of her prominent readers.

Opposing Chadwick's sympathetic view is the critic Q.D. Leavis. In
the spring issue of *Scrutiny*, 1944, Leavis reviewed various books that had
emerged from the Catholic revival, including Georgina Battiscombe's
biography. She polemically attacked Christian critics for their confusion
of ideology with literary merit, while pillorying Yonge for her "anti-Life"
ideology ("Charlotte Yonge," 236). Unlike "the fanatic Bunyan or the spin-
sters Miss Austen and Miss Edgeworth," Charlotte Yonge lacked "any
sympathy for and even recognition of the natural sources of healthy life"
(235). In spite of the vituperative tone that characterized *Scrutiny* at its
least attractive, Leavis is making a case that needs to be answered; for,
like Hutton but more insistently, she forces her reader to confront the
question of the relationship between ideology and art, and specifically
the question of the possibility of Christian art. The religious critic is often
caught between an aesthetic judgment and an evaluation of the doctrinal
orthodoxy of a particular work. Leavis's opinion seems to be that religious
critics are acceptable as long as they are totally indistinguishable from
any other kind of critic, and she challenges readers to identify which of
Scrutiny's regular contributors are Roman Catholic (341n1). With hind-
sight, one can say that Leavis is in the powerful grip of an ideology whose

principal prophet is D.H. Lawrence. The assumption throughout the essay is that the able-bodied and sexually active are superior to the disabled and celibate: Leavis's ideology might be said to be a mirror-image of Yonge's. To point this out, however, is not to answer the case that Leavis argues, which is that for Yonge the Church was a "substitute for living" rather than "an illumination of life" (236) and that her fiction consists of simplistic Sunday school tales rather than a genuine response to life's complexity. I will return to these questions later in the chapter, since they are aspects of the more fundamental question about the nature of fiction and the relationship between literature and religion.

While Yonge has not figured prominently in feminist criticism, there has been considerable interest in her novel *The Clever Woman of the Family* (1865), which was Yonge's most overt fictional treatment of the "woman question."[9] In general, however, Yonge's work does not challenge the established structures of Victorian society or the traditional gender roles of the middle-class family; rather, it venerates them to such a degree that even mainstream Victorian critics like R.H. Hutton took her to task. She retained the Tory and feudal social attitudes and the theological certainties of the first generation of the Oxford Movement, even though she lived until the turn of the century, when Anglo-Catholicism had started to absorb both biblical criticism and Christian socialism. This was reflected in the thought of Charles Gore (1853–1932), editor of the collection of essays *Lux Mundi* (1889), which, to the dismay of some older members of the movement, marked the accommodation of Anglo-Catholicism with certain liberal principles.[10] In *Reasons Why I Am a Catholic and Not a Roman Catholic* (1901), a work she did not live to complete, Yonge describes her Catholic understanding of the Anglican church in such a manner that she could have been writing fifty years earlier or more. There is no hint of the increasing sympathy for specifically Roman Catholic beliefs and practices that had developed among many Anglo-Catholics by the end of the nineteenth century.

In *A Literature of Their Own* (1977), one of the most influential works of feminist scholarship, Elaine Showalter discusses Yonge in a rather cursory manner. She largely ignores the Christian argument of *The Heir of Redclyffe*, viewing Guy's death as an act of passive aggression that enables him to punish Philip in the most effective way (*Literature*, 138). Additionally, she confidently asserts that Yonge, like her fellow Tractarian novelists Felicia Skene and Elizabeth Missing Sewell, wanted to be a clergyman (144). Yonge certainly spent her life serving the Church of England, whether through her writing, or her financial support of missionary work, or her Sunday school teaching, but she would no more have wanted to be a clergyman than a soldier. She admired both professions greatly but regarded them as male prerogatives.

The most scholarly feminist analysis of Yonge is Catherine Sandbach-Dahlström's *Be Good Sweet Maid: Charlotte Yonge's Domestic Fiction* (1984). This monograph stresses the interplay of different literary genres in Yonge's fiction, notably between romance and domestic realism, and argues that "a fruitful dramatic tension exists in Charlotte Yonge's novels between the representation of the 'fallen' world's sense of an empirical reality that obeys its own human laws and the implied author's belief in a world ruled by an immanent Divine Spirit" (21). Sandbach-Dahlström stresses the importance of understanding Yonge's dogmatic beliefs in order to understand her fiction, and she admits that any dissonance between the realistic genre and the dogmatic purpose is likely to be the product of the modern critic's inability to accept Yonge's own beliefs. However, she reads several of the novels in a way that uncovers "evidence for a muted protest in the careers of the rebellious or erring heroines" (172). A similar approach is taken by June Sturrock, who surveys Yonge's work along with a wide range of contextual materials. Sturrock finds that, while Yonge was by no means a feminist, her fiction reflects concerns similar to those of the Victorian women's movement from the 1850s to the 1870s, particularly on the issues of educational reform, women's work, and women's political and legal status. Like Sandbach-Dahlström, Sturrock finds a "muted protest" in Yonge's work. *The Clever Woman of the Family*, for example, "celebrates the domestic and religious lives of women; but it also explores and vindicates a fierce and frustrated yearning for useful work" ("*Heaven*," 48).

These studies, Sturrock's in particular, have shown how Yonge's fiction is crucially involved not only in the religious politics of her time but in its sexual politics. Other analyses of Yonge's fiction focus on the theological influence of the Oxford Movement; still others approach Yonge from the perspectives of literary theory and Victorian studies. The books by Joseph Baker and Raymond Chapman, however, are now rather dated in terms of their critical approach. Elliot Engel's article on *The Heir of Redclyffe* emphasizes its Tractarian connections but takes a narrow approach, concentrating on a very few aspects of the topic. Gavin Budge's more recent article is insightful but primarily concerned with the philosophical background, and with making an argument about the theory of realism in

twentieth-century literary criticism. Barbara Dennis's book *Charlotte
Yonge (1823–1901): Novelist of the Oxford Movement* (1992) promises "a
fresh appraisal of Charlotte Yonge as the novelist of the Oxford Movement" (5). Dennis has unearthed some interesting new evidence based
on unpublished letters, and she has numerous valuable observations, but
the book lacks an overall argument, and its value is anecdotal. It does
not offer a coherent appraisal of Yonge as a Tractarian novelist.[11] The following discussion of *The Heir* seeks to synthesize these various discussions
of Yonge's fiction, in order to show how *The Heir* is in fact the exemplary
novel of the Oxford Movement.

-◄◦►-

Yonge's connection with John Keble and Tractarianism is well known.
Indeed, her book *Musings over the "Christian Year"* (1872) and her history
John Keble's Parishes (1898) are important sources of information about
Keble's parish ministry. At the beginning of *Musings* Yonge describes
Keble's arrival in the parish: "I was twelve or thirteen years old at the
time of his appointment to Hursley Vicarage, and had begun to study
the 'Christian Year,' so that it was with awe and reverence for the first
poet I had ever seen that I looked at him from the first" (i–ii). The turning
point in her life was her preparation for confirmation:

> At fifteen I became a catechumen of Mr Keble's, and this I would call
> the great influence of my life did I not feel unworthy to do so; but of
> this I am sure, that no one else, save my own father, had so much to
> do with my whole cast of mind.
>   Otterbourne Rectory is united with Hursley, so that the Rector of
> the one is the Vicar of the other; but having a parish church of our
> own, it was as a sort of outlying sheep that I was allowed to be prepared
> by him for the confirmation of the year 1838. I went to him twice a-
> week from August to October, and after the first awe, the exceeding
> tenderness and gentleness of his treatment made me perfectly at home
> with him. I fancy I was his first young lady scholar, and that he was
> rather feeling his way, for I have heard from later pupils of a fuller and
> more minute instruction, beginning sooner and continuing longer
> than mine. That, however, was everything to me. Starting from a child's
> technical familiarity with the Catechism and Bible, and from the misty
> theology of one *taught* orthodoxly, but confused by the indiscriminate
> reading of Tract Society books (then children's only Sunday fare), he

opened to me the perception of the Church, her Sacraments and her foundation, and prepared me to enter into the typical teaching of Scripture ...

It must have visibly impressed and excited me considerably, for his two warnings, when he gave me my ticket, were, – the one against much talk and discussion of Church matters, especially doctrines, the other against the danger of loving these things for the sake merely of their beauty and poetry – aesthetically he would have said, only that he would have thought the word affected. (*Musings*, iiv)

Keble was professor of poetry at Oxford from 1831 to 1841, and his lectures, written and delivered in Latin – the usual practice until Matthew Arnold was elected to the professorship in 1857 – were published in 1844 with the title *De Poeticæ Vi Medica: Prælectiones Academicæ*.[12] (They were not translated into English until 1912). M.H. Abrams was one of the first scholars to discuss Keble's lectures at length, and in *The Mirror and the Lamp* (1953) he commented that they have received "remarkably scanty attention" (145). This is no longer the case, as a number of scholars have followed Abrams's lead in exploring the nature and influence of Tractarian poetics, notably Stephen Prickett, G.B. Tennyson, and Geoffrey Rowell.[13] Here I will outline only those points that are embodied in *The Heir of Redclyffe*, where Charles Edmonstone refers to Guy reading the *Praelectiones* (91), and where the "healing power of poetry" is stressed.

Keble's *Lectures* (p. 9) contains a fulsome dedication to William Wordsworth,

TRUE PHILOSOPHER AND INSPIRED POET
WHO BY THE SPECIAL GIFT AND CALLING OF ALMIGHTY GOD
WHETHER HE SANG OF MAN OR OF NATURE
FAILED NOT TO LIFT UP MEN'S HEARTS TO HOLY THINGS
NOR EVER CEASED TO CHAMPION THE CAUSE
OF THE POOR AND SIMPLE
AND SO IN PERILOUS TIMES WAS RAISED UP
TO BE A CHIEF MINISTER
NOT ONLY OF SWEETEST POETRY
BUT ALSO OF HIGH AND SACRED TRUTH

The principal task of the *Lectures* is to set out a sacramental theory of poetry that reconciles Wordsworthian Romanticism with the theology of the Oxford Movement, in effect turning Wordsworth into a Tractarian poet. In his most rhapsodic passages Keble takes a very high view of poetry, and in the dedication he virtually equates Wordsworth with an inspired prophet.

One of the most striking things about the *Lectures* is the way that Keble's description of the effect of poetry parallels theological accounts of the operation of the sacrament of penance or reconciliation. As G.B. Tennyson notes, Abrams's parallels between Keble and Freud ignore the fact that the burdens Keble repeatedly refers to are not psychological repressions: "Context in the *Lectures* and knowledge of the previous writings of the Tractarians make clear that what is moving the poet to artistic expression (as it moves all men to their limited degrees of 'poetry') is the yearning for God" (*Poetry*, 60). For Keble, poetry provides relief by expressing "any strong current of thought or feeling" that carries the poet away (*Lectures* 1:19). Because civilization restrains the immediate and direct expression of whatever comes into our minds, "it comes about that those to whom, most of all, utterance would be the relief from a burden are altogether restrained by a sort of shame, far from discreditable, nay rather, noble and natural, from any such relief" (1:20). Like the forgiveness of sins, poetry has been ordained by the Almighty as "comfort for sufferers" (1:21). In its use of rhythm and meter and in its ability "to recall, to renew, and bring vividly before us pictures of absent objects," poetry "exhibits, assuredly, wonderful efficacy in soothing men's emotions and steadying the balance of their mind" (1:21). The use of the word "soothing" is significant here, for in his Advertisement to *The Christian Year* Keble refers to "that *soothing* tendency in the Prayer Book, which it is the chief purpose of these pages to exhibit" ("Advertisement," vi; Keble's emphasis).[14] As Stephen Prickett notes, Keble uses the word "soothe" in a stronger sense than its present-day use; for it retains shades of its older meaning of "to prove or show to be true; to assert or uphold a truth"; "to give support," "encourage," or "confirm" (*Romanticism*, 112–13). Perhaps it has some of the same meanings as "comfort," in the sense of the "Comfortable Words" of the *Book of Common Prayer*. Once again, this reinforces the analogy between poetry and confession; for the Comfortable Words give comfort precisely because they assure us of the forgiveness of sins. For example: "If any man sin, we have an Advocate with the Father, Jesus Christ the righteous; and he is the propitiation for our sins. 1 *St John* 2.1." In fact, the Comfortable Words are part of the absolution in the *Book of Common Prayer*. Keble's own view of the purpose of his poetry is also found in the Advertisement: "The object of the present publication will be attained, if any person find assistance from it in bringing his own thoughts and feelings into more entire unison with those recommended and exemplified in the Prayer Book" (v–vi).

The key to understanding Tractarian poetics is that poetry works indirectly, by analogy. The doctrine of reserve, expressed most fully in Isaac Williams's two tracts (*Tracts for the Times*, nos. 80 and 87), is a key concept in the theology and aesthetic theory of the Oxford Movement. In terms of poetics, it essentially means that authors do not speak directly about what most concerns them, partly because to do so would violate the decorum that surrounds the sacred, and partly because one can only speak of things divine by indirection, perceiving them through the veil of our worldly experience. For this reason, Keble is able to trace an analogy between the poetry of the largely pre-Christian authors he discusses and the more direct revelation of divine truth in the Scriptures. Similarly, in the poetry of *The Christian Year*, Keble traces an analogy between nature and revelation, following the logic of Joseph Butler's *Analogy of Religion* (1736). Bishop Butler explained his principle of analogical reasoning as follows:

> Hence, namely from analogical reasoning, Origen has with singular sagacity observed, that *he who believes the Scripture to have proceeded from him who is the Author of Nature, may well expect to find the same sort of difficulties in it as are found in the constitution of Nature.* And in a like way of reflection it may be added, that he who denies the Scripture to have been from God upon account of these difficulties, may, for the very same reason, deny the world to have been formed by him. On the other hand, if there be an analogy or likeness between that system of things and dispensation of Providence, which Revelation informs us of, and that system of things and dispensation of Providence which Experience together with Reason informs us of, *i.e.*, the known course of Nature; this is a presumption that they have both the same author and cause; at least so far as to answer objections against the former's being from God, drawn from anything which is analogical or similar to what is in the latter, which is acknowledged to be from him; for an Author of Nature is here supposed. (4; Butler's emphasis)

The poetic implications of this doctrine are explained more succinctly in one of the best-known poems of *The Christian Year*, "Septuagesima

Sunday," where nature is presented as a book that can be read by a reader with a "Christian heart" (42, line 4). In *The Heir of Redclyffe*, nature is frequently presented as a revelation of God's purpose, especially for Guy and Amy.

One of the consequences of Keble's theory is that the poets themselves may not be aware of the full significance of what they write. Defending his mode of reading Homer, Æschylus, and other ancients, he notes that "it has not seldom pleased the divine Power that even the weightiest and truest oracles should be delivered by the mouth of men, who were the very foes of religion, they being all the while unconscious of the full force of their utterance" (*Lectures* 1:400). Virgil's account of the prophetic sibyl is taken by Keble to be an allegory of the way that human beings learn about the divine: "We can draw no more fitting meaning from this fable, in my judgement, than to suppose the poet to imply that the sole way by which the knowledge of divine things is conceded to mortal men, is that they shall collect from every quarter the traces and fragments of it which have been thrown into confusion by the storm and stress of our daily lives and have been scattered in all directions. Moreover, he not obscurely implies that there will be no repairing of this disaster, nor will these fragments of truth ever be arranged and made serviceable to mankind, save by constant, devoted prayerfulness" (2:463-4). The poetic imagination, and its ordering activity, is here closely linked to the spiritual life. Both are means of perceiving the divine order beyond the chaos of daily life; attentive reading of poetry is allied to "constant, devoted prayerfulness" as an attitude towards experience.

Some of Keble's remarks concerning Robert Southey's poem *Thalaba* (1801) will serve as a final example of the way that poetry works according to Tractarian poetics. In the *Lectures*, Keble makes a few scattered references to modern literature, including one to Southey. He notes that the surface tendency of *Thalaba* "is ... to commend to us the Ottoman faith and the monstrosities of Mahomet." However, the poem gives pleasure, "even to those who are whole-heartedly devoted to the pure and sacred Truth: mainly and especially, if I mistake not, by reason of the implied, underlying comparison which the reader's mind spontaneously institutes for itself" (2:314). The Christian believer should read *Thalaba* in the same way that he or she reads classical literature, "and thus a true religious reserve is carefully protected: genuine piety is not exposed to the eye of men and the full light of publicity, yet it is present, hidden behind a veil, at one time and place the veil of ancient Greek worship, at another that of modern errors" (ibid.). Charlotte Yonge spoke positively about *Thalaba* in a letter of 1850, although she expressed reservations about Southey's treatment of the Catholic faith and concluded that "he was not in earnest" (in C. Coleridge, *Yonge*, 161). In *The Heir of Redclyffe*, Guy is "enchanted" by his first reading of *Thalaba* and in it he "found all manner of deep meanings, to which the sisters listened with wonder and delight" (*Heir*, 116). Laura, like one of the more literal-minded readers to whom Keble objects in his *Lectures*, points out in the course of a discussion of the "deep meanings" of *Thalaba* that "Southey did not see all this himself, and did not understand it when it was pointed out" (ibid.).

In a passage from the concluding lecture that I have already quoted in part, Keble makes his boldest statements about the relationship between poetry and religion, showing how they overlap and reinforce one another:

> For, while Religion seeks out, as I said, on all sides, not merely language but also anything which may perform the office of language and help to express the emotions of the soul; what aid can be imagined more grateful and more timely than the presence of Poetry, which leads men to the secret sources of Nature, and supplies a rich wealth of similes whereby a pious mind may supply and remedy, in some sort, its powerlessness of speech; and may express many things more touchingly, many things more seriously and weightily, all things more truly, than had been possible without this aid. Conversely, should we ask how, pre-eminently, "came honour and renown to prophetic bards and their poems", it is Religion that has most to be thanked for this. For, once let that magic wand, as the phrase goes, touch any region of Nature, forthwith all that before seemed secular and profane is illumined with a new and celestial light: men come to realize that the various images and similes of things, and all other poetic charms, are not merely the play of a keen and clever mind, nor to be put down as empty fancies: but rather they guide us by gentle hints and no uncertain signs, to the very utterances of Nature, or we may more truly say, of the Author of Nature. And thus it has come to pass, that great and pre-eminent poets have almost been ranked as the representatives of religion, and their sphere has been treated with religious reverence. In short, Poetry lends Religion her wealth of symbols and similes: Religion restores these again to Poetry, clothed with so splendid a radiance that they appear

to be no longer merely symbols, but to partake (I might almost say) of the nature of sacraments. (*Lectures* 2:481)

The effect of this passage is to suggest that poetry must be taken very seriously indeed. Keble was using words with characteristic precision when he promised at the beginning of his long course of lectures that he would "maintain the religious reverence due to a subject so serious, I had almost said so sacred" (1:13). Religion is poetic in the way that it influences us, not in the sense that we should treat religious matters aesthetically, for Keble warned against that and unlike later Anglo-Catholics was never interested in ritual, but in the sense that both religion and poetry soothe and comfort, and both reveal something of divinity to fallen humanity. Poetry may be the handmaiden of religion, but religion also serves poetry by giving it its splendid significance. Poetry is thus virtually sacramental in its effect, a source of divine grace.

The background of Keble's poetics illuminates much of significance in *The Heir of Redclyffe*. Yonge's own views on the relationship between secular learning and literature and divine revelation are well illustrated in the preface to her *Conversations on the Catechism* (1859–63). In her reference to the "unconscious allegory" of literature, she echoes Keble:

It has been the attempt to show, at least by hints, how all branches of secular study are truly subservient to the one great lesson, and may be illustrated by the true Light. Thus, as far as space and the limited knowledge of the author would permit, Mythology and History have been examined for rays of truth, for illustration of prophecy, for the course of the Divine dealings with the chosen, and for examples of good or evil; and thus again material science and modern discovery have been brought in both with a view of grappling with their perversion towards scepticism, and their real testimony to the Eternal Truth and Almighty Providence, their voice of praise. Light literature has sometimes been mentioned, either for the sake of illustration, or to mark the unconscious allegory that pervades all that is truly good. (*Conversations* 1:vi)

Art and learning are thus seen as subservient to divine truth, but this does not mean, as Q.D. Leavis suggested, that Yonge's culture is bigoted and narrow. Kathleen Tillotson demonstrated the range of her reading and her abilities as a literary critic (see "Charlotte"), and reading *The Heir of Redclyffe* one is struck by the variousness of the literary, artistic, and musical culture that pervades the Edmonstones' home and especially the lives of its young people. Manzoni and de Fouqué figure prominently among the literary figures, but there are also references to Malory, Cervantes, Shakespeare, Bishop Butler, Byron, Keble, Dickens, Tennyson, and others.

Like Keble, Yonge seeks to transform the legacy of Romanticism in *The Heir of Redclyffe* and to put its Wordsworthian aspect to the service of Tractarian Anglicanism, while rejecting the Byronic side of the Romantic movement. Georgina Battiscombe sums up the effect of *The Heir* in the following way: "The trend of the day was towards prosaic and strenuous living, yet romanticism was still the prevailing literary fashion, romanticism associated with the names of the vicious Byron, the atheistical Shelley, and such novelists as poor Caroline Lamb. Romanticism, in short, was bad. Charlotte took its reformation in hand, and in the character of Guy she turned romanticism into a respectable church-going creed ... no one before Charlotte had associated romance with everyday life as it was lived in the year 1853" (*Yonge*, 73).

Guy Morville is in some ways a version of the Byronic hero. He lives in a crumbling Gothic mansion on a cliff overlooking a dangerous harbour, which is described by Philip early in the novel as "more like a scene in a romance than anything real," with a "great quadrangle where the sun never shone" (*Heir*, 10). Furthermore, he is the inheritor of the Morville temper, an attribute that is expressed in a portrait of a wicked ancestor of the Restoration. In her *History of Christian Names* (1884), Charlotte Yonge notes that Sir Guy was one of the knights of the Round Table, and that Guy has been a favourite name; however, "'Gunpowder Treason' gave a sinister association to the sound of Guido Fawkes, and the perpetual celebrations of the 5th of November, with the burning of Guy Fawkes in effigy, have given a meaning to the term of Guy, that will probably continue long after the last tar-barrel has flamed and the last cracker exploded over his doom" (228). To make sure that the reader is aware that Guy's first name is that of the notorious conspirator against church and state, Charles Edmonstone makes a pun on his name before he has even seen him, suggesting to his sister Charlotte that, on meeting him, she should exclaim "What a guy!" (15). Shortly thereafter he comments that he is "tired of the sound of his name! One fifth of November is enough in the year" (*Heir*, 21). Guy bears the family name of Hugo Morville, one of the four knights who murdered Thomas à Becket, the archbishop of Canterbury, in 1170. Recounting the event in a history book intended for children, Yonge describes the state of the murderers after they retreated to Morville's castle in Cumberland: "They found themselves regarded with universal execration; their servants shrank from their presence, and, in the exaggerations of tradition, it was said that the very dogs would not approach them" (*Cameos*, 156). She also describes the beatific expression of the martyred saint, who looks "as if he had calmly fallen asleep" (155). It is significant that Guy will die a similarly beautiful death, which is a sign of his sanctity; after seven centuries the curse has been expiated.

Guy's temper is repeatedly emphasized throughout *The Heir*, although what little anger we see seems thoroughly justified. Guy declares that he resembles "old Sir Hugh's portrait at home" (*Heir*, 55). Old Sir Hugh, a courtier during the reign of Charles II, appears to have been guilty of forgery and of bribing Judge Jefferies to sentence a rival to death; he compounded these crimes by currying favour with William of Orange. In the manner of a Gothic hero Guy tells the Edmonstones, "It is my firm belief that such a curse of sin and death as was on Sintram rests on the descendants of that miserable man" (71). This belief is confirmed when Guy learns the full story of how his grandfather had been the cause of Guy's father's death. However, Guy's Byronic inheritance of temper and doom is not an irrevocable destiny; for as Laura tells him, "The doom of sin and death is on us all, but you should remember that if you are a Morville you are also a Christian" (ibid.). Here the hereditary taint is associated with the curse of original sin, and Guy's Romantic quest becomes the pilgrimage by which he fully realizes and accepts the redemption for that sin wrought by Christ and subdues himself to God's will. In his struggle with sin, another painting provides him with inspiration, this time the literary description of a Raphael Madonna: "Dwell on the form of the Child, more than human in grandeur, seated on the arms of the Blessed Virgin as on an august throne. Note the tokens of divine grace, His ardent eyes, what a spirit, what a countenance is His; yet His very resemblance to His mother denotes sufficiently that He is of us and takes care for us" (45). This poetic recreation of an artistic representation of the incarnation reminds Guy that because God became man, redemption is possible for everyone. The novel tells the story of how Guy, far more deeply than the other characters, realizes the significance of the promise of redemption.

Guy is a Victorian version of Sir Galahad, a knight who quests for his own sanctification through mastery of himself. We know from a letter that Charlotte Yonge wrote to her friend Marianne Dyson, who ran a boarding school for girls, that the character of Guy Morville reminded Charlotte's mother of that most romantic of the Tractarians, Hurrell Froude (1803–36), which, Charlotte wrote, "I hope is a sign that I have got the right sow by the ear" (in C. Coleridge, *Yonge*, 170). Froude was a flamboyant character whose early death prompted his friends to publish his literary *Remains* (1838, 1839), works whose hostility to Protestantism helped to fan the flames of opposition to the Oxford Movement. Froude's character was described as follows by an early historian of the Movement: "Froude was a Tory, with that transcendental idea of the English gentleman which forms the basis of Toryism. He was a High Churchman of the uncompromising school, very early taking part with Anselm, Becket, Laud, and the Nonjurors. Woe to any one who dropped in his hearing such phrases as the dark ages, superstition, bigotry, right of private judgment, enlightenment, march of mind, or progress" (Mozley, *Reminiscences* 1:227). Guy is not of course a clergyman, nor particularly well read in theology, but rather a Christian knight who lives up to his duties, which Yonge sees in quite feudal terms. In his veneration of Charles I and his romantic love of Sir Thomas Malory's *Morte D'Arthur* (c.1469), Guy's kinship to Froude is particularly apparent. He also resembles Froude in his moral scrupulousness; Mare and Percival note that Guy Morville and Hurrell Froude, in the journal published as part of his *Remains*, "show the same morbid consciousness of sin over the slightest fault" (*Best-seller*, 106). Significantly, however, Guy matures spiritually, and is able to perform his duties without excessive self-recrimination.

Neither Guy nor his cousin Philip Morville has living parents, which emphasizes the fact that each is being tested to see how he will deal with the world on his own resources, assisted only by God's grace. The novel really centres on the contrast between these two men, and Catherine Wells-Cole has shown how, in its portrayal of Philip, *The Heir* critiques Victorian ideals of "authoritative manhood" ("Yonge Men," 77). As in many Victorian novels, there is a dearth of older authority figures. Mr Edmonstone is a weak and ineffectual parent, easily swayed by others. As a result, Philip is able to assume a great deal of authority, which, given the lack of Christian humility for which his father once rebuked him, proves to be his downfall. Guy, on the other hand, chooses Mrs Edmonstone as a spiritual counsellor. She teaches him that self-denial is not enough; he must consider what others want him to do, and what duties are required by his position in society. When she makes him realize that he has disappointed others by not going to a ball, her spiritual counsel echoes that of John Keble, whose advice always recognized the demands of family and social duties. Thus, for example, Keble advised a lady, "an entire stranger":

> Your question about dancing, &c., is of a kind which, I believe, the best advisers are used to answer conditionally. Such things, they say, are not bad in themselves, but in the abuse of them; and I suppose it very often happens that persons, if they use them at all, find them so instrumental to one bad feeling or another, that their wisest course, if they can choose, is to refrain from them. But I can conceive cases where it would be unloving, or undutiful, to act strictly in this rule; where, for example, the wish of parents is concerned. I can even conceive cases where it would be more real self-denial to go to such a party than to stay away from it. (*Letters*, 57)

This passage is remarkably similar to the advice Guy receives from Mrs Edmonstone, and is one example of the influence John Keble had on his most famous parishioner, and of the harmony of their minds on spiritual and ethical matters.

Guy's chivalrous love of Amy is also part of his spiritual pilgrimage. It is significant that he refers to her as his Verena, after their fervent readings of Friedrich de la Motte Fouqué's *Sintram and His Companions* (1814). This somewhat bizarre romance, translated into English by Julius Hare in 1820, was a favourite book of the Tractarians, and Barbara Dennis usefully discusses its influence on *The Heir* in the introduction to her Oxford World's Classics edition (xiv–xvi). Verena is the saintly mother of Sintram, the accursed hero who eventually achieves his redemption after a testing sojourn at a castle in the wasteland of the Mondenfelsen, which Amy's imagination connects with the craggy landscape of Redclyffe, where Guy spends his solitary Christmas, and where he conquers temptation.

Guy's banishment from the Edmonstones' home, significantly named Hollywell, forms part of the archetypal pattern of the chivalric or romantic quest; furthermore, it occurs because Guy's sense of honour prevents him from clearing himself of the accusation of gambling. He does not want to reveal his uncle's vices, nor can he betray the secret of the Miss

Wellwoods, who are trying to found an Anglican sisterhood. As a result, Guy goes into exile at Redclyffe; he is delivered from this "waste land" first when he conquers temptation by thinking of his social duty in a neglected parish that forms part of his estate, and then when he rescues the crew of a wrecked ship in one of Charlotte Yonge's typical narrations of romantic heroism. By the time he is reconciled with the Edmonstones, Guy has proven himself to be a model Young England squire.

Critics writing about Charlotte Yonge have often noted the lack of overt reference to religious dogma, the reluctance to name Jesus Christ or the sacraments of the Church directly, and the avoidance of controversial content of the sort that is often found in both Tractarian and anti-Tractarian novels. Barbara Dennis writes of *The Heir* that "there is not a word of dogma, or an identifiable reference to the [Oxford] movement in it" (*Charlotte Yonge*, 56). However, as Dennis's discussion suggests, though I think not strongly enough, the novel is saturated with the assumptions, cultural preferences, ethical values, and ecclesiastical practices, in short with the whole ethos, of Tractarianism. If the doctrine of reserve prevents these things from being overtly named, they are there just below the surface. Indeed, one could see sacramentalism as the organizing principle of *The Heir of Redclyffe*.

At the level of its narrative events, the novel is punctuated by references to the sacraments of the Church. Mrs Lavers, the landlady of the inn where Guy's mother died in childbirth, was responsible for making sure that Guy was baptized, and she preserved the china bowl that was used for the purpose as though it were a sacred object (291). Guy and Amy receive Holy Communion at their wedding, and again after Guy has made his confession and received absolution as he lies dying. The daily offices of the Church and the Holy Communion comfort Guy in his time of testing. Throughout the novel, then, Yonge stresses that "soothing tendency" of the *Book of Common Prayer* mentioned by Keble. Furthermore, the characters in the novel live their lives according to the calendar of the Church, that Christian year of feasts and fasts by which, in the Catholic tradition, time is sanctified. Keble's book of poems is essentially a verse commentary on this way of measuring time, and significant events in *The Heir* occur in relation to Christmas, Easter, Ascension Day, and Michaelmas. Guy's twenty-first birthday, his coming of age, is not celebrated with festivities because it occurs in Holy Week.[15]

The treatment of art and nature in *The Heir* is similar to that in Keble's poetry and poetics, and it is perhaps the most intellectually significant part of the novel; for here Charlotte Yonge makes her own contribution to several Victorian cultural debates. Guy is a potentially Byronic hero whose passions are chastened by his religious principles; he achieves both a Wordsworthian spiritual harmony with nature and a Victorian domestic bliss that is imbued with a romantic attractiveness of its own. One of Yonge's most notable and most widely praised achievements is that in Guy Morville she makes doing one's duty and mastering one's passions seem exciting and romantic. She does this by endowing them with the aura of chivalric heroism, while retaining a recognizably mid-Victorian domestic setting. Writing shortly after Yonge's death, Ethel Romanes noted that she had "an extraordinary gift for investing the dullest situations, the most commonplace occupations, not merely with interest, or with gentle satire, but with romance" (*Appreciation*, 178); she was "almost the first storyteller who dared to write of the Religious Life as a normal development" (4).

Yonge's novel originated in an idea of Marianne Dyson's, who had herself tried to write a story depicting two characters, "the essentially contrite and the self-satisfied" (C. Coleridge, *Yonge*, 162). By means of this contrast between the humility of Guy and the self-righteousness of Philip, Yonge criticizes what she sees as the worldly standards of achievement that dominated Victorian society in the 1850s. Philip is self-satisfied and interfering, but because these qualities are combined with an assertive will, intelligence, and a strong and attractive physique, he holds sway over almost everyone in the novel. Philip is the model gentleman, able to adapt his conversation to any audience (*Heir*, 85). He is indispensable to Mr Edmonstone and Lord Kilcoran in practical matters, a thoroughly accomplished man of the world, with good family connections; he has also demonstrated a certain nobility of character by sacrificing his university career for the sake of his sisters after the death of their father. Yet, as Ethel Romanes perceptively notes, Philip "is a perfect type of Philistine before Mr Matthew Arnold had made Philistinism known to us" (*Appreciation*, 67). He is dismissive of *Le Morte D'Arthur*, while Guy, anticipating later Victorian taste, admires it. Philip regards Guy's musical abilities with suspicion since he connects them with Guy's inferior social connections on his mother's side. He also suggests that Guy is out of his depth reading Butler's *Analogy*, which had a key influence on Tractarian theology and was incidentally a work that Matthew Arnold spoke of with respect, even if he saw it as outmoded (see his essay "Bishop Butler and the Zeit-Geist" in *Complete Prose* 8:11–62). Philip says that he has never spent much time over Butler himself (*Heir*, 144). He is like the worldly gentleman described by John Henry Newman in *The Idea of a University* and elsewhere: the product of a highly civilizing and admirable liberal education but without the infusion of divine grace that would render him a true Christian. His lack of feeling for music marks him as hard-hearted, while he is willing to substitute his own private judgment for the accepted behaviour in determining whether he and Laura should keep their engagement secret. He thus combines a negative aspect of Romanticism, reliance on the self, with a failure to experience religion genuinely as a matter of the heart. He is a Mr Worldly Wiseman, who is a thorough success in the eyes of others but whose own father, before his death, diagnosed his key failing: "Did he not remember his return home for the last time before that when he was summoned thither by his father's death? He had come with a whole freight of prizes, and letters full of praises; and as he stood, in expectation of the expression of delighted satisfaction, his father laid his hand on his trophy, the pile of books, saying, gravely, – 'All this would I give, Philip, for one evidence of humility of mind'" (521).

Philip's failings are mirrored in his worldly, confident sister Margaret Henley, who represents Yonge's critique of the feminine version of philistinism. She is a bluestocking who follows the superficial standards of taste in the literary marketplace, setting herself up as the arbiter of culture in the fashionable watering-place of St Mildred's: "She was, in fact, the leading lady of the place – the manager of the book-club, in the chair at all the charitable committees, and the principal person in society, giving literary parties, with a degree of exclusiveness that made admission to them a privilege" (210). From this vantage point she criticizes Elizabeth Wellwood, the saintly Tractarian lady who seeks to found a sisterhood, and whom the narrator characterizes with the same biblical phrase that Charlotte Mary Yonge quotes at the end of her memoir of John Keble, a "burning and shining light."[16] Margaret and Philip thus represent the secular, calculating, fashion-conscious bourgeoisie, who were seen by the Tractarians and by less-orthodox prophets such as Carlyle as having lost sight of the true realities, which are spiritual rather than material. It is not surprising that their childhood home is called Stylehurst. In many ways Philip is presented as an admirable person, but due to the lack of humility that his father perceived, he relies too much on his own judgment and does not see that he is guided by self-interest.

It is clear that for Yonge science and literature should, and if properly used would, serve Christian truth. In Dr Henley, a fashionable physician, and his dilettantish wife Margaret, we see science and culture as ends in themselves, unconnected to any larger and spiritual vision of human possibility. These two characters thus resemble two different courses of study in a university that does not teach theology, the one subject that, according to Newman's Platonic vision of Oxford in *The Idea of a University*, can give unity to all others. Margaret embodies the kind of corrupt literary taste that Wordsworth and Keble criticized, and Guy seeks relief from the superficial society offered by Mrs Henley by retreating, like Wordsworth, to the surrounding countryside: "There was something in a fine landscape that was to him like a friend and companion" (246).

The key cultural reference in the contrast between Guy and Philip is the poetry of Byron. For John Keble, Byron had "sullied his splendid powers by many serious vices, inexcusable in any one, to say nothing of a great poet" (*Lectures* 1:258). Keble praised Byron's "ardent and profound" poetical gift and lamented his failure to become "a minister and interpreter of the mysteries that lie hid in Nature." Instead Byron gave a picture of his own twisted personality, which Keble blamed on the affliction of "an ill-balanced mind" (2:339).[17] Another Tractarian poet, Isaac Williams, wrote that "the subtle poison of ... [Byron's] books did me incalculable injury for many years; the more so as the infidelity was so veiled in beautiful verse and refined sentiment" (*Autobiography*, 7). Byron figures twice in *The Heir of Redclyffe*. Early on, while Guy is still forming his character and chafing under Philip's condescension, Philip cautions him not to let Byron get hold of him: "it is bad food for excitable minds" (*Heir*, 87). Later in the novel there is a discussion during which Guy says that he has never read Byron's *Childe Harold*. Philip is irritated that Guy actually heeded his earlier caution and suggests that his warning referred only to "his perversions of human passions, not to his descriptions of scenery" (399). Guy shows himself a true disciple of Keble when he says, "I should be more unwilling to take the word of a man like that to interpret nature than anything else, except Scripture" (399). The danger, he explains, is that if one's ears are filled with the wrong way of reading nature, one might not hear its true voice (400). Guy thus sees nature as a book that can reveal moral lessons and teach us the will of God. To underscore the point, the narrator, recalling Guy's earlier outburst of rage towards Philip, draws a conclusion that Guy does not himself fully realize: "Who could have told where the mastery might have been in the period of fearful conflict with his passions, if he had been feeding his imagination with the contemplation of revenge, dark hatred, and malice, and identifying himself with Byron's brooding and lowering heroes?" (399). This is the most explicit piece of literary criticism in *The Heir of Redclyffe*, and it clearly connects Guy's reading, his experience of nature, and his journey towards sanctification.

Guy himself writes poetry, and this seems more important in establishing that he has a poetic sensibility than that his verses have merit. There are several ways in which Guy and Amy especially live poetically, in the sense of reading literature and the book of Nature as signs, "almost sacraments," of God's presence. The allegory is prepared for by an epigraph to the novel from Keble's *Lyra Innocentium* (1846) equating the harshness of the end of winter, preceding the season of flowers, with the personal austerities that "must the way of bliss prepare."[18] This imagery is used to represent Mrs Edmonstone's first suspicion that Guy and Amy may be falling in love: "It was Amy, not Eveleen, who was constantly with Guy. Reading and music, roses, botany, and walks on the terrace! She looked back, and it was still the same. Last Easter vacation, how they used to study the stars in the evening, to linger in the greenhouse in the morning nursing the geraniums, and to practise singing over the school-room piano; how, in a long walk, they always paired together; and how they seemed to share every pursuit or pleasure" (175–6). Similarly, the wedding of Guy and Amy is accompanied by nature imagery that presages Guy's death and the spiritual triumph that his death represents. As the couple drive away, Amy is "startled by a long cluster of laburnums, their yellow bloom bent down and heavy with wet, so that the ends dashed against her bonnet, and the crystal drops fell on her lap." Guy says to her, "Why, Amy, the Hollywell flowers are weeping for the loss of you!" (389). This image from pastoral elegy foreshadows the fact that Guy will not return from his wedding journey. In the following paragraph, the receding storm is accompanied by "a wide-spanned rainbow," a sign of God's covenant and of the divine grace that infuses Guy's saintly death (389).

Early in the novel, the Edmonstone children and their friends play a parlour game called "Definitions." Guy defines happiness as "gleams from a brighter world, too soon eclipsed or forfeited" (41). There is a Wordsworthian quality to this definition, with its intimation of the transcendental, and Guy's spiritual quest leads him towards a fuller vision of this brighter world. Catherine Sandbach-Dahlström, who has usefully

traced the romance archetypes in *The Heir*, notes that Guy is always associated with youthfulness, spring, and the sun (*Be Good*, 35). The most
significant crisis in Guy's spiritual pilgrimage comes in chapter 16, when
he receives Mr Edmonstone's letter accusing him of gambling. The epigraph to this chapter, again from *Lyra Innocentium*, equates the sun burning behind a cloud to the hidden presence of God:

> So waits the Lord behind the veil,
> His light on frenzied cheek, or pale,
>   To shed when the dark hour is gone. (*Heir*, 222)

In his anger, Guy resolves to challenge Philip in order to make him suffer
for his falsehoods, but then he sees the setting sun. This sight becomes a
religious vision; for "the good angel so close to him for the twenty years
of his life, had been driven aloof but for a moment, and now, either that,
or a still higher and holier power, made the setting sun bring to his mind,
almost to his ear, the words, – 'Let not the sun go down upon your wrath,
Neither give place to the devil' [Ephesians 4:26–7]" (225). After a powerful
struggle, Guy brings himself through prayer and contemplation of the
suffering of Christ to forgive Philip. By the time the sun has set, his victory
has been won. The imagery of light is continued later in the novel on the
wedding journey. After Guy has nursed Philip through the crisis of his
fever, he tells Amy that "the shipwreck was a gleam, the first ray that
came to cheer me in those penance hours, when I was cut off from all"
(420). Guy's own death occurs as the sun rises: "The light streamed in at
the open window, and over the bed; but it was 'another dawn than ours'
that he beheld" (468). This passage is also linked to Guy's meditation on
the transience of earthly happiness, as he rows on the bay at Redclyffe.
Taking his words from the Collect for Ascension Day, he says to himself,
"In heart and mind thither ascend, and with Him continually dwell"
(372). Yonge is suggesting through these passages that Guy's goodness
has become too great for him to remain in this world.

Like Wordsworth, like Keble, Guy is attached to his home, to the craggy
landscape around Redclyffe, and above all to the sea. There is a strong
Romantic sense of place in *The Heir of Redclyffe*, and an emphasis on
continuity between past and present. Stylehurst, in spite of the implications
of its name, is connected with the virtues of Archdeacon Morville, which
do not exist in the same way in his surviving children, while Guy's virtues

stand out during his retreat to the world of Redclyffe, still largely feudal, beyond the reach of the railway. There is a suggestion that if only Guy and Philip had met at Stylehurst they might have been reconciled earlier and more easily; for it is there that Philip is seen at his best, "so deeply, securely fixed is the love of the home of childhood in men of his mould, in whom it is perhaps the most deeply rooted of all affections" (519). It is to the Stylehurst parish church, on a communion Sunday, that Guy goes after his outburst of anger and achievement of self-mastery, and the "pardon and peace" that he receives are linked in Wordsworthian manner with the pastoral tranquillity of the old country graveyard (247). The passage is reminiscent of the descriptions of the country churchyard in Book 6 of Wordsworth's *Excursion*, which I will discuss in chapter 5. In contrast with these pastoral settings, or with the Anglican stronghold of Oxford, St Mildred's embodies the spirit of modernity: "St Mildred's was a fashionable summer resort, which the virtues of a mineral spring, and the reputation of Dr Henley, had contributed to raise to a high degree of prosperity. It stood at the foot of a magnificent range of beautifully formed hills, where the crescents and villas, white and smart, showed their own insignificance beneath the purple peaks that rose high above them" (209–10). St Mildred's resembles the "fashionable watering-place" of Sandbourne in Hardy's *Tess of the D'Urbervilles* (1891), which has sprung up next to the ancient landscape of "the enormous Egdon Waste" (*Tess*, 363).

One topic that recurs frequently in nineteenth-century literature is the relationship between earthly love, specifically of an erotic or romantic nature, and the love of God. This is a common theme in the literature of doubt, where an illicit sexual love is often connected, as the sign or cause or consequence, with the loss of faith. Examples may be found in Froude's notorious *Nemesis of Faith*, Geraldine Jewsbury's *Zoe*, and, going further back, George Sand's operatic *Lélia*. Arnold's poetry, Trollope's *Bertrams*, and George Eliot's *Adam Bede* treat the same topic, and it arises, with sardonic wit and tragic irony, in the fiction of Thomas Hardy.

Charlotte Yonge's presentation of romantic love is problematic for modern readers not least because of her veneration of authority, in particular the authority of parents – something that troubled her Victorian readers as well. Clearly she could not conceive of having to forsake father and mother for the sake of Christ. She insists that romantic love, however high-minded, is idolatrous if it is not subservient to a consciousness of God – which for Yonge is a consciousness of moral duty. This is brought out in the contrast between Laura and Amy Edmonstone. A reference to Petrarch by Charles Edmonstone establishes that the choice of Laura's name is not accidental (*Heir*, 104), and her uncritical veneration of the priggish Philip is described in language that clearly indicates its idolatrous nature: "How was it meantime with Laura? The others were laughing and talking round her, but all seemed lost in the transcendent beam that had shone out on her" (121). Shortly afterwards Laura's behaviour within the family is analyzed during her cousin Eveleen's visit: "Laura made such sensible comments that Eveleen admired her more than ever; and she, knowing that some were second-hand from Philip, others arising from his suggestions, gave him all the homage paid to herself, as a tribute to him who reigned over her whole being" (143).

In obvious contrast, Amy's love is dutiful, and she immediately rushes to tell her mother after she reaches an understanding with Guy. As a classic example of the Victorian "domestic angel," she is able to assist Guy in his spiritual progress, so that their love blends with a higher love: "Not till then did he understand his own feelings, and recognize in her the being he had dreamt of. Amy was what made Hollywell precious to him. Sternly as he was wont to treat his impulses, he did not look on his affection as an earthborn fancy, liable to draw him from higher things, and, therefore, to be combated; he deemed her rather a guide and guard whose love might arm him, soothe him, and encourage him" (187). Once again we see the key word "soothe" in this description of Amy as a kind of chivalric heroine. Her full name is Amabel, which, like "Guy," is discussed in Yonge's *History of Christian Names*. Yonge notes that the name means "lovable" and is the English version of the French "Aimable," one of a series of names descended from the Latin *amo* (*Names*, xxiii, 181–2).

Nature and love of home are analogous to and intimately connected with the love of God in the world of Charlotte Yonge. Guy's youthful attractiveness of manner and enthusiasm are signs that he will overcome the hereditary Morville temper, as promised in the epigraph to chapter 2, from *The Tempest*: "If the ill spirit have so fair a house / Good things will strive to dwell with't" (in *Heir*, 15). Charlotte Yonge provides an image of her own art in one of her minor characters, the painter Mr Shene, who is based on William Dyce, the High Church artist (*Heir*, 607n). Mr Shene makes a sketch of Guy for a painting of Sir Galahad, seeing in the mid-Victorian baronet the holiness of the romantic medieval knight who sought the Grail. Another useful image of Yonge's art may be found in

Keble's *Lectures*, in an analysis of what seems an unpromising subject, the odes of Pindar: "His verse is most aptly likened to the song of the lark: since this little bird pre-eminently recalls something of the essential tone of lyric verse by its untrammelled, joyous, and perennial strain. Further, the lark is not mute even amid bare and barren fields, but soars up to the sky with joyous trill from its nest, wherever it may be: in this just like Pindar himself, who from the most straitened and (it may happen) obscure beginnings, delights to soar to lofty, noble themes" (2:155). In the mundane world of the Victorian domestic novel, Yonge is able to soar to the heavens by seeing analogues of the mercy and love of God, and to display the whole system of Tractarian spirituality by hints, implications, and analogies. Her achievement is to take the imagery and some of the experiences validated by Romanticism and to anchor them in the quotidian world of her own class and time, in what Keble famously termed "the trivial round, the common task" (from "Morning," line 53, in *Christian Year*, 4). As David Brownell notes, "The Christian life is never simple or easy in Yonge's world because her firm grasp on the real world always underlies her religious emotions, and she refuses to idealize the details of life, even at the most solemn moments" ("Two Worlds," 169). The world is as treacherous a place to Yonge as it is to Christina Rossetti; but whereas Rossetti concentrates more on the dangers and snares, resisting the temptation to see God in nature, Yonge shows a world transfigured by love and signs of the divine. One can trace two distinct tendencies within the Oxford Movement: the more austere one of Edward Pusey, which manifests itself in a poem like Rossetti's "The World," and the Wordsworthian theology of John Keble, which delights in the Book of Nature, and which finds literary expression in Yonge's greatest work.

In the course of her long career Charlotte Yonge appealed to a wide variety of readers and wrote a number of very good novels; *Heartsease* and *The Daisy Chain* are among her more significant works. Her success results at least in part from her ability, which numerous critics have acknowledged, of making goodness seem both attractive and interesting. In *The Heir of Redclyffe* she achieved this in a story of mythic proportions that is anchored in the whole sweep of English history from Thomas à Becket through the Civil War to her own era. At the same time the book is deeply enmeshed in the religious and cultural controversies of the 1850s.

The fact remains, however, that Yonge is not generally considered to be in the first rank of Victorian novelists. Is this simply a question of her literary talent, or, harking back to Q.D. Leavis's criticisms, does her overt Christian purpose detract from the literary value of her fiction? Is the idea of a "Christian novel" an oxymoron? *The Heir* succeeds by combining a detailed portrait of life in a middle-class family with numerous elements of romance, but there are limitations on Yonge's vision. As noted earlier, her veneration of parental authority prevented her from exploring the potential conflict between the commands of a parent and the commands of God. Her good characters simply obey the parent. Furthermore, the sins and temptations faced by Yonge's characters tend to be those of childhood, even in the case of her adult characters. To take Georgina Battiscombe's example, "nowhere, in all her innumerable books, is anyone tempted to commit adultery" (*Yonge*, 74). There is not the kind of insight into sin that we find in Dostoevsky. Nor is there much empathy for the outcast. There is always the sense with Yonge that she is above all a lady; her Christianity, however sincere and even at times profound, is unable to leap over class divisions. She admires those priests who work among the poor, but her novels never attain a vision of the most radical implications of the doctrine of the incarnation and all that is meant by the sense of Christ's offering of himself. Joseph Baker made this point effectively when he said that Yonge's religion "is not mysticism, but churchgoing raised to the nth degree" (*Novel*, 111). On the other hand, Yonge's work for the Oxford Movement transcended the mere propagandist fiction of other Tractarian novelists, and it has endured among "common readers" to the present day. Perhaps, like some devotional poetry, its appeal is much greater to those who share Yonge's beliefs, and perhaps too the most searching explorations of the meaning of Catholic faith should be sought in the spiritual autobiography, rather than in the novel. Nevertheless, I am convinced that *The Heir of Redclyffe*, Yonge's theological romance, is a significant achievement of Victorian literature, and an important Christian novel.

FOUR

"FROM ST PAUL TO PECKSNIFF": *TROLLOPE'S BERTRAMS* AND ARNOLD'S GOD

It is very hard to come at the actual belief of any man. Indeed how should we hope to do so when we find it so very hard to come at our own.

Anthony Trollope,
"The Clergyman Who Subscribes to Colenso"

IN THE COURSE OF A PUBLIC LECTURE on Victorian literature, I once heard a speaker – who was obviously seeking a suitably pejorative term – refer to Christianity as a "Eurocentric" mode of thought. She was corrected in the question period, but her mistake is in some ways understandable. The history of western colonialism and the prominence of the bishop of Rome may obscure both the Middle Eastern origins and the global spread of Christianity. Furthermore, nineteenth-century liberalism had the effect, and sometimes the explicit aim, of modernizing Christianity, removing it from its origins and infusing it with the values of contemporary European national cultures. Matthew Arnold was among those who contributed to this trend. In *God and the Bible* (1875), Arnold summed up his view of the present state of Christianity in one of his well-known epigrams: "At the present moment two things about the Christian religion must surely be clear to anybody with eyes in his head. One is, that men cannot do without it; the other, that they cannot do with it as it is" (in *Complete Prose* 7:378). The liberalizing tendency in nineteenth-century English and German Christianity was often ethnocentric in nature, as we see in the following passage from a letter that Arnold wrote to his mother on Christmas Day, 1867: "Bunsen used to say that our great business was to get rid of all that was purely Semitic in Christianity, and to make it Indo-germanic; and Schleiermacher that in the Christianity of us western nations there was really much more of Plato and Socrates than of the wild Bedouins with Joshua & David – and on the whole, Papa worked in the direction of these ideas of Bunsen and Schleiermacher, and was, perhaps, the only powerful Englishman of his day who did so. In fact he was the only deeply religious man who had the necessary culture for it" (*Letters* 3:207). In Thomas Arnold's doctrine the church, ideally, should be identical with the nation, a view that would certainly have encouraged ethnocentric tendencies in his thought.[1] For this reason, too, Thomas Arnold was opposed to the idea of giving Jews full citizenship privileges (Stanley, *Life* 2:28).

Matthew Arnold followed the anthropological thought of his time in using the linguistic categories of nineteenth-century philology as indicators of racial differences. In this, Ernest Renan was one of his principal guides, as Frederic Faverty showed in *Matthew Arnold: The Ethnologist* (1951).[2] Arnold's use of racial categories is most apparent in *On the Study of Celtic Literature* (1867), in which he distinguishes between the Teutonic and the Semitic spirits and notes that "even in the sphere of religion, that sphere where the might of Semitism has been so overpowering ... the tendency is in Humboldt's direction; the modern spirit tends more and more to establish a sense of native diversity between our European bent and the Semitic bent, and to eliminate, even in our religion, certain elements as purely and excessively Semitic, and therefore, in right, not combinable with our European nature, not assimilable by it" (in *Complete Prose* 3:301). Such statements seem sinister in view of Germany's subsequent history of aggression, and especially given the explicit anti-Semitism of those Christian theologians who developed a justification in theological terms for the policies of the Nazi regime. Faverty gives a judicious summary of Matthew Arnold's racial theories, saying that "to the unfounded assumptions of the racial hypothesis Arnold lent the weight of a distinguished name" (*Ethnologist*, 191). He concludes that "perhaps it is enough to say of him, as he said of the average Englishman, that he walked diligently by such light as he had, but took too little care that the light he had was not darkness" (192). When commenting on Arnold's use of these categories, and his rhetorical contrasting of Hebraism and Hellenism in *Culture and Anarchy*, one should be aware of his deep appreciation of the Hebrew scriptures, in which he found a concept of righteousness that was one of his most recurrent points of reference. Also, as Ruth apRoberts has noted, he had some significant connections with Jewish intellectuals, including Emanuel Deutsch and the Rothschild family (*Arnold*, 163–75). Like many nineteenth-century thinkers, Arnold's attitude to Judaism was complex, a mixture of admiration, understanding, and prejudice. There is more to be said on Arnold and Judaism, but for my purpose it suffices to say that while Arnold's ethnocentrism is troubling to a twenty-first-century reader, there are far more questionable figures in liberal theology.[3]

I do not intend to add to the large volume of commentary on Arnold's religious writing.[4] Instead, I shall look at the way some of his ideas and their implications were anticipated and explored in fictional form by Anthony Trollope. Arnold's religious thought may be summed up as an attempt to continue his father's Broad Church theology, but based on a far more sceptical or positivistic view of scripture and revelation. Matthew Arnold is important because of his popularity and influence: it is through him that many educated Englishmen became aware of the German theological tradition that began with Schleiermacher, and of the attitude to Christianity exemplified in Renan's *Life of Jesus* (1863). Arnold's *Literature and Dogma* is the only one of his major prose works conceived from the beginning as a book, rather than as a series of articles (*Complete Prose* 6:451n). R.H. Super estimates that it must have sold in excess of one hundred thousand copies: "It was, in the eyes of most of Arnold's contemporaries (though perhaps not the most intelligent of them), his chief claim to literary greatness" (*Complete Prose* 6:454n). Arnold is also important as an example of someone who desperately tried to combine a devout religious sensibility (the way that he read the Bible and other religious texts strongly resembles Catholic spiritual practice) with a sceptical "modern" habit of mind that precluded belief in anything supernatural or miraculous. He was thus a religious modernist, but one who had a deep love for the institution of the Church conceived of in effect as a poetic structure. Ironically, given Arnold's hostility to many aspects of the Oxford Movement, he shared this conception of the Church of England with his godfather, John Keble.[5]

In *Literature and Dogma*, Arnold uses some of his most sardonic irony to describe an Anglican ritualist celebration of the mass. The whole context of the passage is interesting, in relation both to Arnold's overall theological assumptions and to Trollope's portrayal of faith and doubt. Arnold argues that the problem with doctrines such as the Roman Catholic understanding of the mass or the Protestant idea of justification is that they cannot be proven: "This is the real objection both to the Catholic and to the Protestant doctrine as a basis for conduct; – not that it is a degrading superstition, but that it is *not sure*; that it assumes what cannot be *verified*" (*Complete Prose* 6:361). Here Arnold confuses faith or belief with knowledge, thereby inadvertently revealing the reason why his whole theological project is necessary. According to him, a basis for conduct can only be valid if it is empirically verified, so that in a late essay, "The Study of Poetry," he is able to say that Christianity is declining because "our religion has materialised itself in the fact, in the supposed fact; it has attached its emotion to the fact, and now the fact is failing it" (*Complete Prose* 9:161). He assumes, like many scientists, that religious faith is impossible after the scientific revolution and the Enlightenment; unlike those scientists, however, as A.O.J. Cockshut notes in one of the most perceptive analyses of Arnold's religious writings, he did not conclude that humanity had to learn therefore to live without religion. Referring to the introduction to *God and the Bible*, Cockshut writes that Arnold felt closer to the evangelists Dwight L. Moody and Ira D. Sankey than he did to the Victorian scientist and dogmatic atheist W.K. Clifford, even though the former embodied everything Arnold was attacking in *St Paul and Protestantism* (1870), while the latter shared Arnold's rejection of "a personal God, dogma and miracle" (Cockshut, *Unbelievers*, 68). To return to Arnold's description of High Church worship, he notes in *Literature and Dogma* that for a long time Christians did not worry that dogma assumes that which cannot be verified:

And there are still, and for a long time yet there will be, many to whom it does not occur. In particular, on those "devout women" who in the history of religion have continually played a part in many respects so beautiful but in some respects so mischievous, – on them, and on a certain number of men like them, it has and can as yet have, so far as one can see, no effect at all. Who that watches the energumens during the celebration of the Communion in some Ritualistic church, their gestures and behaviour, the floor of the church strewn with what seem to be the dying and the dead, progress to the altar almost barred by forms suddenly dropping as if they were shot in battle, – who that observes this delighted adoption of vehement rites, till yesterday unknown, adopted and practised now with all that absence of tact, measure, and correct perception in things of form and manner, all that slowness to see when they are making themselves ridiculous, which belongs to the people of our English race, – who, I say, that marks this can doubt, that for a not small portion of our religious community a difficulty to the intelligence will for a long time yet be no difficulty at all? (*Complete Prose* 6:361)

Arnold was not without sympathy for Anglican ritualism in certain forms (see Honan, *A Life*, 351–2) but was opposed both to the dogmatic basis of Anglo-Catholicism and to the more fervent excesses of ritualist practice. I wonder whether the reference to devout women was an allusion to the religious practices of his own wife, who was once described as "a zealous and consistent High Churchwoman of the Tractarian School" (in Honan, *A Life*, 187).

In the preface to *Last Essays on Church and Religion* Arnold asks rhetorically, "Will there never arise among Catholics some great soul, to perceive that the eternity and universality, which is vainly claimed for Catholic dogma and the ultramontane system, might really be possible for Catholic worship?" (*Complete Prose* 8:162).[6] This remark has been much ridiculed,[7] and indeed it is nonsensical, from the point of view of simple indifference to religion and from that of orthodox belief. Nevertheless, it captures the essence of Arnold's approach to matters ecclesiastical and theological. Catholic worship represented to Arnold a form of poetry, which like other forms of poetry might be capable of many different interpretations. It is thus not surprising that in the late essay "The Study of Poetry" he speaks of religion being replaced by poetry.[8] Those acquainted in more detail with Roman Catholicism might also remember that in the "Stanzas from the Grand Chartreuse" Arnold displayed a vagueness about the specific practices of Catholic worship that mirrors the lack of close analysis in much of his literary criticism.[9]

Arnold wrote three books on the Bible with the overall aim of reconstituting Christianity in the context – or, as he would have said, in accordance with the *Zeitgeist* – of a scientific age. Thus, he rejected from the beginning all concepts of the miraculous and the supernatural, and most of the received language used to talk about God, in order to insist on "the natural truth of Christianity" (*Complete Prose* 6:143) and thereby give to the Bible "a real experimental basis" (6:151). He had already begun to sketch out this basis in *St Paul and Protestantism* (1869-70), where he declares that the epistles of St Paul should be read as literary discourse, not science. To Arnold, the historical error of the Protestant reading of St Paul can be explained as follows: "What in St Paul is secondary and subordinate, Puritanism has made primary and essential; what in St Paul is figure and belongs to the sphere of feeling, Puritanism has transported into the sphere of intellect and made thesis and formula. On the other hand, what is with St Paul primary, Puritanism has treated as subordinate: and what is with him thesis and belonging (so far as anything in religion can be said to belong) to the sphere of intellect, Puritanism has made image and figure" (*Complete Prose* 6:8).

To Arnold, religion is primarily a matter of conduct, which he insists is "three-fourths of human life" (6:173). Like Friedrich Schleiermacher and other theologians of the Romantic movement he locates the sources of religion in human feelings. In *Literature and Dogma* Arnold writes:

> Religion, if we follow the intention of human thought and human language in the use of the word, is ethics heightened, enkindled, lit up by feeling; the passage from morality to religion is made when to morality is applied emotion. And the true meaning of religion is thus, not simply *morality*, but *morality touched by emotion*. And this new elevation and inspiration of morality is well marked by the word "righteousness." Conduct is the word of common life, morality is the word of philosophical disquisition, righteousness is the word of religion. (*Complete Prose* 6:176)

God, Arnold insists both in *Literature and Dogma* and in the later *God and the Bible*, is not a magnified man (a statement that is in itself quite orthodox) but rather, as far as we can have knowledge of God, "simply *the stream of tendency by which all things seek to fulfil the law of their being*" (6:189), so that the germ of religious consciousness in ancient Israel was "a consciousness of *the not ourselves which makes for righteousness*" (6:196; Arnold's emphasis). Like Renan, Arnold combines these liberal tenets with the implied, and sometimes explicit, claim to understand Jesus better than the disciples were able to, and sometimes perhaps better even than Jesus understood himself. Indeed, readers of Arnold's books on the Bible might legitimately conclude that Arnold believed himself to be the first person really to understand what Jesus was getting at. His poem "Rugby Chapel" suggests that his father, Thomas Arnold, was a kind of Moses figure preparing the way for the later revelation of the latter-day Matthew, his son, as well as being himself Christlike:

> If, in the paths of the world,
> Stones might have wounded thy feet,
> Toil or dejection have tried
> Thy spirit, of that we saw
> Nothing – to us thou wast still
> Cheerful, and helpful, and firm!
> Therefore to thee it was given
> Many to save with thyself;
> And, at the end of the day,
> O faithful shepherd! to come,
> Bringing thy sheep in thy hand.
> (*Poems*, 450, lines 134–44)

As W. David Shaw notes with an irony worthy of Arnold himself, "If Arnold admires everything about Catholicism except its Christianity, he admires everything about biblical typology except its doctrinal content. Moses is no longer a type of Christ ... He is now a type of Dr Thomas Arnold and his agnostic son, who uses the biblical type to prefigure a new religion of culture and man" (*Lucid Veil*, 145).

If Arnold represents the logical conclusion of a liberalizing tendency that took nothing on faith but retained nonetheless a deep and conservative attachment to the institution and practices of the religion it was intellectually undermining, Trollope provides us with a prescient fictional analysis of the psychology and sociology of this tendency. In his little-known novel *The Bertrams*, a young Englishman who is thinking of the Church as a career makes a tour of the Middle East in search of his father, who is an English diplomat of questionable moral character. The tour is also in a sense a search for a Heavenly Father, as George Bertram first finds his religious vocation in a moment of revelation on the Mount of Olives and then relinquishes it when his enthusiasm is mocked by a woman to whom he is attracted.

The Bertrams was published in 1859, the same year as Darwin's *Origin of Species*, although it is set in the 1840s, and it alludes both to the Oxford Movement and to the political upheaval surrounding the repeal of the Corn Laws in 1846. In his *Autobiography*, Trollope denigrated *The Bertrams*, saying, "I do not know that I have ever heard it well spoken of even by my friends," and noting that the plot "was more than ordinarily bad" (125, 126). Nevertheless, it is a novel with a great deal to interest any student of the Victorian period, and it is by no means as lacking in merit as Trollope implied. One of its distinctive features is that it combines the political themes of Trollope's Palliser novels with the religious material of his Barchester novels. It has been described as "the most intellectual" of Trollope's forty-seven novels (Mullen and Munson, *Companion*, 42). Trollope is not always taken seriously as a thinker, although there have been several studies of the contribution of his novels to ethical thought.[10] W. David Shaw has discussed the role of reserve in Trollope's work in relation to the issue of mysteries of identity;[11] as storytellers, his narrators are reserved about intellectual questions and even more so about metaphysical and theological issues. Such matters are not the normal stuff of fiction, as Trollope knew, and perhaps he also knew of various embarrassing attempts to prove otherwise. At the same time, Trollope's novels, especially *The Bertrams*, do have theological implications, and in *The Bertrams* the doctrine of reserve, which was discussed in the previous chapter, is itself the object of scrutiny.

In the discussion that follows, I compare Trollope's treatment of theology in *The Bertrams*, specifically his treatment of biblical criticism and its effects, with the argument in Matthew Arnold's books on the Bible. Trollope's collection of sketches, *Clergymen of the Church of England* (1866), provides another useful reference point. Trollope was well aware of the effect on the Victorian church of both the Oxford Movement and biblical criticism, and in *The Bertrams* he exposes the vulnerability of the liberal attempt to resolve the dilemmas resulting from these developments. As a realistic novel that includes a trip to Jerusalem, *The Bertrams* can also be seen as a commentary on the Middle Eastern romance of Benjamin Disraeli's *Tancred, or The New Crusade* (1847).

The Bertrams is critical of the preoccupation with competition and professional success in the mid-Victorian world; as in many of his novels, Trollope contrasts the struggle for existence in London with the more humane and chivalric values that survive in pockets of rural England. Past and present are similarly contrasted in another novel of 1859, George

Eliot's *Adam Bede*, which is also concerned with the foundations of religious belief. Eliot, of course, conceals a demythologizing humanism
beneath the representation of Methodist and Anglican piety in her rural
England of 1799–1800. Her treatment of theology in this novel will be
the focus of my next chapter.

Trollope begins *The Bertrams* with an essay-like prologue entitled "Vae
Victis" (Woe to the Vanquished) in which he argues that although mid-
Victorian England is superficially an "age of humanity" (1), human feelings
are disregarded in the competitive world of middle-class life, where "success is the only test of merit" (3). The prologue makes significant use of
biblical allusion to add to the force of the argument. In the world Trollope
represents, the biblical text "To him that hath shall be given; and from
him that hath not shall be taken even that which he hath" is given a literal
and materialistic interpretation (2).[12] This competitive ideology has
reversed the wisdom of the Bible. Trollope rewrites Ecclesiastes 9:11 in
the following passage: "Let us get rid of the fault of past ages. With us,
let the race be ever to the swift; the victory always to the strong. And let
us always be racing, so that the swift and strong shall ever be known
among us" (2). The Pauline race for the incorruptible crown (1 Corinthians
9:25) has in effect been turned into a rat race, or more accurately a horse
race; for Trollope combines his biblical allusions with metaphors from
other fields of activity, including the turf, thus implying the difficulty of
distinguishing between worldly and religious motivations, a recurrent
theme in the novel. As well as being topical, the horse-racing metaphor
alludes to the role that chance plays in the lives of the characters. The
problem that George Bertram struggles with throughout the book is that,
while he is sceptical about the existence of the incorruptible crown and
so cannot wholeheartedly pursue it, he is not single-minded enough to
pursue worldly success at all costs, as his friend Henry Harcourt does. As
with Thackeray's use of the parable of Dives and Lazarus in *Vanity Fair*,
Trollope's biblical allusions highlight the dearth of charity in the self-
proclaimed "age of humanity"; meanwhile, the ironic inversion of biblical
precepts indicates the difficulty that the characters, especially George,
have in living according to Christian values, given the combined effect
on those values of Mammon and the intellectual critique of religion.

The Bertrams focuses on the fortunes of a group of young people,
among them George Bertram and Arthur Wilkinson – two latter-day
English knights, as their names suggest. At the end of the first chapter,

in a striking example of the competition Trollope has been talking about, they receive their university examination results: while Wilkinson only gains second-class honours, Bertram achieves a double first and tries to decide whether to enter the Church, read for the bar, or pursue a career as a writer, a seat in Parliament being one of his more distant goals. In the end, his future is decided on his trip to the Middle East. Before turning to Trollope's Jerusalem chapters I shall look briefly at the very different Middle Eastern trip in Disraeli's *Tancred*; for, as Ruth apRoberts notes, *Tancred* is a kind of popularized version "of the comparative approach to religion" (*Arnold and God*, 175) and must to that extent have been instructive to its first English readers. In a more modest and sceptical way, Trollope attempts the same task in portions of *The Bertrams*.

Tancred is a romance rather than a realistic novel. Instead of treating religious questions with reserve, it recounts, with a mixture of ironic comedy and fervent seriousness, the young Lord Montacute's pilgrimage to the Holy Land, where his ancestor had journeyed as a crusader. Tancred Montacute's religious aspirations have been disappointed by the inadequate counsel of the Anglican clergy he has encountered in England, and he resolves to travel to the Middle East because he believes that it is only there that God has ever spoken, or will ever speak, to human beings. Telling his father of his desire to visit the Holy Sepulchre, he says: "It is time to restore and renovate our communications with the Most High. I, too, would kneel at that tomb; I, too, surrounded by the holy hills and sacred groves of Jerusalem, would relieve my spirit from the bale that bows it down; would lift up my voice to heaven, and ask, What is DUTY, and what is FAITH? What ought I to DO, and what ought I to BELIEVE?" (55).

Tancred passes a solemn night of vigil in the Holy Sepulchre but without revelation, whereas on Mount Sinai he is vouchsafed a vision of divinity, a "mighty form" that waves "a sceptre fashioned like a palm tree" and identifies himself as "the angel of Arabia" (290). The angel's parting words to Tancred are "Cease, then, to seek in a vain philosophy the solution of the social problem that perplexes you. Announce the sublime and solacing doctrine of theocratic equality. Fear not, faint not, falter not. Obey the impulse of thine own spirit, and find a ready instrument in every human being" (291). The rest of the novel is largely concerned with political intrigue and adventure that, for a present-day reader, conjures up nothing so much as the world of Indiana Jones. Tancred certainly does not seem endowed with a new spiritual purpose as a result of his revelation; instead, he becomes involved in a complex geopolitical plot that seems to have a racial basis. Nevertheless, Disraeli does make some theological points in this novel. The Church of England, as represented by Tancred, is placed amidst the various churches of the Mediterranean world, which in turn are seen in the context of the other monotheistic religions of the Middle East. In particular, as though in direct refutation of Thomas Arnold's insistence on the radical disjuncture of Christianity and Judaism, Disraeli emphasizes the continuities between the two faiths.

While George Bertram's pilgrimage is far more secular and only in the most attenuated and ironic form to be described as a new crusade, Trollope, like Disraeli, presents the Middle East as the land of faith, the place where his young English heroes confront the question of their vocation in life. Similarly, both novelists use the multicultural nature of the Middle East to present the English church as it were from the outside, which makes *The Bertrams* quite different from Trollope's Barchester novels.

The Jerusalem chapters in *The Bertrams* are the most explicitly religious passages in Trollope's fiction, and they include some effective satire of the irreverence of English tourists, for example as they eat a boiled ham amidst Jewish tombs in the valley of Jehoshaphat, or stand "on the very altar-step while the priest is saying his mass" (100). Trollope drew on his own travels on post office business to write this part of the novel.[13] The central contrast in this section is between, on the one hand, the "traditionary falsehoods" (82), the churches and holy sites that have accumulated over the centuries, so that when you are within the walls of the Holy City "all is ... unbelievable, fabulous, miraculous; nay, all but blasphemous" (83), and, on the other hand, the natural landscape that still speaks to the piety of the Protestant Englishman. It is significant that Trollope uses the word "miraculous" in conjunction with the adjectives "unbelievable" and blasphemous"; nearly twenty-five years later Arnold wrote, as though presenting an element of his faith, that "our popular religion at present conceives the birth, ministry, and death of Christ, as altogether steeped in prodigy, brimful of miracle; – *and miracles do not happen*" (in Arnold, *Complete Prose* 6:146; Arnold's emphasis).[14]

George's objection to Jerusalem is in good part aesthetic: not only are the holy sites repugnant to his English taste but they are contained in a dirty and uncomfortable city. "George Bertram had promised himself that the moment in which he first saw Jerusalem should be one of intense mental interest," but instead he finds himself riding uncomfortably "down a steep, narrow, ill-paved lane, with a half-formed gully in the middle, very slippery with orange-peel and old vegetables, and crowded with the turbans of all the Eastern races" (*Bertrams*, 67). As a result, the first thing he does in the holy city is to swear at his horse. By contrast, Disraeli's *Tancred* does not identify natural beauty with religious experience. As he journeys from Jerusalem to Bethany he reflects, "What need for nature to be fair in a scene like this, where not a spot is visible that is not heroic or sacred, consecrated or memorable" (*Tancred*, 183).

Trollope's presentation of religious feeling in *The Bertrams* can be illustrated effectively by the contrast between two different sacred sites, the Church of the Holy Sepulchre, where warring Christian factions are kept apart by Muslim guards, and the Mount of Olives, which is where George has the religious experience that leads him to his short-lived determination to enter the Church. He does not enjoy his visit to the Church of the Holy Sepulchre, an event that Trollope describes in some detail. George is first confronted by the spectacle of the various competing churches, Roman and Eastern, with their respective altars, none of which is reserved for his own Church of England. Disraeli made a similar observation in *Tancred*; in describing the hero's vigil at the Holy Sepulchre, the narrator comments, "Yet the pilgrim is not in communion with the Latin Church; neither is he of the Church Armenian, or the Church Greek; Maronite, Coptic, or Abyssinian" (*Tancred*, 169).

In fact, there was a newly consecrated Anglican bishop of Jerusalem in the 1840s, the product of a cooperative venture undertaken by of the Church of England and the German Lutheran church and masterminded by Thomas Arnold's friend Christian Bunsen, a Prussian diplomat who had served in Rome and London, and who was a prolific amateur biblical scholar and theologian. While it embodied a practical example of the elder Arnold's state Protestant imperialism, the establishment of the Jerusalem bishopric was one of the events that determined John Henry Newman's decision to convert to the Church of Rome.[15] It made the notion that the Church of England was one branch of the whole Catholic church far less tenable, since there was already an indigenous Orthodox church in Jerusalem.[16] The first occupant of the new see was Dr Michael Solomon Alexander (1799–1845), a converted Jew, and he was consecrated in 1841. The whole story of the Jerusalem bishopric reads like something invented by Benjamin Disraeli: it was undertaken partly as a result of Britain's desire for influence in Turkey, partly because of the millennial hopes of certain Evangelical clergy, and partly to further the Prussian sovereign's effort to introduce episcopacy into the German church.[17] Having refused to travel on a ship called the *Infernal*, the new bishop was carried to his see on a British warship with the only slightly less objectionable name *Devastation* (Chadwick, *Victorian Church* 1:190). The Evangelical novelist Mrs Tonna addressed a public letter to the bishop requesting that he have his sons circumcised (Wolff, *Gains*, 206). Appropriately enough, Disraeli has the bishop of Jerusalem welcoming Tancred's clerical travelling companion. Trollope does not bring the issue into *The Bertrams*, but he does mention the bishop of Jerusalem in *The Eustace Diamonds* (1873) in a somewhat disreputable context. He ordains the fraudulent Jewish convert, the Reverend Mr Emilius, who in *The Prime Minister* (1876) is shown to be not only a bigamist but a murderer. As a further historical note, it is worth mentioning that the Prussian involvement in the Jerusalem bishopric did not last. The Anglican church in Jerusalem was more successful at "converting" Arab Christians than Jews and Muslims, and Edward Said discussed the curious historical irony whereby, in the twentieth century, the parent church suggested, with the same paternalism with which the see had been established, that it would be well for the Palestinian Anglicans, along with other groups of Arab Protestants, to rejoin the Orthodox church, thus negating the history by which they had been formed (Said, *Culture*, 39–41).

Unlike Disraeli's hero, who pays for the privilege of a solitary vigil in the Church of the Holy Sepulchre, George Bertram's visit to the sepulchre itself is made in the company of various pilgrims:

> Those who were there around him seemed to be the outcasts of the world, exactly those whom he would have objected to meet, unarmed, on the roads of Greece or among the hills of Armenia; cut-throat-looking wretches, with close shaven heads, dirty beards, and angry eyes; men clothed in skins, or huge skin-like-looking cloaks, filthy, foul, alive with vermin, reeking with garlic, – abominable to an Englishman. There was about them a certain dignity of demeanour, a natural aptitude to carry themselves with ease, and even a not impure taste for colour among their dirt. But these Christians of the Russian Church hardly appeared to him to be brothers of his own creed.
>
> But he did put his hand on the slab of the tomb; and as he did so, two young Greeks, brothers by blood – Greeks by their creed, though

of what actual nation Bertram was quite unable to say – pressed their lips vehemently to the marble. They were dirty, shorn about the head, dangerous-looking, and skin-clothed, as we have described; men very low in the scale of humanity when compared with their fellow-pilgrim; but, nevertheless, they were to him at that moment objects of envy. They believed: so much at any rate was clear to him. By whatever code of morals they might be able to govern their lives, whether by any, or as, alas! might be too likely, by none, at least they possessed a faith. Christ to them was an actual living truth, though they knew how to worship him no better than by thus kissing a stone, which had in fact no closer reference to the Saviour than any other stone they might have kissed in their own country. (73–4)

This is a complex passage, which depicts sympathetically George's feeling of racial superiority, yet recognizes that the Orthodox pilgrims, the "outcasts of the world," are precisely those for whom the gospel was originally preached. Furthermore, George envies them for the simple and fervent religious faith that he is unable to share. Our attitude to George's experience depends in part on our view of religious faith. If faith is the most important thing, then the pilgrims are better off than George, just as Newman had suggested – to the horror and contempt of Thackeray – that a religious but unethical beggar-woman was better off than an ethical but unbelieving gentleman. But the nature of faith is ultimately mysterious and therefore incommensurate with a rational understanding of the universe, and Trollope's reader is invited to conclude that faith is possibly something that must be transcended by civilization. Certainly faith is presented here as the possession of the "uncivilized," in George's terms. While George may envy the pilgrims the security of their simple faith, he is like the figures in Arnold's "Stanzas from the Grand Chartreuse" who have gone beyond the possibility of such an attitude and yet are nostalgic for the lost age of faith.

Trollope in part resolves this impasse when he describes another form of religious experience, one more suitable to an educated English gentleman. This occurs in the Romantic solitude of the Mount of Olives, outside the city itself. There, in that natural setting, George has what might be called a liberal Protestant epiphany, a kind of Wordsworthian revelation, which Trollope refrains from describing in detail. The closest he comes is to say of the Mount of Olives that "if there be a spot in that land of wondrous memories which does bring home to the believer in Christ some individualized remembrance of his Saviour's earthly pilgrimage, that certainly is it" (76–7). Trollope's narrator declares that to reflect on why it is that the Mount has this atmosphere of authenticity is not appropriate to "these light novel pages" (78). As we saw in *Vanity Fair*, the exercise of reserve is in keeping with the decorum of the novel genre, but Trollope does something that Thackeray does not, explicitly referring the reader to another book that reflects at some length on the edifying atmosphere of the Mount of Olives: A.P. Stanley's *Sinai and Palestine in Connection with Their History* (1856). Stanley, the disciple and biographer of Thomas Arnold, makes a contrast similar to Trollope's between the streets of Jerusalem, where "it is useless to seek for traces" of Christ's presence, and the "free space of the Mount of Olives," where it is "impossible not to find them" (*Sinai*, 189). The connections between Wordsworth and Coleridge and the Arnold circle are well known;[18] for Coleridge was a key intellectual influence on the whole Broad Church tendency, particularly on Thomas Arnold's doctrine of the Church, while Wordsworth was the neighbour and friend of the Arnold family. A.P. Stanley, far more than Matthew Arnold, was heir to Thomas Arnold's intellectual and theological legacy. In Stanley's account of his trip to Palestine as well as in Trollope's fictional account of a young Englishman's moment of religious fervour, we find what could be described as a Wordsworthian reading of the Gospels, in which the associations experienced in the natural setting of the Mount of Olives affirm the truth of the narratives of the life of Christ. Something similar can be found in Renan's *Life of Jesus*, though Renan combines his highly sentimental Romanticism with an iconoclastic scepticism, attributing questionable motives to the disciples and to Jesus himself.[19]

Having visited the Mount of Olives, George Bertram "resolved that he would be a clergyman … He would be one of the smallest, one of the least of those who would fight the good fight; but, though smallest and least, he would do it with what earnestness was in him" (*Bertrams*, 81). In the very next paragraph, however, the narrator declares, "Reader! you may already, perhaps, surmise that George Bertram does not become a clergyman. It is too true." The reason he does not is that he falls in love with a young woman who is an embodiment of the spirit of the Enlightenment: "She could speak of sacred things with a mocking spirit, the mockery of philosophy rather than of youth; she had little or no enthu-

siasm, though there was passion enough deep seated in her bosom; she
suffered from no transcendentalism; she saw nothing through a halo of
poetic inspiration: among the various tints of her atmosphere there was
no rose colour; she preferred wit to poetry; and her smile was cynical
rather than joyous" (99). In the face of Caroline Waddington's smile of
reason, George's romantic piety wilts. As Ruth apRoberts notes (*Moral*,
115–16), Trollope portrays the psychological roots of George's later loss
of faith with great insight: "He had not strength of character to laugh at
her description and yet to be unmoved by it. He must either resent what
she said, or laugh and be ruled by it. He must either tell her that she knew
nothing of a clergyman's dearest hopes, or else he must yield to the contempt which her words implied" (*Bertrams*, 122).

Because George's sense of vocation is rooted in an emotional reaction
to a particular place, it cannot survive the fact that Caroline does not
share that reaction. If, to the spiritual man of feeling, the devout woman
is a channel of grace, the sceptical woman, through the same alchemy of
erotic attraction and spiritual influence, has a destructive influence on
religious belief. George finds himself subtly persuaded by Caroline's
mockery, and once more Trollope employs a biblical metaphor: "Still he
thought of the tables of the money-changers, and the insufficiency of
him who had given as much as half to the poor. But even while so thinking, he was tempted to give less than half himself, to set up on his own
account a money-changing table in his own temple. He would fain have
worshipped at the two shrines together had he been able. But he was not
able; so he fell down before that of Mammon" (123). The upshot is that
George decides to read for the bar, but when Caroline postpones their
engagement until he has qualified, George neglects his studies. Instead,
he writes an essay of biblical criticism, in the tradition of Strauss, Feuerbach, and George Eliot, entitled "The Romance of Scripture." Trollope is
particularly interesting on the question of faith and doubt. George

had intended to be honest in his remonstrance; but it is not every man
who knows exactly what he does believe. Every man! Is there, one may
almost ask, any man who has such knowledge? We all believe in the
resurrection of the body; we say so at least, but what do we believe by
it?

Men may be firm believers and yet doubt some Bible statements –
doubt the letter of such statements. But men who are firm believers

will not be those to put forth their doubts with all their eloquence. Such men, if they devote their time to Scripture history, will not be arrested by the sun's standing on Gibeon. If they speak out at all, they will speak out rather as to all they do believe than as to the little that they doubt. (221–2)

Trollope came back to this question in an essay he wrote in 1866 entitled "The Clergyman Who Subscribes to Colenso," which formed the last chapter of his book of sketches, *The Clergymen of the Church of England*.[20] Echoing the passage from *The Bertrams*, he declares there that "it is very hard to come at the actual belief of any man. Indeed how should we hope to do so when we find it so very hard to come at our own?" ("Clergyman," 124). In this essay Trollope acknowledges that liberal theology has created a new world, and that one must live in that world:

If one could stay, if one could only have a choice in the matter, if one could really believe that the old shore is best, who would leave it? Who would not wish to be secure if he knew where security lay? But this new teacher, who has come among us with his ill-defined doctrines and his subrisive smile, – he and they who have taught him, – have made it impossible for us to stay. With hands outstretched towards the old places, with sorrowing hearts, – with hearts which still love the old teachings which the mind will no longer accept, – we, too, cut our ropes, and go out in our little boats, and search for a land that will be new to us, though how far new, – new in how many things, we do not know. Who would not stay behind if it were possible to him? (128)

George Bertram's friend Arthur Wilkinson still felt no need for such a search. As Trollope's narrator comments, "Wilkinson would have been contented to be let alone; to have his mind, and faith, and hopes left in the repose which nature and education had prepared for them" (*Bertrams*, 333). Trollope's novel as a whole, however, might be said to offer a prophetic demonstration of the difficulties involved in Arnold's attempt to construct a demythologized Christianity. For Trollope there is an aporia in which the alternatives seem to be the irrational superstitious faith of the uncivilized, and the flimsy sentimental faith of the educated. He shows the vulnerability of a religion viewed as "ethics heightened, enkindled, lit up by feeling ... *morality tinged by emotion*," as Arnold defined it in *Literature and Dogma* (*Complete Prose* 6:176; Arnold's emphasis). Since he is not given to metaphysical or theological speculation, Trollope exercises the novelist's privilege of declining to resolve the dilemma he presents. Instead, he implies that one should maintain a gentlemanly reserve while following the traditional ways of High Church Anglicanism. Arthur Wilkinson, the average man, performs his clerical duties in an unreflective way and gains a degree of happiness and usefulness that George is denied. George is an extremist, seeing true faith as the most sublime thing in human experience and anything less as a contemptible hypocrisy. Arthur sees what George calls "the whole gamut of humanity from St Paul to Pecksniff" as a continuum, on which he strives to be "nearer to St Paul than to Pecksniff"; George seems to think that everyone who is not a St Paul is merely a Pecksniff (*Bertrams*, 331). Trollope thus seems to recommend that one should deal with the challenge of the liberal critique by acknowledging it intellectually, while exercising reserve about speaking on theological matters so as to minimize the disruptive effect. This is the same strategy that Trollope adopted in the sphere of politics, famously saying, "I consider myself to be an advanced, but still a conservative Liberal" (*Autobiography*, 291). George's rationalistic logic destroys any possibility of faith by expecting human beings to behave in a totally consistent manner. He exclaims to Arthur: "Your flocks do not believe, do not pray, do not listen to you. They are not in earnest! In earnest! Heavens! if a man could believe all this, could be in earnest about it, how possibly could he care about other things?" (*Bertrams*, 335). George is "angry with himself for not believing, and angry with others that they did believe" (333). Arthur is content to let some things be matters for faith rather than knowledge, and to regard "prayer to God" as a sufficient "fountainhead" of faith (334).

Thomas Arnold's solution was rather different and stands in the tradition of which Schleiermacher was both a source and the major figure. As Karl Barth notes, "The nineteenth century brought with it many deviations from Schleiermacher, and many protests against him; often his ideas were distorted to the point of unrecognizability, and he was often overlooked and forgotten. But in the theological field it was nevertheless his century" ("Schleiermacher," 425). Barth further notes that Schleiermacher based his theology in "pious feeling," or "pious self-awareness" (454) and that for him "The kingdom of God ... is utterly and unequivocally identical with the advance of civilization" (435). In Thomas Arnold, this emphasis on the progress of civilization finds expression as the doctrine of accommodation, which views God's revelation as unfolding progressively. The Bible could thus be viewed as at once the word of God and the product of a different time, subject to the limitations of that time, since God's revelation had to accommodate itself to those limitations and adapt itself to the state of human knowledge at the time when it entered history. He thus distinguishes between the "truth of revelation" and the "inspiration of the historical record of it" (Thomas Arnold, "Interpretation," 415). As a result, certain divine commands, such as the injunction to Saul to slaughter all of the Amalekites (1 Samuel 15) – the kind of biblical story that made Thackeray so hostile to the Old Testament – could be understood as commandments that were given "to persons differently circumstanced from ourselves" and thus no longer directly binding, though instructive by analogy (389). The danger, of course, is that in the senior Arnold's theology the progress of Christianity and the progress of civilization become identified, logically justifying an imperial mission to disseminate a more advanced understanding of the gospel.[21] For Matthew Arnold, the doctrine of accommodation is transformed into the notion of the *Zeitgeist*, that mysterious force that determines what is and is not possible and reasonable to be thought and felt. By following the *Zeitgeist* and by reading the Bible as a literary structure, as a series of poetic statements tending to promote virtue, Arnold sought to resolve George Bertram's problem of belief, and to set out a form of Christianity that George would have been able to accept. A similar explanation is provided in Robert Browning's "A Death in the Desert." In that poem, the dying St John articulates an evolutionary understanding of Christian belief, explaining how it has been accommodated to the needs of the hearers:

> I say, that as the babe, you feed awhile,
> Becomes a boy and fit to feed himself,
> So, minds at first must be spoon-fed with truth:
> When they can eat, babe's-nurture is withdrawn.
> I fed the babe whether it would or no:
> I bid the boy or feed himself or starve.
> I cried once, "That ye may believe in Christ,
> Behold this blind man shall receive his sight!"

I cry now, "Urgest thou, *for I am shrewd*
And smile at stories how John's word could cure –
Repeat that miracle and take my faith?"
I say, that miracle was duly wrought
When, save for it, no faith was possible.
Whether a change were wrought i' the shows o' the world,
Whether the change came from our minds which see
Of the shows o' the world so much as and no more
Than God wills for His purpose, – (what do I
See now, suppose you, there where you see rock
Round us?) – I know not; such was the effect,
So faith grew, making void more miracles
Because too much: they would compel, not help.
          · (In Browning, *Dramatis Personae*, 85–6, lines 453–73)

Trollope is more cautious than Arnold or Browning, and in his depiction of the failure of George's short-lived religious vocation he shows the limitations of such liberal versions of Christianity. In part this is no doubt the result of the cautious and conservative tone of Trollope's mind. The eloquent first chapter of *The Bertrams*, with its scepticism about the extent to which Victorian England really does represent an age of humanity, sets the tone for the whole novel. Those who compete according to the rules of the race, seeking only worldly success, are in the end the unhappiest: Henry Harcourt is driven to suicide and Caroline must suffer the guilt of her part in his death. Clearly for Trollope Christianity is something other than the progress of civilization. On the other hand, Trollope was very much a man of his time. It is significant that, unlike many of the other major Victorian novelists, he did not usually set his novels in an earlier generation; on the contrary, they are highly topical in their cultural allusions and political references. One of the few theological books that Trollope had in his library was *Essays and Reviews* (Mullen, *Trollope*, 253). As "The Clergyman Who Subscribes to Colenso" shows, Trollope knew that the results of biblical criticism had to be faced. If we had a choice, he argued, we would remain where we were; instead, we must "cut our ropes, and go out in our little boats" ("Clergyman," 128). Here Trollope uses a metaphor common in Matthew Arnold's poetry. The difference between Arnold and Trollope lies in Trollope's notion of reserve. It was best, he thought, not to talk of such things very much and allow the changes to occur beneath the cover of the old forms; that way their effect could be minimized. Furthermore, as we have seen, he hinted that the pursuit of truth could not be the only motive at work in those who spoke so much about the problems of belief. Trollope too may have believed in the *Zeitgeist*, but unlike Arnold he had no interest in speculating about it.

The Bertrams is a fascinating depiction of Victorian faith and doubt, set with Trollope's keen sense of history in the 1840s, the decade of the Oxford Movement, of Mary Ann Evans's translation of David Friedrich Strauss's *Life of Jesus Critically Examined* (1846), and of J.A. Froude's sceptical *Nemesis of Faith*. With his profound understanding of the psychology of faith and doubt, Trollope gave us a sense of what it felt like to be an individual grappling – at a particular historical moment – with what in intellectual history are sometimes seen as merely abstract theological questions. Instead of wrestling with the *Zeitgeist*, as Arnold did in his religious prose, Trollope enabled us to experience with his characters the effects of that mysterious time-spirit at work among them.

FIVE

"FEELING'S A SORT O' KNOWLEDGE": GEORGE ELIOT'S RELIGION OF HUMANITY

Instruction in religion, meaning that piety itself is teachable, is absurd and unmeaning. Our opinions and doctrines we can indeed communicate, if we have words and our hearers have the comprehending, imagining power of the understanding. But we know very well that those things are only the shadows of our religious emotions, and if our pupils do not share our emotions, even though they do understand the thought, they have no possession that can truly repay their toil.   Friedrich Schleiermacher, *On Religion*

——◀◯▶——

THE PROCESS BY WHICH MARY ANN EVANS became George Eliot is one of the best known of the Victorian loss-of-faith stories. As a young woman of nineteen, Mary Ann was a fervent evangelical. This can be seen in her correspondence with her friend and former teacher Maria Lewis, to whom she wrote in May 1839: "The authors of the Oxford Tracts ... evince by their compliments to Rome, as a dear though erring Sister, and their attempts to give a romish colour to our ordinances, with a very confused and unscriptural statement of the great doctrine of justification, a disposition rather to fraternize with the members of a church carrying on her brow the prophetical epithets applied by St John to the Scarlet beast, the Mystery of iniquity, than with pious non-conformists" (*George Eliot Letters* 1:26). As a staunch Protestant, she saw the catholicizing tendencies of the Tractarians as a form of fraternizing with the enemy. Not surprisingly, her moral views were derived from her religious opinions. In a particularly interesting letter of 16 March 1839, for example, she discusses the reading of novels, an activity frowned on by strict evangelicals:[1]

> I am I confess not an impartial member of a jury in this case for I owe the culprits a grudge for injuries inflicted on myself. I shall carry to my grave the mental diseases with which they have contaminated me. When I was quite a little child I could not be satisfied with the things around me; I was constantly living in a world of my own creation, and was quite contented to have no companions that I might be left to my own musings and imagine scenes in which I was chief actress. Conceive what a character novels would give to these Utopias. I was early supplied with them by those who kindly sought to gratify my appetite for reading and of course I made use of the materials they supplied for building my castles in the air. (*Letters* 1:22)

The use of the word "Utopias" is interesting, for we see the mature George Eliot using it in an important discussion of aesthetic teaching with her Positivist admirer Frederic Harrison. The forensic metaphor also reappears in the celebrated statement of Eliot's realistic theory of fiction in chapter 17 of *Adam Bede*. In the second paragraph of that chapter, she acknowledges that the artist's mirror is "doubtless defective"; nevertheless, she writes, "I feel as much bound to tell you, as precisely as I can, what that reflection is, as if I were in the witness-box narrating my experience on oath" (*Bede*, 175).

Within three years of writing these letters to Maria Lewis, Mary Ann Evans had become acquainted with sceptical biblical criticism, notably Charles Hennell's *Inquiry Concerning the Origin of Christianity* (1838), which seems to have been the work that precipitated her refusal to go to church with her father on 2 January 1842 (Ashton, *A Life*, 36). Hennell's inquiry was instigated by his sister Caroline's marriage to Charles Bray, into whose circle in Coventry Mary Ann was welcomed after she and her father moved to the outskirts of the city in 1841. In response to Bray's sceptical views, Charles Hennell undertook to examine the scriptural evidence for the divine origin of Christianity. As he explains in his preface, he gradually came to the conclusion "that the true account of the life of Jesus Christ, and of the spread of his religion, would be found to contain no deviation from the known laws of nature, nor to require, for their explanation, more than the operation of human motives and feelings, acted upon by the peculiar circumstances of the age and country whence the religion originated" (*Inquiry*, iv).[2] His rationalist approach is accompanied by a liberal optimism about human progress. Although he rejects the idea of any kind of inspired status for the Bible, he seeks to reassure those of a religious temperament: "The cause of progressive mental improvement may at length require that such narrations should be placed amongst the things of romance rather than of history: but this being done, the imagination may still delight itself by contemplating them in what now appears to be their true and proper light; and the more freely, from its being now unchecked by the necessity of explaining and reconciling those absurdities and inconsistencies which must belong to them when viewed as matters of fact" (322). If the gospels are to be viewed as imaginative romance, George Eliot's novels can be seen as alternative romances, often typologically connected to the Christian scriptures, that sought to delight the imagination by showing "the operation of human motives and feelings," with careful attention to "the peculiar circumstances of the age and country," that is, to the social and cultural context in which her characters lived. Throughout her fiction she recognizes, as she wrote in *Felix Holt, The Radical* (1866), that "there is no private life which has not been determined by a wider public life" (43).

In 1844 Mary Ann Evans began her intellectual career by undertaking the translation of David Friedrich Strauss's *Das Leben Jesu, kritisch bearbeitet* (1835), working from the fourth edition of 1840. Her translation was published anonymously in three volumes in 1846 as *The Life of Jesus, Critically Examined*. She followed this with reviews of several English contributions to biblical criticism. These reviews form part of the significant corpus of intellectual journalism that she produced between 1851 and 1856, along with her translation of Ludwig Feuerbach's *Essence of Christianity* (1854). The latter appeared under the name "Marian Evans," the spelling of her name she adopted in 1851 (Ashton, *A Life*, 80).

George Eliot's fiction is central to any discussion of theology and the novel in the Victorian period. The relationship of her fiction to biblical criticism and, more generally, to philosophical ideas has been explored in considerable depth by a number of scholars.[3] Building on their work, I look at an issue that remains problematic – the nature of Eliot's relationship to Christianity; for the views she presents in her novels seem different from those documented in her essays and letters.

The connection between Eliot and Matthew Arnold has been discussed by U.C. Knoepflmacher, but it deserves further consideration. In her early fiction Eliot was doing what Arnold did in his religious books, namely, articulating a non-dogmatic version of Christianity that she shows operating within the institution of the Church. Unlike liberal divines, however, and even unlike Strauss, she did not regard the Church as the institution from which to develop and support a new ethical imperative capable of standing up to scientific scrutiny. It is significant that, apart from *Daniel Deronda*, all of Eliot's novels are set in a past that is at least one generation removed from her own time. Knoepflmacher astutely observes, "George Eliot's humanism contended that the 'essential' ethos of Christianity could live on in the 'idea of humanity as a whole,' but it failed to present her with an actual vehicle for this positive, and Positivist, morality" (*Humanism*, 60–1). The tragedy of *The Mill on the Floss* (1860) can be seen as the result of this failure. In three subsequent novels, *Romola* (1863), *Felix Holt, The Radical*, and *Middlemarch*, the most enduring vehicle seems to be a maternal nurturing woman who combines the characteristics of the Christian Madonna, the Victorian domestic angel, and the Comtean inspiring woman. Art is important in *Romola* and politics in the other two novels (*Middlemarch* toys with the idea of utopian communities and they both address the question of electoral reform), but the characters of Romola, Esther, and Dorothea, a triptych of noble Victorian ladies, dominate the conclusions of these novels. Viewed against this background, George Eliot's use of Judaism in *Daniel Deronda* and the visionary role given to Mordecai seem all the more striking. Following other commentators on the religious aspect of Eliot's fiction, I concentrate on *Adam Bede*, the novel in which Eliot sets out most fully her secular gospel, boldly rewriting the sacred scripture. It is, moreover, a far greater literary achievement than is often realized, a work whose complex patterning throws up new combinations and juxtapositions with every reading.

Peter C. Hodgson has undertaken a theological interpretation of George Eliot's fiction in *The Mystery beneath the Real* (2000). Hodgson argues against the humanistic reading of Eliot by scholars such as Knoepflmacher and Rosemary Ashton and suggests that her affinities with Feuerbach have been overemphasized. I think he is right in his assertion that Eliot remained "a deeply religious thinker" (*Mystery*, ix) in spite of abandoning orthodox Christianity. Hodgson makes it clear that he is writing as a theologian, not as a literary critic, and one cannot object if he finds George Eliot's works useful for one of his primary tasks in his book, that of rethinking religious faith for the postmodern age (ix). However, when he makes statements about Eliot's own religious position Hodgson seriously understates the extent of her breach with Christianity. He refers to Eliot's "nonconformist, noncredal, nonpracticing form of Christian belief" (174), a formulation that has little meaning in the Victorian context, and not a great deal more today. At times he seems to baptize all displays of altruism or acts of solidarity with human suffering as vestigial forms of Christianity. Unlike Mary Ward, George Eliot did not long for the Church of England to change so that she could again be a part of it. Nor did she maintain the kind of ambivalent continuing relationship with it that, in their different ways, both Matthew Arnold and Walter Pater did. Thus, while my reading of the religious dimension of Eliot's fiction converges at times with Hodgson's, he sometimes ignores significant *literary* evidence that contradicts his theological argument.

In a letter to the publisher John Blackwood describing George Eliot's proposed *Scenes of Clerical Life* (1858), George Henry Lewes, who was Eliot's common-law spouse, said that it would "consist of tales and sketches illustrative of the actual life of our country clergy about a quarter of a century ago; but solely in its *human* and *not at all* in its *theological* aspect" (in Eliot, *Letters* 2:269; Lewes's emphasis). Lewes distinguished the series from the recently "abundant religious stories polemical and doctrinal," comparing them instead to Goldsmith and Austen. Each of the three tales that Eliot wrote embodies the lesson that human sympathy is more important than dogmatic teaching and emphasizes the ties that exist between the clerical protagonist and his parishioners. For the unremarkable Amos Barton, it is the death of his wife that overcomes the fault-finding of the people of Shepperton: "His recent troubles had called out their better sympathies, and that is always a source of love" (*Scenes*, 62). Maynard Gilfil's love story, which took place in the dim and distant past, is the source of his friendly bond with his parishioners, a kind of buried life that emerges as a love of humanity, in spite of Gilfil's rather crotchety character. In the more ambitious "Janet's Repentance," the narrator analyzes the effects of the coming of Evangelicalism to the town of Milby, describing its consequences as the inculcation of "that idea of duty, that recognition of something to be lived for beyond the mere satisfaction of self, which is to the moral life what the addition of a great central ganglion is to animal life" (228). The story resembles an evangelical novel of religious controversy in its structure, as Mr Tryan wins over the townspeople before dying a Christian death, but George Eliot presents his religious beliefs in demythologizing human terms, as she does more clearly in *Adam Bede*. In spite of Lewes's description, Eliot did not entirely avoid the theological aspect of clerical life.

Notwithstanding her interest in clerical lives, one would not expect George Eliot to have been very sympathetic to John Henry Newman, given the company she kept, and the views she held. However, Eliot's earnest ethical idealism prompted the following reaction in 1864:

> I have been reading Newman's Apologia pro Vita Suâ, with such absorbing interest that I found it impossible to forsake the book until I had finished it. I don't know whether the affair between him and Kingsley has interested you, or whether you have shared at all my view of it. I have been made so indignant by Kingsley's mixture of arrogance, coarse impertinence and unscrupulousness with real intellectual *in*competence, that my first interest in Newman's answer arose from a wish to see what I consider thoroughly vicious writing thoroughly castigated. But the Apology now mainly affects me as the revelation of a life – how different in form from one's own, yet with how close a fellowship in its needs and burthens – I mean spiritual needs and burthens. (*Letters* 4:158–9)

Here we see clearly Eliot's habitual distinction between the outward form of spiritual life and its real "essence." This distinction is fundamental to Feuerbach's humanized version of Christianity and central to Eliot's fiction, especially *Adam Bede* and *Silas Marner* (1861). To her, Newman's dogmatic beliefs and allegiance to Rome were secondary, a matter of "form"; what was essential was the inner experience of the spiritual life, which was a matter of "needs and burthens," or, as she repeatedly termed it in *Adam Bede*, human suffering and human sympathy. The *Apologia* affected her as "the revelation of a life," a description that might be applied to each of her novels. In the presentation of human lives in fiction, she sought to reveal something about the truth of their experience of suffering and community, a humanistic essence of the revelation that for Christians is authoritatively contained in the life of Jesus Christ as recorded in the four Gospels.

In *Adam Bede* George Eliot is far more self-conscious than she is in *Scenes of Clerical Life* in her methods of showing the spiritual significance of the life of her protagonist. The narrator of *Adam Bede* is generally regarded as male;[4] for the identity of "George Eliot" was still a mystery when the novel was published, and it is named for its male protagonist, not for either of the eligible young women who feature in it. This fact has been seen as another form of "camouflage," like the pseudonym, the novel's real story being that of two paired, contrasted, but ultimately interchangeable women. This was the dominant reading among feminist critics in the 1980s and 1990s.[5] Without quarrelling with the insights of this school of criticism, I focus my discussion on the title character, Adam Bede the carpenter. Since he is, typologically, both Adam and Christ, Adam Bede is meant to typify human experience, and the novel can be read as the story of his spiritual life, with its "needs and burthens," another version of that life of everyman or woman of which Eliot found an example in Newman's *Apologia*. It is true that there are concealed stories about female characters that are of great interest in *Adam Bede*, notably in the chapters describing Hetty's flight, and these qualify my reaction to the novel as a whole. It is important to recognize, however, that Eliot is trying to construct a myth of the typically human, and that Adam Bede is the central figure in that myth. I read the novel as his spiritual biography and as a secular scripture that seeks to give that biography a potentially universal significance.

Sandra Gilbert and Susan Gubar's concept of camouflage, set out in *The Madwoman in the Attic* (1979), could be extended to Eliot's presentation of religious belief in *Adam Bede*. In spite of her own agnosticism, she describes the lives of her Anglicans and Methodists of sixty years ago in such a way that Christian readers might well have assumed that she shared their beliefs. The spiritual lives of the characters are explored in sympathetic detail, and the contrasting modes of worship of the Methodists and the Anglicans are depicted with loving care and at considerable length. In particular, Dinah's biblically saturated discourse is a remarkable creation, demonstrating the centrality of the sacred text in her thinking and expression. The narrator's rationalizing commentary, meanwhile, as he looks back from his own time in mid-century (just before the publication of *Essays and Reviews*) provides a perspective that allows the sceptical or agnostic reader to place the beliefs of Adam and Dinah in a particular historical moment and to assume, as Eliot did, that

the intellectual progress of humanity has made it impossible for an educated person to feel or believe as they did.[6] For example, in the course of
a careful exposition of the behaviour of Methodists at the end of the eighteenth century, aimed at readers with a bias against Methodism, the narrator comments about Seth's love of Dinah: "He was but three-and-twenty,
and had only just learned what it is to love – to love with that adoration
which a young man gives to a woman whom he feels to be greater and
better than himself. Love of this sort is hardly distinguishable from religious feeling. What deep and worthy love is so? whether of woman or
child, or art or music" (*Bede*, 37). The passage ostensibly links Seth's feelings to the religious feelings Dinah has evoked by her preaching. From
the perspective of Feuerbach, on the other hand, it suggests that "religious
feeling" is really another name for the various forms of human attachment
and sympathy. Such a reading is reinforced a page later, when the narrator
admits that the characters of the novel are not part of the modern world
of 1859: "They believed in present miracles, in instantaneous conversions,
in revelations by dreams and visions; they drew lots, and sought for Divine
guidance by opening the Bible at hazard; having a literal way of interpreting the Scriptures, which is not at all sanctioned by approved commentators" (38). Eliot then offers an analogy that bolsters the suggestion
that she is using Methodism as a metaphor for a humanistic outlook:
"The raw bacon which clumsy Molly spares from her own scanty store,
that she may carry it to her neighbour's child to 'stop the fits,' may be a
piteously inefficacious remedy; but the generous stirring of neighbourly
kindness that prompted the deed, has a beneficent radiance that is not
lost" (38). This implies that the supernatural aspects of religion, believed
in by the majority of the characters in the novel, are "piteously inefficacious" remedies, which should nevertheless be respected for the human
goodness that they embody and produce.

An excellent discussion of the way that Eliot camouflaged her true
religious views can be found in an outstanding critical essay by her contemporary Richard Simpson (1863). The liberal Roman Catholic Simpson
notes how the pseudonym "George Eliot" played a vital role in the establishment of Marian Evans's career as a novelist: "It would have been difficult even for so able a writer to gain the public ear as a professedly religious
and even clerical author, if the same name had been signed to the *Clerical
Scenes* in 1858 and to *Adam Bede* in 1859, as had been signed to transla-
tions of Strauss's *Life of Jesus* in 1846, and of Feuerbach's *Essence of Chris-*

tianity in 1853" ("Novels," 222–3).[7] For Eliot, he argues, a positivist religion must be based on Christianity: "It must be exhibited as the inner substance, which, having ever existed as a germ within the shell of Christianity, will be displayed in all its fresh ripeness when the dead husk drops away" (224). Thus the mid-Victorian positivist can quite consistently "have a hearty sympathy with the orthodoxy of the uneducated, or, what comes to the same thing, of past generations of educated men" (225). Summing up the general part of his article, Simpson comments, "It is no small victory to show that the godless humanitarianism of Strauss and Feuerbach can be made to appear the living centre of all the popular religions" (225).

It is a critical commonplace that George Eliot is a Wordsworthian novelist. On her twentieth birthday she wrote to Maria Lewis that she had "been so self-indulgent" as to buy a complete edition of Wordsworth in six volumes (published by Moxon in 1836–37). Though she wished that the poet could have found "less satisfaction in terrene objects," she had "never before met with so many of my own feelings, expressed just as I could like them" (*Letters* 1:34). *Adam Bede* pays homage to another of Eliot's favourites, Sir Walter Scott: it was set, like Scott's *Waverley*, sixty years in the past, which placed the action of the novel in 1799, a year after the publication of Wordsworth's *Lyrical Ballads* (1798). This allowed Eliot to have Arthur Donnithorne encounter the book as a recent publication (*Bede*, 65).[8] The epigraph to *Adam Bede* is from Book 6 of Wordsworth's poem *The Excursion* (1814):

> So that ye may have
> Clear images before your gladden'd eyes
> Of nature's unambitious underwood
> And flowers that prosper in the shade. And when
> I speak of such among the flock as swerved
> Or fell, those only shall be singled out
> Upon whose lapse, or error, something more
> Than brotherly forgiveness may attend.
> (Lines 651–8, in Wordsworth, *Works*, 661)

One of the central tenets of the realist aesthetic that George Eliot shared with the Pre-Raphaelite Brotherhood was the importance of "clear images" in establishing a convincing mimesis of reality that was at the same time infused with ethical idealism. This was memorably expressed in a passage in the journal she kept on a trip to Ilfracombe, in Devon, to study natural history with George Henry Lewes. Having likened the banks in the Ilfracombe lanes to pictures by Holman Hunt, she added: "I never before longed so much to know the names of things as during this visit to Ilfracombe. The desire is part of the tendency that is now constantly growing in me to escape from all vagueness and inaccuracy into the daylight of distinct, vivid ideas. The mere fact of naming an object tends to give definiteness to our conception of it – we have then a sign that at once calls up in our minds the distinctive qualities which mark out for us that particular object from all others" (*Letters* 2:251). There is a scientific, positivist quality to this statement; Eliot goes well beyond Wordsworth, who is often vague or indistinct in his visionary moments (the "*something* far more deeply interfused" of "Tintern Abbey" is a good example), as he seeks to convey an experience that has no particular name. Eliot's emphasis on what is verifiable and quantifiable makes her mistrustful of the poetics that the Tractarians derived from Wordsworth. It is interesting to note the context from which Eliot took her epigraph. Book 6 of *The Excursion* begins with a panegyric by the Poet to the State and the Church, addressing the latter in terms that the Tractarians would have endorsed:

> – Hail to the State of England! and conjoin
> With this a salutation as devout,
> Made to the spiritual fabric of her Church;
> Founded in truth; by blood of Martyrdom
> Cemented; by the hands of Wisdom reared
> In beauty of holiness, with ordered pomp,
> Decent and unreproved. (Lines 6–12)

Furthermore, the passage that constitutes the epigraph to *Adam Bede* is in fact spoken by a Priest, in the course of a discourse to the Solitary containing numerous stories of rural love, rivalry, and tragedy much like the stories of the characters in *Adam Bede*. The difference is that the Priest speaks for a transcendent God, who exists beyond the world of time. As several critics have shown in detail,[9] *Adam Bede* is dominated by time, whether the time of the clock, the agricultural seasons, the church year, or a term of pregnancy. The accumulation of all these different measures of time creates the impression that there is no transcendent view of time, except perhaps in the voice of the all-seeing narrator, who knows in precise detail the minute particulars of this story of sixty years ago. On the other hand, in *The Excursion*, a motto on a sundial speaks of the existence that transcends time: "*Discerning mortal! Do thou serve the will / Of Time's eternal Master, and that peace, / Which the world wants, shall be for thee confirmed!*" (6:519–21; emphasis in the original). In the secularizing world of *Adam Bede*, such images tend to have a human reference, for example in the first chapter when Adam sings Thomas Ken's Morning Hymn:

> Let all thy converse be sincere,
> Thy conscience as the noonday clear;
> For God's all-seeing eye surveys
> Thy secret thoughts, thy works and ways. (*Bede*, 13)

Here "God's all-seeing eye" seems to refer to the surveillance of the rural community, for eventually all the secrets of the characters, their illicit meetings, hidden jewellery, and concealed pregnancies, are known to all. Another all-seeing figure is the narrator, whose imagination allows him to be a "licensed trespasser" (71) taking the reader into all the domestic interiors that are described in turn in the early part of the novel. Wordsworth's rural community in *The Excursion* resists the rationalizing tendencies of the modern world, and his Priest is content to trust in Providence, and to acknowledge that "human life abounds / With mysteries" (*Excursion* 6:562–3). George Eliot may take her epigraph from Book 6 of *The Excursion*, but it is carefully chosen to declare her faith in the "clear images" that come from replacing myth by history and reducing supernatural belief to its constituent human emotions. The narrator of *Adam Bede* understands many things that remain mysterious to the characters, and thus Eliot implies that human knowledge and wisdom fill the place Wordsworth leaves to God.

If "Holy Scripture containeth all things necessary to salvation," as we are told in article six of the Thirty-Nine Articles,[10] then the Bible is qualitatively different from all other books, and the revelation of God in Jesus Christ is a unique event. The individual Christian's task is the imitation of Christ, the sanctification of the self, but this is not a process that can be completed in earthly time or human life. The humanizing versions of typology adopted in Victorian novels, however, are concerned only with this-worldly existence, and they therefore introduce new understandings of the incarnation, which, as A.S. Byatt perceptively notes, have a close relationship to theorizing about the form of the novel (Byatt, "Introduction," xxv).[11] It makes an important difference whether characters are all seen in relation to one ideal story, or whether that privileged narrative is but one highly influential example of the endless human quest to discover truth. Eliot struggled throughout her career with the problem of the relation of her fictional characters to ethical ideals.

Before looking at Adam Bede as a typical figure, it may be helpful to consider briefly his immediate fictional precursor, the Reverend Edgar Tryan in "Janet's Repentance," one of the *Scenes of Clerical Life*. Like Janet, and unlike Jesus, Edgar Tryan has sins to repent of, but by the time he comes to Milby he is a heroic figure whose self-giving ministry arouses the devotion of a predominantly female circle of admirers, and he takes on the role of a Christ figure in the community, to the extent that he has a triumphal entry into Milby before dying a sacrificial death. When Janet sends for Mr Tryan in her distress, after her abusive husband's behaviour has escalated, the narrator explains Tryan's influence as the "blessed influence of one true loving human soul on another" (*Scenes*, 263) and refers to the fact that ideas "sometimes … are made flesh; they breathe upon us with warm breath, they touch us with soft responsive hands, they look at us with sad sincere eyes, and speak to us in appealing tones; they are clothed in a living human soul, with all its conflicts, its faith, and its love. Then their presence is a power, then they shake us like a passion, and we are drawn after them with gentle compulsion, as flame is drawn to flame" (263). Here, Eliot draws on the doctrine of the incarnation but restricts her attention to the aspect of it that is available to any human being who makes divine love manifest, the aspect of embodying idea in flesh. In a further passage of rationalizing commentary, the narrator undercuts the idea of a supernatural source for Mr Tryan's ministrations: "There are unseen elements which often frustrate our wisest calculations – which raise up the sufferer from the edge of the grave, contradicting the prophecies of the clear-sighted physician, and fulfilling the blind clinging hopes of affection; such unseen elements Mr Tryan called the Divine Will, and filled up the margin of ignorance which surrounds all our knowledge with the feelings of trust and resignation" (271). Tryan's relationship with Janet coincides with the onset of his decline into tuberculosis, and their growing sublimated love for one another supersedes their sense of divine presence, which is replaced for each by the presence of the other. In one scene, the unexpected apparition of Mr Tryan when Janet is thinking about him seems to be a repetition of the appearance of Christ on the road to Emmaus: "It seemed very natural to her that he should be there. Her mind was so full of his presence at that moment, that the actual sight of him was only like a more vivid thought" (296). Similarly, as Tryan's health declines, Janet's meetings with him take on the character of the Christian's encounter with Christ in the sacraments. She feels "gratitude that his influence and guidance had been given her, even if only for a little while – gratitude that she was permitted to be with him, to take a deeper and deeper impress from daily communion with him, to be something to him in these last months of his life" (298). For both Janet and Edgar Tryan, the "Divine Presence" (290, 298) is transformed into the presence of the beloved, and for Janet, after Tryan's death, this lives on both as memory and as maternal love for her adopted child. George Eliot summed up this transformation epigrammatically in one of her letters: "Heaven help us! said the old religions – the new one, from its very lack of that faith, will teach us all the more to help one another" (*Letters* 2:82).

By way of analyzing George Eliot's transformation of the doctrine of the incarnation, it is helpful to look at a letter she wrote in 1866, in response to a long and enthusiastic letter from the Positivist Frederic Harrison, who had advised her on the complex legal aspects of the plot of *Felix Holt, The Radical*. Harrison had suggested to Eliot that it might be her task to write a literary work in which "the grand features of Comte's world might be sketched in fiction in their normal relations though under the forms of our familiar life" (Eliot, *Letters* 4:287). Eliot's reply, which is both thoughtful and tactful, is well-known as a statement about the nature of aesthetic teaching, but it is also relevant to the question of the typicality of literary characters and their relation to the figure of Jesus Christ:

That is a tremendously difficult problem which you have laid before me, and I think you see its difficulties, though they can hardly press upon you as they do on me, who have gone through again and again the severe effort of trying to make certain ideas thoroughly incarnate, as if they had revealed themselves to me first in the flesh and not in the spirit. I think aesthetic teaching is the highest of all teaching because it deals with life in its highest complexity. But if it ceases to be purely aesthetic – if it lapses anywhere from the picture to the diagram – it becomes the most offensive of all teaching. Avowed Utopias are not offensive, because they are understood to have a scientific and expository character: they do not pretend to work on the emotions, or couldn't do it if they did pretend. (4:300)

The key statement here is that Eliot seeks "to make certain ideas thoroughly incarnate," so that they seem to have revealed themselves "first in the flesh and not in the spirit." This was the way that Janet Dempster experienced the teaching of Edgar Tryan. By way of contrast in Hardy's *Jude the Obscure* we shall see a world in which there is only flesh, and no spirit, so that the realm of ideas is continually subverted by the physical desires of the characters, even though Jude seeks to make certain ruling ideas incarnate in his own life.

George Eliot's critical understanding of Christianity, and in particular her sceptical attitude to the biblical narratives, was the product of her distinctive path of earnest intellectual inquiry. When a Baptist minister recommended by Miss Franklin, the proprietor of the school that Mary Ann Evans had attended, sought to recommend books to combat her scepticism, he could not name one book on Christian evidences that she had not already read (Ashton, *A Life*, 46). George Eliot had an intellectual career before she wrote any of her fiction. Once she did begin to write fiction, she realized that the ideas with which she had so energetically been occupied – which in the context of her exchange with Harrison would include the fundamentals of Comte's Positivist philosophy, although not the dogmatic apparatus of his Religion of Humanity – had to be made thoroughly incarnate, "*as if* they had revealed themselves to me first in the flesh and not in the spirit." Thus, a plurality of aesthetic manifestations replaces the unique event of the Christian creed (*et homo factus est*); in the terms employed by Matthew Arnold, poetry replaces religion. In Eliot's view a work of art must not be overtly didactic, unlike the "avowed Utopia," which belongs to the realm of political philosophy rather than that of art. In her early evangelical phase, Eliot had used the term "Utopia" disparagingly to refer to the daydream world that was a sign of her dissatisfaction with the real world and consequently of her resistance to the divine will; now she saw a Utopian vision as part of the effort to transform and ameliorate the conditions of the only world she believed in, the material phenomenal world that is scientifically verifiable. For fiction to work on the emotions, however, and thereby to play its part in transforming this world, the ideas it contains had to be concealed, unavowed, and thoroughly incarnate in the flesh and blood of believable characters.

In *Mimesis* (1953), Erich Auerbach traced the realistic impulse in western literature back to the biblical texts; in exploring George Eliot's aesthetic of fiction we see that her realism is an aspect of her displacement of Christian theology. This is evident in her description of a realistic Dutch painting in the celebrated digression on realism in chapter 17 of *Adam Bede*: "I turn without shrinking, from cloud-borne angels, from prophets, sibyls, and heroic warriors, to an old woman bending over her flower-pot, or eating her solitary dinner, while the noonday light, softened perhaps by a screen of leaves, falls on her mob-cap, and just touches the rim of her spinning-wheel, and her stone jug, and all those cheap common things which are the precious necessaries of life to her" (177). This passage puts the picture of the old woman into a sequence of heroic or inspired paintings and finds an equal share of divinity in the domestic and humble. The reference to the noonday light further suggests a transfiguring gaze, as though the realist painter or writer in effect brings out the true divinity concealed within the scene. The discovery of spiritual significance in the commonplace locates George Eliot in a nineteenth-century tradition that extends from Wordsworth to James Joyce's epiphanies. In her concern to dignify the lives of ordinary people, Eliot's realism draws on the Christian doctrine that all human beings are created in the image of God.

Adam Bede is named for the first man, whose sin is redeemed by Christ, and for the Saxon monk who wrote the history of the early English church. He is thus Everyman, every sinful man, and a typical example of an outstanding English man. He is also an exemplary workman, first seen in the carpenter's workshop, which both establishes an immediate link to Jesus Christ, the second Adam, and presents Adam as a Carlylean hero akin to the Abbot Samson, another medieval monk, in Thomas Carlyle's *Past and Present*. The opening chapter of *Adam Bede*, with its mixture of realism and typological symbolism, not to mention its setting in a carpenter's shop, might be thought of as a verbal equivalent to John Everett Millais's painting *Christ in the House of His Parents* (1849–50). Adam's occupation and position as an artisan who has a chance of succeeding his master as well as various employment possibilities among the local gentry, make him a useful central character; for he has a wide range of social movement in the world of Hayslope and its environs, in terms of the people with whom he is likely to come into contact, and in terms of his own eventual upward mobility. As the narrator, a natural historian of English life, tells us, "Those were times when there was no rigid demarcation of rank between the farmer and the respectable artisan, and on the home-hearth, as well as in the public-house, they might be seen taking their jug of ale together; the farmer having a latent sense of capital, and of weight in parish affairs, which sustained him under his conspicuous inferiority in conversation" (*Bede*, 97).

At the beginning of his spiritual biography, Adam is of a rigid and somewhat judgmental nature, but his weak point is his susceptibility to Hetty Sorrel's feminine charm; hence the "very old story" of Adam's temptation in the garden, when amidst the apple-tree boughs he thinks that Hetty is showing signs of love for him (221). He does not realize that she has already fallen, having strayed into the dark wood where the allusions are all to classical erotic tales rather than to biblical types. Both Adam and Hetty, for different reasons, have to learn the truth of the cross, that all human beings are destined one day for suffering; in their different ways, we can see them both, in the garden scene, as imprisoned in their own pride and egoism. Hetty believes that Arthur loves her and is going to make her a lady; "It never entered into her mind that Adam was pitiable too – that Adam, too, must suffer one day" (221). Adam, for his part, is caught up in his idea of his own rectitude and deludes himself into thinking that Hetty will love him and make him happy. The reader is aware, as Adam is not yet, of the scenes between Hetty and Arthur in the woods; perhaps, too, an earlier scene is proleptic, as Adam and Seth carry a coffin they have made across the countryside: "It was a strangely-mingled picture – the fresh youth of the summer morning, with its Eden-like peace and loveliness, the stalwart strength of the two brothers in their rusty working clothes, and the long coffin on their shoulders" (51). It is as though sin has brought death into the pastoral landscape, and the coffin foreshadows Thias Bede's death by drowning, the first in a series of images of suffering and death. In spite of Adam's regret at his hardness to his father, however, he does not learn from the experience, for he judges Arthur harshly – Eliot intends us to think overly harshly – for his behaviour towards Hetty. Here the twenty-first-century reader is perhaps more sympathetic to Adam than Eliot had intended, for we tend not to share

Adam's deference to the gentry and are likely to be more thoroughly dem-
ocratic than the implied author of the novel. Because Adam does not
learn from the regret he feels at his father's death, he blames Arthur exclu-
sively and must live through a painful experience of suffering when his
engagement to Hetty comes to its tragic conclusion.

Adam's suffering begins with the sight of Hetty and Arthur kissing in
the wood, shortly after his social "exaltation" at the birthday feast. His
life divides into two at the moment he is examining a "curious large
beech," which turns out to be his tree of knowledge of suffering (295). In
general, the emphasis of the novel is on the development of Adam's character through this suffering, but for a time the emphasis shifts to Hetty;
however, once she comes to a consciousness of her wrongdoing and confesses to Dinah, she disappears from the novel. This shift of narrative
perspective, which for a short while significantly deepens our interest in
Hetty as a character, is a complexity in the novel that qualifies Adam's
representative status; it has been valuably discussed in the feminist criticism I have already alluded to. Without seeking to erase the fact that
Hetty and Adam have very different fates, it should also be noted that
the narrator subsumes the suffering of all of the characters in the novel
in the image of a roadside crucifix, "an image of a great agony" that he
remembers from his European travels (363). His point is to emphasize
that human life is often discontinuous with the life of the natural world,
a point already implied earlier in the novel, in the "strangely-mingled
picture" of the two brothers carrying the coffin through the bucolic landscape (51), or in the narrator's comment that "there is no hour that has
not its births of gladness and despair, no morning brightness that does
not bring new sickness to desolation as well as new forces to genius and
love. There are so many of us, and our lots are so different: what wonder
that Nature's mood is often in harsh contrast with the great crisis of our
lives?" (292).

The description of the crucifix comes at the beginning of a section
that focuses on Hetty's experiences, reminding the reader that human
suffering can occur in the loveliest pastoral landscape, and thereby informing us that Hayslope should not be read as an idyll or an Eden: "Such
things are sometimes hidden among the sunny fields and behind the
blossoming orchards; and the sound of the gurgling brook, if you came
close to one spot behind a small bush, would be mingled for your ear
with a despairing human sob. No wonder man's religion has much sorrow

in it: no wonder he needs a Suffering God" (364). Here the narrator's camouflage of Christian piety makes his discourse resemble that of the Priest in *The Excursion*, moralizing on the fate of the parishioners now buried in "the Churchyard among the Mountains." Wordsworth, however, does not insist in the way that Eliot does on the separateness of human experience and the natural world. In Eliot's narrative commentary, there is also a hint of the voice of the natural historian of religion, tracing, like Feuerbach, the psychological origin of the image of the crucified God amidst the objective conditions of human existence.

Hetty's experiences of extremity include a repetition of the scene of the Nativity, as she spends a night in a rough shed attached to a sheepfold before giving birth to her child, an episode that is not directly narrated. Unlike the Virgin Mary she is alone, and she causes the death of her child in an ironic repetition of the slaughter of the innocents. The direct narration of Hetty's experiences ends with her still on the road, and the narrator follows a question about what her fate will be with an uncomfortable address to his male readers: "God preserve you and me from being the beginners of such misery!" (389). After this the narrative perspective shifts back to Hayslope and to Adam in particular.

Adam's experience at the trial in Stoniton, his suffering as a result of his inability to do anything in the face of the unalterable situation produced by Arthur's actions, is presented by George Eliot in a series of sacramental and typological images. Adam is transformed in such a way that after this experience he is virtually reborn as a different person; thus, as the narrator comments, "deep, unspeakable suffering may well be called a baptism, a regeneration, the initiation into a new state" (425). In addition to baptism, there is a re-enactment of the Last Supper in the bread and wine that Adam shares with Bartle Massey in the "upper room in a dull Stoniton street" (420). This meal portrays the human essence of the meaning of the eucharist in Feuerbachian terms and is also a last supper before Adam's rebirth as a new man when he is able to face his suffering. Adam's rediscovery of his capacity to love, when he becomes conscious that Dinah has replaced Hetty as the object of his affection, is described as being like "a resurrection of his dead joy" (501), and to make the typological significance clearer, this realization is preceded by Lisbeth looking at a picture in Adam's Bible, "that of the angel seated on the great stone that has been rolled away from the sepulchre" (498). The chapter in Book Sixth describing the harvest supper also begins with vague religious imagery: the beautiful setting sun "was enough to make Adam feel that he was in a great temple, and that the distant chant was a sacred song" (515).

The ending of *Adam Bede* is often treated as a kind of afterthought, and Adam's marriage to Dinah – the result, according to Eliot's "History of *Adam Bede*," of a suggestion by George Henry Lewes (Eliot, *Letters*, 2:503) – is dismissed as a typical Victorian happy ending.[12] Whether or not it was part of Eliot's original design, the marriage is integral to the novel's vision of a thoroughly secularized version of Christianity. When we first see Dinah, she is like a consecrated virgin in her wish to live for God alone.

Stephen Prickett, looking at the chapter entitled "The Two Bed-Chambers," provides an astute analysis of the contrast between Dinah and Hetty, noting that here the biblical resonances differ from traditional typology in being "totally internalized," referring to "events of consciousness, states of mind" ("Romantics," 211), rather than to external actions (as with Henry Fielding's repetition of the parable of the Good Samaritan in *Joseph Andrews* [1742], or, to use Prickett's own example, Austen's use of typology in *Mansfield Park*). Both Dinah and Hetty are locked up in projections of their own consciousness. Hetty, looking at herself in the mirror, is absorbed in her romantic fantasies about marrying Arthur and becoming a lady; Dinah, seated at the window, communes with the supernatural being whom she projects as a personification of her own loving nature.[13] From early on in the novel, the narrator provides a rationalizing explanation of her sense of divine presence, suggesting for example that the divine guidance that she seeks to rely on is really a combination of intelligence, tact, and empathy: "And do we not all agree to call rapid thought and noble impulse by the name of inspiration" (*Bede*, 113). The description of Dinah as endowed with a Pre-Raphaelite attractiveness and sweetness of spirit that makes her a version of the *schöne Seele* (beautiful soul) of German Romantic literature results in a literary creation very different from the aunt whose story Eliot used as her source, and whom she described as being not at all like Dinah, but "a very small, black-eyed woman, and … very vehement in her style of preaching" (*Letters* 2:502–3).

There is an interesting parallel between Dinah's role and that of Isabella in *Measure for Measure*. Like Isabella, Dinah believes that she is called to a celibate life of prayer and service; but less ambiguously than Shakespeare, George Eliot resolves her story by having the religious young woman get married and become a mother. Here she is following Feuerbach's analysis of the monastic life, which he regards as a logical conclusion of orthodox Christian belief, but a deluded way of life if orthodox belief is regarded as an illusion. Thus Dinah is locked up in herself through her belief in a transcendent and supernatural divine being; her marriage to Adam represents her acceptance of the religion of humanity, albeit cloaked in Anglican vestments. In a consideration of "the Christian Significance of Voluntary Celibacy and Monachism," Feuerbach wrote, "Separation from the world, from matter, from the life of the species, is therefore the essential aim of Christianity. And this aim had its visible, practical realisation in Monachism ...Where the heavenly life is a truth, the earthly life is a lie; where imagination is all, reality is nothing" (*Essence*, 161). Thus, "the unworldly, supernatural life is essentially also an unmarried life" (164). The conclusion of *Adam Bede* makes it clear that Dinah is choosing between earthly and heavenly love, between the religious beliefs of the past and the humanism of the future, and that her marriage to Adam is, in the title of a book George Eliot had once reviewed, an example of "The Progress of the Intellect." In this respect one can draw a parallel between Eliot and Charles Kingsley, who both believed in human progress and saw marriage as having a profoundly spiritual significance. Nevertheless, the conclusion of *Adam Bede* shows that Dinah pays a price in marrying Adam, losing her autonomy and public role. Similarly in *Middlemarch*, Eliot explores at length the consequences of inadequately considered marriages.

Adam's courtship of Dinah is preceded by that of his brother Seth, who contributes to the theme of secularizing religious discourse by twice expressing his romantic feelings for her through the language of Methodist hymns. In the first instance, he confesses to Dinah that he cannot help applying to her the words of a hymn, "She is my soul's bright-morning star; / And she my rising sun" (36), substituting the female pronouns for "Thou," addressed to God, in the original by Isaac Watts. As Valentine Cunningham suggests in his note on this passage, such a substitution of the earthly love for Christ would have been quite blasphemous to a pious Methodist and is thus not very realistic (in *Bede*, 560n). It is rather an example of something one finds recurrently in Victorian fiction, the substitution of erotic love for love of God, or the conflation of the two. Much later, when Adam departs to bring back Hetty, as he thinks, from Snowfield, Seth again repeats a hymn to himself: "Dark and cheerless is the morn / Unaccompanied by thee" (*Bede*, 391), and here again the words could apply to the absence of earthly lovers in the lives of either of the brothers at that moment, rather than to the prospect of the absence of God's merciful presence.

When Adam proposes to Dinah, she feels that her love for him is replacing her love of God, and it is clear that she must choose between Adam, the new type of Christ, and the traditional image of the Suffering God. She tells Adam, "It's hard to me to turn a deaf ear ... you know it's hard; but a great fear is upon me. It seems to me as if you were stretching out your arms to me, and beckoning me to come and take my ease, and live for my own delight, and Jesus, the Man of Sorrows, was standing looking towards me, and pointing to the sinful, and suffering, and afflicted" (509). She represents her dilemma as a version of the parable of Dives and Lazarus, a parable that is implicitly alluded to elsewhere in the novel in imagery of "a great gulf" fixed between Hetty's fate as an outcast and "the bright hearth and the warmth and the voices of home" (386).[14] In the case of Dinah's dilemma, the gulf is really that between Christianity and the religion of humanity, though as feminist critics have noted, the issue is complicated by the fact that Dinah has more autonomy and freedom of speech in her role as a Methodist preacher than she will as Adam's wife. She is seen in the epilogue no longer preaching, but rather waiting in the same posture that Adam's mother had assumed at the beginning of the novel.

Adam's courtship of Dinah is preceded by her desire to return to the hills of Stonyshire and her ministry among the poor. She tells Mrs Poyser, "I feel drawn again towards the hills where I used to be blessed in carrying the word to the sinful and desolate" (475). Mrs Poyser's reply is an exasperated "You feel!" (475). Mrs Poyser seems to share the view of Marian Evans the progressive intellectual that religion is not simply a matter of feeling, but that feeling must be subjected to the test of reason. As Valentine Cunningham suggests in annotating another passage in the novel, Eliot was particularly acerbic in her comments on feeling and religion in her essay "Evangelical Teaching: Dr Cumming" (see *Bede*, 559n), where she wrote, "In accordance with this we think it is found that, in proportion as religious sects exalt feeling above intellect, and believe themselves to be guided by direct inspiration rather than by a spontaneous exertion of their faculties – that is, in proportion as they are removed from rationalism – their sense of truthfulness is misty and confused" (Eliot, *Writings*, 145).

When Adam goes to meet Dinah near Snowfield to see if she will marry him, he waits for her on a hilltop, with typological resonances of God meeting Moses, or of the transfiguration. Indeed, when he speaks to her before she sees him, "She was so accustomed to think of impressions as purely spiritual monitions, that she looked for no material visible accompaniment of the voice" (*Bede*, 532). However, it is Adam the man who is speaking, and this suggests through the typological symbolism that for Dinah an earthly marriage covenant will take the place of the direct voice of God; henceforth Adam, the suffering man who has learned to love, will replace Jesus Christ, the Suffering God with whose cross she had previously so strongly identified. The sense of religious and ethical progress, as part of the overall development of civilization, is much more clearly expounded in Eliot's essays than in her fiction, but it is strongly implied here too. One can draw parallels with Tennyson's *In Memoriam*, where the references to Hallam as a forerunner of the new race of human beings, and as a kind of cosmic evolutionary Christ figure, make a similar point in a more overt manner. Like *Adam Bede*, *In Memoriam* also uses a wedding to provide a conclusion to a work full of religious questioning and typological symbolism.

A brief overview of Adam Bede's religious experiences might help to clarify the meaning of the religion of humanity that Eliot presents in the novel. Adam's religion is a mixture of rationality, ethical strictness, and devout feelings, which as a result of his essentially conservative temperament are attached to the prescribed formulas and liturgy of the Church of England. He retains some peasant superstitions, we are told, but "if a new building had fallen down and he had been told that this was a divine judgment, he would have said 'May be; but the bearing o' the roof and walls wasn't right, else it wouldn't ha' come down'" (50). Unlike that of Dinah and Seth, Adam's religion does not involve dogmatic assertions, nor is it reliant on direct access to the supernatural. He disapproves of the doctrinal emphasis of Mr Ryde, Irwine's successor as rector in Hayslope (181). A further hint of Adam's beliefs and values comes in the Carlylean "lay-sermon" he preaches during an argument with Seth about Methodism, to the amusement of some of his fellow workers:

There's such a thing as being over-speritial; we must have something beside Gospel i' this world. Look at the canals, an' th' aqueducs, an' th' coal-pit engines, and Arkwright's mills there at Cromford; a man must learn summat beside Gospel to make them things, I reckon. But t' hear some o' them preachers, you'd think as a man must be doing nothing all's life but shutting's eyes and looking what's a-going on inside him. I know a man must have the love o' God in his soul, and the Bible's God's word. But what does the Bible say? Why, it says as God put his sperrit into the workman as built the tabernacle, to make him do all the carved work and things as wanted a nice hand. And this is my way o' looking at it: there's the sperrit o' God in all things and all times – week-day as well as Sunday. (9)

At another point in the novel, Adam sounds like Matthew Arnold as he tells the narrator, "It isn't notions sets people doing the right things – it's feelings" (180). He is also like Arnold in the way that he experiences the liturgy of the Anglican church as a kind of poetry that acts on his feelings: "to Adam the church service was the best channel he could have found for his mingled regret, yearning, and resignation; its interchange of beseeching cries for help, with outbursts of faith and praise – its recurrent responses and the familiar rhythm of its collects, seemed to speak for him as no other form of worship could have done" (199). In *Progress of the Intellect* (1850), Robert William Mackay wrote not only that knowledge is moral but that we would "at last discover it to be religious" (quoted in Eliot, *Writings*, 36). In *Adam Bede*, the reverse of this statement seems to be true as well; towards the end of the novel, Adam says to to Dinah that "feeling's a sort o' knowledge" (509). For once Adam sounds like a Methodist, as he contradicts the more rational position he usually adopts and the perspective voiced by Mrs Poyser; if indeed he is speaking for the implied author, then George Eliot is voicing a rather different position here from that of Marian Evans. Knowledge is not merely positive, rationally ascertainable truth; there is a knowledge of the heart, of feeling, as exemplified in Adam Bede's Arnoldian relationship to his church. It is perhaps because he is an Anglican that this position is possible; for the Church of England anchors religious feeling in a tradition and in the consent of the community. Dinah is brought into the community of Hayslope by her marriage to Adam. She is also brought within a traditional family structure, which means that her unusual freedom comes to an end. However, for George Eliot, the female writer in 1859, the novel is a substitute for the sermon on the green or the afternoon service in the parish church. If Dinah is suspended from preaching at the end of the novel, Mary Ann Evans grows up to be a novelist, teaching the compassion of the religion of humanity through the aesthetic design of her unavowed utopia.

It remains to look at *Adam Bede* in relation to George Eliot's intellectual career as a translator and disseminator of biblical criticism and in the wider context of the theological ferment that resulted from the higher criticism in the first half of the nineteenth century. The grounding of religious truth in subjective feeling rather than in objective fact was widespread throughout this period. It could be found, as *Adam Bede* itself suggests, in the spirituality of Methodism, with its influences from German Pietism; for the same reason, it was a characteristic of the theology of Friedrich Schleiermacher. Even for John Henry Newman, religious assent was the product of converging probabilities rather than of a definite proof. For the George Eliot who reviewed works of biblical criticism and dissected the preaching of Dr Cumming, any religious doctrine that was not scientifically verifiable was to that extent false, and the progress of civilization was the result of the growing expanse of positive knowledge. Schleiermacher, however, was able to make feeling the basis of a Christian dogmatics. For him, "piety in its diverse expressions remains essentially a state of Feeling" (*Faith* 1:11) and dogmatic propositions arise "solely out of logically ordered reflection upon the immediate utterances of the religious self-consciousness" (1:81).[15]

As demythologizers, Strauss and Feuerbach went further than Schleiermacher, creating a radical break with the tradition of Christian hermeneutics and piety. Feuerbach's position is straightforward: in worshipping God, human beings have hypostatized their highest image of themselves: "God as a morally perfect being is nothing else than the realised idea, the fulfilled law of morality, the moral nature of man posited as the absolute being" (*Essence*, 46). Feuerbach's aim in *The Essence of Christianity* is a thoroughgoing humanization of philosophy and religion, so that human beings can stand on their own two feet and realize their destiny without false consciousness (hence, it is often remarked, both Freud and Marx can be seen to follow in the footsteps of Feuerbach). For Feuerbach, the mystification results from a kind of grammatical misunderstanding: "Now, when it is shown that what the subject is lies entirely in the attributes of the subject; that is, that the predicate is the true subject; it is also proved that if the divine predicates are attributes of the human nature, the subject of those predicates is also of the human nature" (25).

It is more difficult to comment in summary form on Strauss. His vast *Life of Jesus* was influential at least in part because of the exhaustive manner in which it dissected each element of the Gospel narratives, suggesting over and over again not only that particular incidents have no supernatural basis but that they may have no verifiable historical basis at all, being rather the mythological expression of some fundamental philosophical truth. Strauss's standard of history is that of a scientific positivist, but he argues that his work of critical analysis leaves intact the true significance of the gospel. Like Feuerbach, he claims to be concerned with identifying an "essence" of Christianity; for Strauss this essence lies in a mythological meaning that preserves more of the content of traditional teaching than does Feuerbach's humanization. According to Strauss, "The supernatural birth of Christ, his miracles, his resurrection and ascension, remain eternal truths, whatever doubts may be cast on their reality as historical facts" (*Life*, lii, preface to first German edition). In a key section of the concluding chapter to the fourth edition (the one Eliot translated), Strauss addresses a question that is still of relevance today, the "Relation of the Critical and Speculative Theology to the Church" (781–4). He says that there are four options open to the "critical theologian" who regards the gospel narratives "for the most part as mere mythi" (782). The first three options are, for Strauss, unsatisfactory. The first, attempting to elevate the Church to the point of view of the speculative theologian, will fail "because to the Church all those premises are wanting on which the theologian rests his speculative conclusions" (782). The theologian who exercises the second option of speaking to the Church in the terms of the popular conception of Christianity held by the Church runs the risk of appearing to be a hypocrite (783). The third option for the theologian is to forsake the ministerial office (783). There remains, however, the possibility of a fourth option, namely, that "in his discourses to the church, [the theologian] will indeed adhere to the forms of the popular conception, but on every opportunity he will exhibit their spiritual significance, which to him constitutes their sole truth, and thus prepare – though such a result is only to be thought of as an unending progress – the resolution of those forms into their original ideas in the consciousness of the church also" (783).

Throughout this discussion, Strauss's commitment to his rationalist method means that the theologian's perspective is invariably assumed to be correct. The logical result of his fourth option would be the destruction of the whole basis for the Church's existence, so that ultimately Strauss and Feuerbach are not so different, and Schleiermacher's description of the theologian's dilemma and divided loyalties – which Strauss refers to at the beginning of the section – is more acute than Strauss will admit.[16] Even today the piety of the Church and the conclusions of critical biblical scholarship are at odds – inevitably given their divergent purposes and loyalties. Biblical scholars are concerned with the methodology and integrity of a critical discipline that has evolved criteria of rational analysis; believers, on the other hand, are concerned with the integrity of their religious experience, which is mediated by the tradition of a church and a sacred text, both in some sense claiming a divine authority. The integrity of that experience cannot be made subject to the dictates of professional theologians, to be modified according to whatever theory they currently regard as most accurate. On the other hand, theology, and especially Anglican theology, has always made the test of reason one of its canons. Thus the tension with which Strauss concludes his *Life of Jesus* is one that remains a necessary part of Christian life and thought.

Matthew Arnold's resolution of the same dilemma was that of the religious modernist. He thought that religious dogmas had to be cast aside when they did not meet positivist standards of verifiability, but he wanted to preserve the institutional structure and the liturgy of the Church. Most of all he wanted to teach his readers to read the Bible poetically. As we have already seen, Arnold defined religion as morality tinged with emotion, which is close to Adam Bede's explanation of why people act morally: "It isn't notions sets people doing the right thing – it's feelings" (*Bede*, 180). Similarly, Adam's account of religious feelings is like an account of being moved aesthetically: "There's things go on in the soul, and times when feelings come into you like a mighty rushing wind … Those are things as you can't bottle up in a 'do this' and 'do that;' and I'll go so far with the strongest Methodist ever you'll find" (181). Like Arnold in *St Paul and Protestantism*, Adam protests against attempts to turn such feelings into the form of exact science: "religion's something else besides doctrines and notions" (181–2). As Richard Simpson put it, expressing what he regarded as Eliot's theological position, "With her, doctrines are but names for sentiments" ("Novels," 247). Similarly, Charles Hennell regarded Christianity as "a system of elevated thought and feeling" based not upon "the uncertain evidence of events which happened nearly two thousand years ago" but upon "an evidence clearer, simpler, and always at hand, – the thoughts and feelings of the human mind itself" (*Inquiry*, viii).

These similarities between the religious views of Matthew Arnold and

Eliot's protagonist imply that there is a less-radical critique of Christianity in *Adam Bede* than we have found in Eliot's non-fiction prose; there is a similar ambiguity in Eliot's religious views as they are expounded through her life in letters to various correspondents. Certainly she withdrew from the fierce hostility to institutional religion that marked the early days of her loss of faith, during her "holy war" with her family. A letter of 6 December 1859 to François d'Albert-Durade, with whom she had boarded in Geneva ten years earlier, expressed an attitude closer to that of Arnoldian agnosticism than anything found in her journalism:

> When I was at Geneva, I had not yet lost the attitude of antagonism which belongs to the renunciation of *any* belief – also, I was very unhappy, and in a state of discord and rebellion towards my own lot. Ten years of experience have wrought great changes in that inward self: I have no longer any antagonism towards any faith in which human sorrow and human longing for purity have expressed themselves; on the contrary, I have a sympathy with it that predominates over all argumentative tendencies. I have not returned to dogmatic Christianity – to the acceptance of any set of doctrines as a creed, and a superhuman revelation of the Unseen – but I see in it the highest expression of the religious sentiment that has yet found its place in the history of mankind, and I have the profoundest interest in the inward life of sincere Christians in all ages. Many things that I should have argued against ten years ago, I now feel myself too ignorant and too limited in moral sensibility to speak of with confident disapprobation: on many points where I used to delight in expressing intellectual difference, I now delight in feeling an emotional agreement. (*Letters* 3:230–1)

On the other hand, writing to Barbara Bodichon, who had expressed an inclination towards Roman Catholicism, Eliot emphasized the withholding of intellectual assent in religious belief that was the essence of her agnostic position:

> As for the "forms and ceremonies," I feel no regret that any should turn to them for comfort, if they can find comfort in them: sympathetically, I enjoy them myself. But I have faith in the working-out of higher possibilities than the Catholic or any other church has presented,

and those who have strength to wait and endure, are bound to accept no formula which their whole souls – their intellect as well as their emotions – do not embrace with entire reverence. The highest "calling and election" is to *do without opium* and live through all our pain with conscious, clear-eyed endurance. (*Letters* 3:366, 26 December 1860; Eliot's emphasis)

Adam Bede is closer to the tone and mood of the first of these two passages from Eliot's correspondence, with its great interest in the inward spiritual life of its main characters, from the hard-hearted Hetty, on whom Christian teaching has made no impact whatsoever, to the fervent piety of Dinah and the anachronistically modernist Anglican Adam. *Adam Bede* is not the last word in Eliot's fiction, however, and the writer who advised her friend that it is best to live without opium may have felt that there was a false element in her impersonation of even a modernist Christian in the implied author of her first novel. Richard Simpson had accused positivists of founding morality on falsehood by allowing religions to have a subjective truth even while dismissing their dogmatic claims, although he admired Eliot's art enough, as his sympathetic reading of her novels suggests, to conclude that "the positive good of her sensible ethics outweighs the negative evil of her atheistic theology" ("Novels," 249–50). He suggested condescendingly but perhaps accurately that many readers would not realize the true argument concealed beneath the surface of Eliot's fiction.

One might suggest, more charitably than Simpson, that in her early fiction, and especially in *Adam Bede*, Eliot could not think beyond the impasse created by her emotional agreement with, but intellectual rejection of, Christianity. As Simpson wrote in 1863, the positivist could quite consistently have "a hearty sympathy with the orthodoxy of the uneducated, or, what comes to the same thing, of past generations of educated men" (225). The use of the historical setting allowed her to assume a faith in her characters that she did not share herself, but that was not very helpful to those Victorians who shared her doubts about religious dogmas and were looking for a creed in which they could believe. As I noted earlier, the female protagonists in *Romola*, *Felix Holt*, and *Middlemarch* all undertake that search for themselves. Each of them finds some form of resolution in marriage or domestic responsibilities, after a traumatic experience that tests their resolve. Romola's boat journey repeats Maggie's in *The Mill on the Floss*, but with a happy ending, and it seems to float the character out of the realistic world of Florence into a mythological landscape. Dorothea's dark night of the soul is followed by a humanistic awakening and an unheroic life as a politician's wife. However, the belief in progress that is clear in Eliot's reviews, especially those of R.W. Mackay and W.E.H. Lecky, would naturally have led her to seek a larger vision of the faith of the future. This leads us logically to *Daniel Deronda*, in which she re-examines the religious question from a very different perspective.

Does *Daniel Deronda* represent a significant shift in the portrayal of religion in Eliot's fiction, or is Judaism simply a new figure for the religion of humanity? In the early novels Eliot uses Christian ministers such as Edgar Tryan or Dinah Morris as exemplary characters embodying the working of human sympathy, whereas in *Felix Holt, Middlemarch*, and *Daniel Deronda* she offers a more diminished and critical representation of clerical figures. In these latter novels politics and art take on some of the roles earlier played by the Church and the religious characters. Knoepflmacher sees *Daniel Deronda* as a new departure for Eliot; for in this novel she "moves from the conditional to the categorical" (*Humanism*, 121). He suggests that in *Daniel Deronda* Eliot distrusts the spiritual effects of culture unless it takes an "essentially religious form" and is "a spiritual force which must have both a national location, as well as an international authority" (132). Elinor Shaffer, on the other hand, in her excellent analysis of *Daniel Deronda* in the context of higher criticism, emphasizes its continuity with the earlier work, even if it approaches the same questions with greater subtlety and complexity: "She had at last, after many attempts, found the right Feuerbachian milieu: one saturated with religion, yet essentially secular and modern, where she could unite the primitive ground of religion with the most advanced consciousness of it" ("*Kubla Khan*," 244). In this view, *Daniel Deronda* represents the culmination of the series of "experiments in life" (Eliot, *Letters* 6:216) that constitute George Eliot's fiction.

Biographers and critics of Eliot often quote a celebrated anecdote related by F.W.H. Myers concerning a visit she paid to Cambridge. In the course of the conversation, "stirred somewhat beyond her wont," she commented on how inconceivable was the idea of God, how unbelievable the concept of immortality, "and yet how peremptory and absolute" was the notion of Duty. Myers added that after they parted, he "seemed to be gazing, like Titus at Jerusalem, on vacant seats and empty halls, – on a sanctuary with no Presence to hallow it, and a heaven left lonely of a God" (quoted in Ashton, *A Life*, 333–4). Though the anecdote has been viewed sceptically by Ashton and others, it nevertheless encapsulates a powerful sense of the Victorian loss of faith, which I think is why it is quoted so frequently. But I agree with Knoepflmacher that there is something different about *Daniel Deronda*, for in this novel religious belief is not subject to the same kind of demythologizing narrative commentary as in the earlier fiction. George Eliot is writing a biblical epic for her own time, in which she implies that the sanctuary may not be quite so unhallowed as she had imagined.

Daniel Deronda, the only novel that Eliot set in the immediate present, has always aroused strong reactions in its readers. Some Victorian reviewers were infuriated by Mordecai's discourses and by the way that Daniel not only discovers but embraces his Jewish heritage. Other readers reacted more positively, and the novel was received favourably by the Jewish community in England.[17] Henry James's dialogue review "*Daniel Deronda*: A Conversation" captured both sides of the debate, which has continued to the present day, Rosemary Ashton being one of the most recent to express a negative view of George Eliot's use of Judaism.[18] There has recently been some controversy about the relationship of the novel to Zionism as it developed through the twentieth century.[19] Given the novel's emphasis on communication and its repeated critiques of colonialism and imperialism, I do not think Eliot can be accused of collusion in imperialist endeavours. In a way, her novel is a literary reversal of the project of the Jerusalem bishopric which was discussed in the previous chapter. Judaism in *Daniel Deronda* is valuable both in its own right, as an ancient religious tradition that has retained a degree of vitality that Christianity has not, and as an image of the kind of spiritual renewal that Gentile English society is in need of.

Daniel Deronda is conventionally divided into a "Jewish part" and a "Gentile part," though since Daniel figures prominently in Gwendolen's story it is not easy to keep them separate. David Carroll has usefully suggested that the work is dominated by two different typologies: the social type in the Grandcourt part and the type as spiritual form, based on biblical typology, in the Jewish part (291). Extending Carroll's analysis, one could say that the dominant treatment of Christianity in *Daniel Deronda* is satirical, while Judaism functions as the "pathway" – to use Mordecai's word – of spiritual communication. Eliot portrays the ruling classes of

England as spiritually bankrupt, given to tyranny and reckless gambling. Their spiritual malaise is similar to that diagnosed in Matthew Arnold's *Culture and Anarchy*, and Eliot uses such Arnoldian phrases as "better self" (*Deronda*, 223) or "doing as one likes" (382). Fundamentally, however, she redefines Arnold's Hebraism, so that the Jewish cultural and hermeneutical tradition becomes the source of her idea of epic; thus Hellenism is subsumed within an expanded Hebraism.

Christianity is the official religion of an imperialistic nation that seeks to convert Jews while being ignorant of the fact that the two religions have a common source. Eliot makes this point more explicitly in her last published work, an essay written in the persona of Theophrastus Such entitled "The Modern Hep! Hep! Hep!" (1879), alluding to a cry said to have been used by the Crusaders when attacking Jews. Near the end of that essay, she writes: "Formerly, evangelical orthodoxy was prone to dwell on the fulfilment of prophecy in the 'restoration of the Jews'. Such interpretation of the prophets is less in vogue now. The dominant mode is to insist on a Christianity that disowns its origin, that is not a substantial growth having a genealogy, but is a vaporous reflex of modern notions" (154). To Gwendolen, any form of spiritual life is alien, "and it was as far from Gwendolen's conception that Deronda's life could be determined by the historical destiny of the Jews, as that he could rise into the air on a brazen horse, and so vanish from her horizon in the form of a twinkling star" (*Deronda*, 467). It is not surprising that she does not understand the spiritual roots of her own culture when we contemplate her clergyman uncle. Mr Gascoigne adroitly combines Christian and worldly sentiments and venerates the aristocracy with a religious fervour. He thinks that Grandcourt's courtship of Gwendolen "was a match to be accepted on broad general grounds national and ecclesiastical" (118). More satire of the state of Christianity comes in a passage that employs a favourite topos of the Tractarian novel, the former abbey that has become a country house, in this case the home of Sir Hugo Mallinger. In a flight of Gothic whimsy, Sir Hugo imagines the ghosts of the Benedictines returning to what was once their refectory and is now his dining room. Gwendolen, the unspiritual modern young woman, responds, "It is very nice to come after ancestors and monks, but they should know their places and keep underground" (350). The choir of the monastic church has been turned into the stables for Sir Hugo's establishment (351).

A revealing moment in *Daniel Deronda* comes when the hero is at last reunited with his mother and acquainted with the truth about his mysterious parentage. Daniel, however, is disappointed in this meeting, finding that he must choose between his religious inheritance and the secular experiences of love and artistic self-fulfilment represented by his mother, the singer Alcharisi: "To Deronda's nature the moment was cruel: it made the filial yearning of his life a disappointed pilgrimage to a shrine where there were no longer the symbols of sacredness" (566). Here, the image of the unhallowed sanctuary is used to repudiate some of the sacred ideas of Eliot's earlier novels, and the novel's attempt to transcend the ideas of culture and self-development has troubled many readers, especially feminists who sympathize more with Daniel's mother and her desire for fulfilment than with Daniel and the traditional marriage he makes with Mirah.

Daniel Deronda reverses typological readings of the Bible and history by showing Judaism replacing Christianity as a source of ethical, cultural, and religious inspiration. Far from being superseded by Christianity, Judaism seems open to the future, not just in the sense of the possible restoration of a national existence to the Jewish people but also in the sense that Judaism is open to development in the light of progress in human knowledge and understanding. Furthermore, Eliot is acutely aware of the history of suffering that Jews have endured, and the betrayal of the ideals of Christianity in that history. In "The Modern Hep! Hep! Hep!" she refers to "the men who made the name of Christ a symbol for the spirit of vengeance" (144); the epigraph to chapter 42 of *Daniel Deronda* is a passage from the Jewish historian Leopold Zunz that begins, "If there are ranks in suffering, Israel takes precedence of all the nations" (in *Deronda*, 441). In the same chapter the role of Judaism in the modern world is the subject of a debate at the working-men's club. Mordecai says that "Israel is the heart of mankind, if we mean by heart the core of affection which binds a race and its families in dutiful love, and the reverence for the human body which lifts the needs of our animal life into religion, and the tenderness which is merciful to the poor and weak and to the dumb creature that wears the yoke for us" (453). Similarly, Eliot concludes "The Modern Hep! Hep! Hep!" with an emphasis on the corporate life of the Jewish people: "The effective bond of human action is feeling, and the worthy child of a people owning the triple name of Hebrew, Israelite, and Jew, feels his kinship with the glories and the sorrows, the degradation and the possible renovation of his national family" (155).

Eliot values Judaism for its openness to the future, which is emphasized throughout *Daniel Deronda*. Daniel learns that ancient sources of spiritual vitality still flow; what prevents them from renewing the life of modern England is a kind of cynicism and flippancy that ridicules everything deeply felt. The meeting of Daniel and Mordecai is compared to a scriptural encounter:

> If he had read of this incident as having happened centuries ago in Rome, Greece, Asia Minor, Palestine, Cairo, to some man young as himself, dissatisfied with his neutral life, and wanting some closer fellowship, some more special duty to give him ardour for the possible consequences of his work, it would have appeared to him quite natural that the incident should have created a deep impression on that far-off man, whose clothing and action would have been seen in his imagination as part of an age chiefly known to us through its more serious effects. Why should he be ashamed of his own agitated feeling merely because he dressed for dinner, wore a white tie, and lived among people who might laugh at his owning any conscience in the matter as the solemn folly of taking himself too seriously? – that bugbear in circles in which the lack of grave emotion passes for wit? (*Deronda*, 434)

At the same time, Daniel reflects rationally on his experience with Mordecai and considers it in a more sceptical light. However, through a convergence of feeling and experience, which is given the external sanction of his discovery of his Jewish parentage, he accepts the destiny that seems to have been allotted him. Typologically, he is taking on a messianic role, but one of the differences presented by Judaism, Eliot suggests, is that the incarnation of the ideal in the real is something that can happen at any time. There is not one pivotal moment, as in Christian history, by which time is redeemed; rather each individual is capable of experiencing "one of those rare moments when our yearnings and our acts can be completely one, and the real we behold is our ideal good" (640). Furthermore, the divine unity that is confessed in the *Shemah*, Mordecai explains, is a vision of "the ultimate unity of mankind" (628). Judaism thus offers a kind of ethical and spiritual universalism, and "the nation which has been scoffed at for its separateness, has given a binding theory to the human race" (628). This is expressed towards the end of the novel by the idea of "separateness with communication" (620), which was one of the leading ideas of Daniel's grandfather. It becomes the image through which Eliot reconciles the disparate strands of her novel. Daniel embraces his Jewish ancestry and looks to a future in which he works to restore the national life of the Jewish people. He marries Mirah, a marriage that will serve this end. Yet he has had a decisive spiritual influence on Gwendolen, a Christian and therefore someone who belongs to a religion that is "chiefly a Hebrew religion" (316). Judaism in its separate form needs a centre to enable it to live a full life in the modern world; Judaism in communication with English Christians might provide the means for renewal of English spiritual life.

Perhaps Judaism could function more effectively for George Eliot as an image of a possible spiritual horizon because it is an ethnic identity as well as a religion, so that Daniel, by asking his mother a question, could determine in objective terms whether or not he was a Jew. Perhaps too it was easier for George Eliot to project religious faith, of however tenuous a kind, into another religion, and one to which she had no intention of converting. Even if these conjectures have some validity, it remains true that Judaism became for her an image of the way that English religious life needed to be transformed. The Jewish tradition, in Eliot's view, was clearly characterized by dialogue and dialectic. Daniel Deronda was true to this tradition when he accepted the faith of his fathers and yet would not promise Joseph Kalonymos that he would believe in the same way that they did, telling him, "Our fathers themselves changed the horizon of their belief and learned of other races" (620). Kalonymos replied, "You argue and you look forward – you are Daniel Charisi's grandson" (620).

As noted earlier, Eliot's use of Judaism in *Daniel Deronda* has provoked many arguments since the novel was first published, including most recently arguments concerning issues of gender and nationalism. A Christian theologian has written that Daniel Deronda, and his creator George Eliot, found in Judaism "a genuine moral and religious community that thrives on inner diversity and debate, that has a distinctive mission to humanity as a whole, and that believes in a God who is mysteriously present in every human face, who gives to human beings a diversity of pathways through life, and is the ultimate, incomprehensible, unnameable ground of the unity of all things" (Hodgson, *Mystery*, 138). *Daniel Deronda* ends with a quotation from Milton's *Samson Agonistes* that comments on the death of Mordecai. It is especially appropriate to Eliot's task that the novel should conclude with an allusion to a Jewish hero who fought the Philistines, and that the allusion should be from a dramatic poem in the form of a classical tragedy, written by a Christian poet, and based on a narrative in the Jewish scriptures.

SIX

THOMAS HARDY'S
APOCRYPHAL GOSPELS

On afternoons of drowsy calm
We stood in the panelled pew,
Singing one-voiced a Tate-and-Brady psalm
To the tune of "Cambridge New".

We watched the elms, we watched the rooks,
The clouds upon the breeze,
Between the whiles of glancing at our books,
And swaying like the trees.

So mindless were those outpourings! –
Though I am not aware
That I have gained by subtle thought on things
Since we stood psalming there.

Thomas Hardy,
"Afternoon Service at Mellstock"

—◀○▶—

THE FINAL CHAPTERS OF THIS STUDY of Victorian theology and the
novel look at three late Victorians, Thomas Hardy (1840–1928), Walter
Pater (1839–94), and Mary Augusta Ward (1851–1920). In each of these
novelists we can see the effects of the religious questions raised by Tennyson, Darwin, Matthew Arnold, and the authors of *Essays and Reviews*.
Each of the three has a significant relationship with Christian theology:
both Hardy and Pater contemplated ordination in the Church of England,
while as a young woman Mary Augusta Ward lived in Oxford, where she

was at the heart of the theological debates that were of such interest to the educated Victorian reading public. Furthermore, the anguished religious history of her father, Thomas Arnold, who twice converted to Roman Catholicism, gave her an intimate awareness of the practical consequences of questions of faith and doubt, as the family moved from Tasmania back to England after his first conversion, and to Oxford when Arnold returned to the Anglican fold in 1865. Thus, each of these novelists writes as an insider, as someone intimately acquainted with the theological disputes that were rending the Church of England, and as someone affected personally by them. They all take for granted the existence of liberal biblical hermeneutics in a way that was not possible for writers born earlier in the century. Furthermore, each writes with a strong dose of scepticism, especially when it comes to the other-worldly and the miraculous elements of Christianity. In Hardy's *The Mayor of Casterbridge* (1886), Elizabeth-Jane Henchard, the character who is closest to the values of the narrator of the novel, echoes Matthew Arnold when she tells her stepfather "I don't quite think there are any miracles nowadays" (*Mayor*, 297). This is the same belief – or lack of belief – that causes Robert Elsmere to give up his living.

Of the three writers, Thomas Hardy had the longest journey; for his place of birth and his education meant that in his early years he was somewhat insulated from the liberal theological developments elsewhere. In fact he lived under the unusual combined influence of Evangelical and Tractarian clergy, as well as having significant links with the Baptist church. This has been documented in a number of places, but most extensively by Timothy Hands, whose *Thomas Hardy: Distracted Preacher?* (1989) gives a detailed account of Hardy's religious life until his loss of faith in 1865. Hands's book is only one of a number of recent studies of Hardy's religious beliefs and of the religious attitudes that inform his novels and poetry.[1] In this chapter I focus on the two great late novels, *Tess of the d'Urbervilles* and *Jude the Obscure*, in which Hardy's theological concerns are more overt and extensive than in his earlier novels. I refer to them as Hardy's "apocryphal gospels," since both novels make extensive use of biblical allusions, including comparisons of various characters to Christ, and they are in a sense sceptical versions of the gospel story, setting out Hardy's critique of dogmatic Christianity.

In his influential book *The Secular Pilgrims of Victorian Fiction* (1982), Barry Qualls does not include a detailed discussion of Hardy, whom he sees as the "death" of the tradition he is tracing (15). Qualls writes of Hardy: "His fiction is the great anti-type for the novels of this study. He does not question if we can know God or nature or the godlike, or man's relationship to them; he *knows* man cannot achieve such visions" (192). I agree with Qualls that Hardy radically undermines the tradition of secular scriptures, for *Tess of the d'Urbervilles* and *Jude the Obscure* are in many ways parodies of the attempts of a novelist like Eliot to adapt biblical motifs and Christian ethical paradigms to a world in which God is absent. Nevertheless, Hardy's critique of typology and of liberal theology is written in the same kind of language as the discourses that are being attacked, using the same Christian symbols and biblical references that constitute the language of belief. Hardy's novels are therefore not as secular as Qualls's statement implies. According to Hands, Hardy's fourteen novels contain over six hundred biblical allusions, with the largest number (eighty-seven) occurring in *Tess of the d'Urbervilles* (*Preacher,* 38). Marlene Springer notes that a particular paragraph in *Tess* describing Mr Clare's religious position contains fourteen distinct allusions (*Allusion,* 129–30). Lance Butler writes, "It could be claimed that he works in an ironic mode with Christian symbols, but he uses them so much (and he *increases* his use as he goes on in his novelistic career) that there comes a point at which we must suspect his imitation of becoming flattery" ("Christian Discourse," 188).

It seems to me that there is a significant difference between the novels of Hardy, Pater, and Ward on the one hand, and such early Modernists as Henry James and Joseph Conrad on the other. The former are preoccupied with theological questions and have a world view that is in some sense fundamentally religious, whereas James and Conrad, even if they sometimes raise metaphysical questions or use religious themes and motifs, are fundamentally sceptical secular writers. Among the earlier twentieth-century writers, D.H. Lawrence would follow most logically from Hardy; but even though he uses biblical motifs and reworks Christian concepts, there is little continuity with the kind of Christian orthodoxy I have used as a reference point throughout this study. In part, of course, this is because the Christianity Lawrence draws on stems from a radical dissenting tradition very different from the Anglicanism that, in whatever variety of theology, is the common heritage of the writers I have chosen to study. Furthermore, in his intense religious concern with human relationships, Lawrence breaks with Christianity in a way that even Hardy, who anticipates some of his understanding of the role of eros in human life, does not. Further into the twentieth century, one can find writers who are Christians, or who draw on a Christian tradition, but these writers, coming after what is often described as the end of Christendom, in addition to coming after the Modernist break with tradition, tend not to engage quite as seriously with theological ideas. Theology is simply not a mainstream intellectual discourse in the Western world in the twentieth century in the way that it was in Victorian England. (The twentieth-century Catholic novel, from Evelyn Waugh and Graham Greene to David Lodge and Mary Gordon, is arguably an exception to this generalization.)

Thomas Hardy's ambivalent relationship with Christianity is far more subtle than Chesterton implied in his famous remark that Hardy was "a sort of village atheist brooding and blaspheming over the village idiot" (*Victorian Age*, 143). Hardy's poems provide a variety of perspectives on Christianity, some of which are despairing, bleak, cynical, or harshly critical. "Afternoon Service at Mellstock (Circa 1850)," which I have used as the epigraph to this chapter, seems to me the poem that best captures the contradictory set of attitudes that Hardy had towards Christianity throughout his life. One important component was always the intellectual rejection of the Christian religion, based largely on the assumption that its supernatural claims were contrary to reason and science. Thus, the psalms and prayers that the speaker in "Afternoon Service" remembers with such evident fondness and nostalgia are nevertheless described as "mindless ... outpourings" (*Complete Poems*, 429). Secondly, Hardy often appealed to the ethical dimension of Christianity to be found in Christ's teaching and other biblical passages in order to censure the institutional church for its lack of charity. This is implicit in the notion that the intellectually liberated speaker in the poem has not "gained" since he rejected the beliefs embodied in the afternoon service as a result of his "subtle thought on things." Thirdly, Hardy had a strong affection for the Church of England as a cultural and social institution, even though in his novels he often portrayed its failure to live up to that role. In "Afternoon Service at Mellstock," the church is part of the village landscape, along with the elms and the rooks; the music that the speaker recalls is sung "one-voiced," so that it is an expression of a community gathered together. As Hands observed, the shift from the first person plural to singular in the last stanza charts "the dissatisfying progression from community to isolation"

(*Preacher*, 100). Hardy is caught in the paradoxical, conflicted position that the poem dramatizes, with heart and head, past and present, thoroughly at odds. The only reconciliation of the contradictions is to be found in the literary works, both poems and novels, that dramatize and contain them. This must surely be one of the many reasons why Hardy has such a widespread popular appeal among the great writers of English literature: his novels speak eloquently to a divided sensibility, giving full weight to the emotional cost of intellectual and social change, yet refusing the consolations of a reactionary pose. His characters, too, living this contradiction especially in their erotic lives, are compelling for the same reason.

THE LAODICEANISM OF THOMAS HARDY

Jan Jedrzejewski's *Thomas Hardy and the Church* (1996) valuably chronicles the evolution of Hardy's beliefs, beginning with the period of youthful faith, followed first by his rejection of the supernatural dimension of Christianity, then by "the middle period of outspoken and bitter criticism of all things Christian in the name of compassion and humanity," and concluding with "the final recognition of the significance of the fundamental ethical values of Christianity in the life of human society despite the irrelevance of their ontological basis" (5). Even within this development, however, Hardy's attitudes are rarely straightforward. A useful way to define him would be with the title of one of his weakest but also one of his most revealing novels, *A Laodicean* (1881). The title refers, of course, to Revelation 3:15, where St John is told to write to the church of Laodicea, "I know thy works, that thou art neither cold nor hot: I would thou wert cold or hot." This verse is part of the text of the sermon by which the Baptist minister Mr Woodwell condemns Paula Power's last-minute refusal of baptism (Laodicean, 18). Michael Millgate aptly uses the concept of "Laodiceanism" to comment on Thomas Hardy's contradictory nature. Millgate refers to his "reluctance to adopt absolute or even firm positions" and his "insistence upon the provisionality of his opinions." Part of the reason for this, according to Millgate, is that "the emotions were for Hardy at least as powerful and persuasive as the intellect" (*A Biography*, 220). However, he was not willing to make the emotions an alternative basis for religious belief; for Hardy, belief had to satisfy intellectual tests, no matter how much it promised to fill emotional needs. If this were not the case, he would surely have been a liberal Christian.

Thomas Hardy's early religious formation came in the parish of Stinsford, under the Reverend Arthur Shirley. Shirley's ministry gave him the opportunity of witnessing a Tractarian clergyman modifying the accustomed practices of the parish. In 1856, at the age of sixteen, Hardy articled with a church architect. After leaving home in 1859, he "began to be drawn towards an Evangelical churchmanship which he was later unwilling to acknowledge" (Hands, *Preacher*, 11). As a young man, he seems to have felt the influence of the Gorham controversy over baptismal regeneration,[2] since he is known to have made a particular study of the question of infant baptism (Jedrzejewski, *Thomas Hardy*, 9–11). Hardy's study leaves its traces in the debate between Somerset and Woodwell in *A Laodicean* (59–61). Hardy refers to his goal of taking holy orders in *The Life and Work of Thomas Hardy*, the autobiography that he wrote in the third person and that was published under his wife's name in two volumes (1928 and 1930):

> He formed the idea of combining poetry and the Church – towards which he had long had a leaning – and wrote to a friend in Cambridge for particulars as to Matriculation at that University – which with his late Classical reading would have been easy for him, and knowing that what money he could not muster for himself for keeping terms his father would lend him for a few years, his idea being that of a curate in a country village. This fell through less because of its difficulty than from a conscientious feeling, after some theological study, that he could hardly take the step with honour while holding the views that on examination he found himself to hold. And so he allowed the curious scheme to drift out of sight, though not till after he had begun to practise orthodoxy. (*Life and Work*, 52–3)

We have no record of the process of Hardy's loss of faith, nor is it really possible, as Timothy Hands reminds us, to be sure "how completely he ever possessed it" (*Preacher*, 29). He appears to have experienced some sort of spiritual crisis, or at least a decline in his religious observances, in the mid-1860s, and the passage from Hardy's *Life and Work* quoted above refers to "the views that on examination he found himself to hold" (53), which made him unfit for ordination. Certainly his growing agnosticism would have been encouraged by his perusal of *Essays and Reviews*, published in 1860, which "impressed him much" (*Life and Work*, 37), and of Darwin's *Origin of Species*, which had come out a year earlier. In his *Life and Work*, Hardy claims that "as a young man he had been among the earliest acclaimers of *The Origin of Species*" (158). In spite of these agnostic influences, however, "he was never to lose entirely his imaginative adherence to the Church" (Millgate, *A Biography*, 91).

In Hardy's fiction, the religious beliefs of his childhood and youth are represented not so much by an interest in Evangelical or Tractarian doctrine as by the portrayal of the church as the centre of the village community, and of its largely instinctive and unconscious life. He presents Evangelicalism in *Tess* and Tractarianism in *Jude* as ecclesiastical ideologies that not only do not promote the essential truths of Christianity but are in fact symptoms of the "ache of modernism" as it corrodes the certainties of the community. The presentation of the traditional religion of the rural community is most notable in *Under the Greenwood Tree* (1872), with its opposition between the music of the village choir and the reforms that are introduced by Mr Maybold. There is a persistent trend in the interpretation of Hardy that sees the instinctive life, or the life close to nature, or a pagan life – these terms all describe something similar – as Hardy's ideal, to be opposed to the atomistic life of urban and industrial society and to the life-denying laws of Christianity. This interpretation certainly seems to be licensed by the more pastoral aspects of Hardy's fiction, and especially by *Far From the Madding Crowd* (1874), but it is not nearly as well supported by most of the later novels. Charlotte Bonica has argued persuasively that in fact Hardy's novels show a "profound moral *dis*continuity between man and nature" ("Nature," 859). She documents the pervasive sexuality in Hardy's representation of nature and suggests that it is sexuality that makes it impossible to live naturally, because of the disruptive and unpredictable force of sexual desire. Shirley Stave sought to revive the pagan reading of Hardy from a feminist perspective by couching his work in dualist terms: "The original, unfallen world, the world previously aligned with the agrarian side of the equation, is natural, Pagan, nonpatriarchal, and mythic, while the world that threatens it is cultural, Christian, patriarchal, and historical" (*Decline*, 2). In Stave's argument, Christianity becomes the carrier of modernity and alienation, but this is only partly true in Hardy's fiction. Neither Christianity nor paganism are viable options for Hardy; he differed from many of his contemporaries, as we shall see, in doubting that the place of religion in Victorian society would be filled either by a transformed liberal version of Christianity or by culture, both of which options were advocated by Matthew Arnold in his critical and religious writings.

In several ways, the contrast between Matthew Arnold and Thomas Hardy is instructive. Both men were convinced that faith in traditional Christianity had been rendered impossible in the modern era for those educated in the scientific world view. Both had a deeply conservative love for the rituals, language, and, in Hardy's case, architecture of the English church. Hardy's rejection of orthodox theology is particularly clear in a passage dated 2 July 1865 in his *Life and Work*. He describes reading Newman's *Apologia* and expresses "a great desire to be convinced by him, because H.M.M. [Horace Moule] likes him so much. Style charming, and his logic really human, being based not on syllogisms but on converging probabilities. Only – and here comes the fatal catastrophe – there is no first link to his excellent chain of reasoning, and down you come headlong. Poor Newman! His gentle childish faith in revelation and tradition must have made him a very charming character" (50-1). The missing first link is faith in the supernatural, which Newman takes for granted. For Hardy, as for George Eliot, such faith was a projection of human feelings, needs, and desires. As he wrote in *The Return of the Native* (1878): "Human beings, in their generous endeavour to construct a hypothesis that shall not degrade a first cause, have always hesitated to conceive a dominant power of lower moral quality than their own" (387).

Hardy to some extent shares Arnold's conception of the *Zeitgeist*, that "Time-Spirit" that informs the cultural productions of a particular age and seems to determine the beliefs of that age, or at least of those people whom we think of as typifying it. There are periods, for example, when the existence of religious faith might be taken for granted, and others when it would be difficult if not impossible to do so, the "sea of faith" having retreated from the earth's shore. Beneath the apparent agreement, though, Arnold and Hardy differ significantly. While Arnold is fully alive to the melancholy consequences of the crisis of faith, he remains relatively optimistic. If he sees himself as "Wandering between two worlds, one dead, / The other powerless to be born" (lines 85-6, "Stanzas from the Grand Chartreuse"), or as a critic who is fated to die in the wilderness rather than to enter the promised land ("The Function of Criticism at the Present Time"), it is clear that he hopes with some degree of confidence that the new world will some day be born, and that others will enter that promised land. Hardy sees a more tragic disjunction between human desire and the human intellect. While he advocated greater honesty and freedom in sexual matters, he also recognized that the human heart and head are radically at odds. No rational human system could ever accommodate the vicissitudes of human desire.

Arnold's goal, especially in his religious writings, was to reconstitute Christianity, because although people could not in his view do without it, neither could they find it meaningful in the form in which it was presently constituted. As we have seen, this assumption underlies *Literature and Dogma* and its companion volume, *God and the Bible*. In both, Arnold seeks to give Christianity a verifiable, "experimental" basis by revealing its natural truth, apart from all dogmatic assertions. Hardy rejected this attempt to modernize religion, though with characteristic inconsistency he also more than once suggested that a radically demythologized established church would be a good thing. In a letter to John Morley, he imagined the Church evolving into "an undogmatic, non-theological establishment for the promotion of ... virtuous living" (*Letters* 1:136, 20 November 1885).

Hardy's rejection of Arnold's reconstruction had two distinct causes. As a more thoroughgoing rationalist than Arnold, Hardy would have regarded the rethinking of Christianity in *Literature and Dogma* as intellectually dishonest, a matter of trying to believe in the objectivity of one's own projections. But Hardy's conservative love of tradition also played a part. He would probably have considered it better to face the fact of the death of God and the loss of the whole rich heritage in which belief in God had been enshrined than to seek to save that cultural tradition by grounding it in a radically reconfigured theology. An example of Hardy's response to Arnold occurs in *Life and Work*. Referring to the insincerity of modern literature, he wrote: "When dogma has to be balanced on its feet by such hair-splitting as the late Mr M. Arnold's it must be in a very bad way" (224). Similarly, in a letter to the Positivist Frederic Harrison he noted that "satire I suppose, is bad as a rule, but surely the New Christians (or whatever they are) who, to use Morley's words 'have hit their final climax in the doctrine that everything is both true & false at the same time' are very tempting game – I mean the 'Robert Elsmere' school" (*Letters* 1:176, 17 May 1888).

In addition to the need to reconstruct religion to make it acceptable,

Matthew Arnold asserts the need for intellectual culture, either as an alternative or as a necessary supplement – the relationship between religion and culture in his work is not clear. In this context, the key texts are *Culture and Anarchy* and the critical essays. Arnold's idea of culture involved the nurturing of the critical spirit, not in the interests of any particular ideology or belief but in the form of "a desire after the things of the mind simply for their own sakes and for the pleasure of seeing them as they are" (*Complete Prose* 5:91). For Arnold, however, human beings are meant to develop their spiritual sides in a harmonious manner, but the English, especially the Nonconformists, tend "to sacrifice all other sides of our being to the religious side" (5:238). Culture, or the concern with spiritual perfection, is thus larger than, and contains, religion. Yet in a characteristic about-face, Arnold develops the idea of culture in a religious direction, including in the accumulating definitions of the term a motto from Bishop Thomas Wilson (1663–1755), a hero to the Tractarians. The aim of culture is, in Wilson's words, "To make reason and the will of God prevail!" (in *Complete Prose* 5:91).

Obviously Arnold was so quintessentially the metropolitan professional-class literary intellectual that the kind of experience recorded and valued in Hardy's novels would have been extremely remote to him. As a historian of the way of life of the part of the rural south of England that he called Wessex, Hardy was well aware that the unselfconscious life of the rural community was vanishing, and that the future lay with the intellectually self-conscious characters of the later novels, those who aspire towards Arnoldian culture. This did not mean, however, that Hardy shared Arnold's hopes. Even more deeply than Arnold, he had a sense of two different worlds, and in his pastoral fiction he gives us an unforgettable representation of some of the valuable things that were being lost with the death of the old world. Elsewhere, Hardy directly represents the intellectual culture of the modern spirit. In *A Laodicean*, his "Story of To-Day," we first see Paula Power declaring her rebelliousness and rejection of dogmatic religion by deciding not to be baptized. She becomes fascinated by the history of Stancy Castle, the ancient house her father purchased, and is in danger of falling in love with the medieval past. At the end of the novel, after fire has destroyed Stancy Castle, George Somerset tells her that she will recover from the effects of medievalism; quoting Arnold's essay "Pagan and Medieval Religious Sentiment," she replies: "And be a perfect representative of 'the modern spirit'? ... representing neither the senses and understanding, nor the heart and imagination; but what a finished writer calls 'the imaginative reason'?" (431).[3] This is Hardy's most positive representation of Arnold's ideal of culture. He provides a searching critique of that ideal in *Tess* and *Jude*, and he never endorses the idea that culture can be a substitute religion. Even after the passage I have just quoted Hardy introduces a qualification, as Paula still wishes that the castle had not burned, and that Somerset was "a De Stancy"; the novel thus ends on what Richard Taylor calls "a note of suggestive irresolution" (*Neglected*, 109).

Two aspects of Hardy's fiction are particularly relevant to a theological understanding of his work: his use of biblical allusion, and the relationship between erotic love and religious emotion in his fiction. Both topics are important in *Tess* and *Jude*, but I shall introduce them by way of *The Mayor of Casterbridge* and *Two on a Tower* before turning to the two great novels with which Hardy ended his fictional career. *Two on a Tower*, which is in my judgment the most accomplished of Hardy's minor works, will provide a convenient transition to the later novels.

The Mayor of Casterbridge is saturated with biblical parallels and allusions, the effect of which is to create the appearance of an ordered universe in which nature and human life alike correspond to a typological pattern of divine order, revealed in the Bible. Yet the perceptions and actions of the main characters are often at odds with this pattern. When he proposes to sell Susan and the child, Michael Henchard promises, "I'll take my tools and go my ways. 'Tis simple as Scripture history" (12). As anyone who has studied the Bible for any length of time knows well, scriptural history is far from simple, and the consequences of Henchard's behaviour, from which parallels to biblical stories are repeatedly drawn, are complicated and various.[4] But none of this makes *The Mayor* a particularly Christian novel. If, as Northrop Frye argued, true typology results in the patterns of comedy and romance, the effect of *The Mayor* is more like satire and tragedy. The story unfolds in a twilight world faintly illumined by the afterglow of a light that is all but extinguished, like the moonlit statues of "A Cathedral Façade at Midnight" (Hardy, *Complete Poems*, 703). In one memorable passage Michael Henchard contemplates suicide, but he is prevented by an apparent miracle, the uncanny image of "his actual double" floating as if dead in the dangerous part of the stream where he had planned to drown himself. This leads him to ask Elizabeth-Jane the question that preoccupied many Victorians: "Are miracles still worked, do ye think, Elizabeth?" (*Mayor*, 297). Her answer, already quoted, is that of a the sceptic and doubter: "I don't quite think there are any miracles nowadays" (297). She then accompanies him back to Ten-Hatches-Hole, where she discovers that the double was the effigy used when the townspeople expose his affair with Lucetta in the skimmington ride. Not only does the "miracle" have a naturalistic explanation but it is ironically connected with Lucetta's death; as Henchard bitterly comments, "That performance of theirs killed her, but kept me alive!" (298). If there is any divinity in the world, it seems a malevolent one; though perhaps, as J. Hillis Miller argues, Henchard is merely projecting his own self-destructive tendencies when he talks of an evil providence ruling his life (*Hardy*, 150).

In *Two on a Tower*, Hardy deals with what Glen Irvin has termed "High Passion and High Church." Like Trollope and George Eliot, but with more emphasis on the role of desire and the impossibility of its fulfilment in the world, Hardy analyzes the interaction of the erotic and the spiritual life. Unlike the religious novelists who focus on the erotic, Hardy does not see a continuity between erotic love and spiritual feeling. By dramatizing the difficulties of reconciling faith, sexual desire, and science, he once again provides a sceptical response to Matthew Arnold's belief in the possibilities of culture to bring harmony to the various impulses that compose the self. In his preface, Hardy describes *Two on a Tower* as a "slightly-built romance" in which he sought "to set the emotional history of two infinitesimal lives against the stupendous background of the stellar universe, and to impart to readers the sentiment that of these contrasting magnitudes the smaller might be the greater to them as men" (*Tower*, 3). The life of Swithin as a scientist and the workings of the stars are the subject of a few scattered paragraphs crammed with the knowledge Hardy got up from his scientific sources in order to write the novel. But for the most part he focuses on the "infinitesimal lives," to the great relief of the reader, for whom the interactions of the inhabitants of Welland are indeed likely to be of greater interest than Hardy's attempts at the astronomical sublime or his outline of the professional career of Swithin St Cleve, which is in fact glossed over in parodic biblical language.[5] There is also the implication that the unpredictable and endlessly complex consequences of human sexual attraction are more important ultimately than the knowledge that is derived from scientific observation of the heavens; for the heavens are indifferent to the destinies of human beings. The connection between the astronomical "transit of Venus" and the love affair between Viviette and Swithin is accidental and arbitrary, resulting from the fact that human culture has chosen to represent the power of love by the planet Venus. For most of the novel, however, Swithin is more interested in the former, and Viviette in the latter. Astrologers may have assumed a connection, but in the "new astrology" referred to in Hardy's epigraph from Crashaw, the beloved replaces God, or the planets and stars, as the ruler of the heart.

As Timothy Hands notes, Viviette Constantine is one of Hardy's "*dévotes*," female characters who "are identifiable by the orthodoxy of their religious beliefs and practices" (*Preacher*, 55). She is one of the few people in the parish to attend church on Ash Wednesday (*Tower*, 65), and her brother refers to her as following "the revived methods in church practice" (204). Whereas falling in love with Caroline Waddington results in George Bertram's religious apostasy in *The Bertrams*, Viviette perceives Swithin as having an "early-Christian face" (29) and contemplates the idea of his death with a melancholy pleasure: "If he had died she might have mused on him as her dear departed saint without much sin; but his return to life was a delight that bewildered and dismayed" (75). Viviette's dismay results from the fact that she is not only married but also of a higher social station than Swithin, so that even after the supposed death of her husband, marriage to Swithin seems to her socially inappropriate. Once again Hardy uses Christian imagery to express Viviette's dilemma. Like Lord Angelo in *Measure for Measure*, Lady Constantine cannot concentrate on her devotions in church: "Heaven had her empty words only, and her invention heard not her tongue" (50). The bushes at the base of the tower where Viviette and Swithin meet are described in a bizarrely arresting simile as "scratching the pillar with the drag of impish claws as tenacious as those figuring in St Anthony's temptation" (60). Viviette's alternation between sexual passion and Tractarian devotion is explicitly analyzed by the narrator:

> Lady Constantine, by virtue of her temperament, was necessarily either lover or *dévote*, and she vibrated so gracefully between these two conditions that nobody who had known the circumstances could have condemned her inconsistencies. To be led into difficulties by those mastering emotions of hers, to aim at escape by turning round and seizing the apparatus of religion – which could only rightly be worked by the very emotions already bestowed elsewhere – it was, after all, but Convention's palpitating attempt to preserve the comfort of her

creature's conscience in the trying quandary to which the conditions
of sex had given rise. (141)

This passage certainly suggests that the roots of religious feeling are sexual,
and it further implies that Viviette's devotion is really a displacement of
sexual desire and a projection of her need to reconcile her erotic feelings
with the official sexual morality of her society.

The novel contains several other passages, however, that, taken together,
suggest that Viviette's feeling for Swithin is the source of a genuine spiritual growth. This does not prevent the tragic fate that is in store for her;
if anything, it heightens our sense of the tragedy. Viviette's second unhappy
marriage is the result of the incompatibility of the morality of the official
church – represented above all by Bishop Helmsdale – and the expression
of a true self-emptying charity in Viviette. She passes, in Pauline terms,
from the old dispensation to the new, from law to charity. Her dilemma
seems to be resolved by the apparent death of Sir Blount, after which she
looks at the Ten Commandments inscribed on the wall of the church,
"and the Table of the Law opposite, which now seemed to appertain to
another dispensation, glistened indistinctly upon a vision still obscured
by the old tears" (79). Now that she feels free to love, the stern commandments on the wall do not seem to apply, as her vision of them is obscured
by the tears of pious sensibility.

Later in the novel, the full significance of this passage is unfolded. Viviette learns that her marriage to Swithin was not valid, since Sir Blount
was at that time still alive, and she also learns of the strange conditional
inheritance that Swithin forfeited by marrying her. (If anyone wanted
to accuse Hardy of incredible plot contrivances, this might be the novel
to choose as an example.) She wonders whether she should save her honour by making herself his legal wife: "As a subjectively honest woman
alone, beginning her charity at home, there was no doubt that she ought.
Save thyself was sound Old Testament doctrine, and not altogether dis-
countenanced in the New. But was there a line of conduct which transcended mere self-preservation, and would it not be an excellent thing
to put it in practice now?" (229). She resolves to sacrifice her own happiness to further Swithin's interests and enables him to travel abroad to
pursue his studies. The irony is that in spite of her resolution, her passion
for Swithin remains, and in their final meeting she yields "to all the passion of her first union with him" (238) and becomes pregnant. This results
in her desperate marriage to the bishop, who reflects that Viviette is a

"good and wise woman" who "perceived what a true shelter from sadness" he offered her, "and was not the one to despise Heaven's gift" (261). The marriage is arranged by Louis Glanville, in a comic scene during which he visits the cathedral close of Melchester, "level as a bowling-green, and beloved of rooks, who from their elm perches on high threatened any unwary gazer with the mishap of Tobit" (254). This esoteric and scatological reference (see Apocrypha, Tobit 2:10) introduces an element of burlesque. The whole scene is a parody of the world of *Barchester Towers*. Viviette's marriage to Bishop Helmsdale was too much for some of the first readers of *Two on a Tower*; the review in the *St James Gazette*, for example, suggested that the marriage of Viviette and the bishop "may even be regarded in certain quarters as a studied and gratuitous insult aimed at the Church" (quoted in Ahmad, "Introduction," xxi), a charge to which Hardy responded somewhat disingenuously in his 1895 preface: "the Bishop is every inch a gentleman" (*Tower*, 3).

When Swithin returns to England three years later, although his ardour towards Viviette has cooled, "he believed that all her conduct had been dictated by the purest benevolence to him; by that charity which 'seeketh not her own.' Hence he did not flinch from a wish to deal with loving-kindness towards her – a sentiment perhaps in the long run more to be prized than a lover's love" (280). Viviette's religiosity, he realizes, has metamorphosed into a true forgetting of self on his behalf; with savage irony, however, Hardy has Viviette die of joy at Swithin's declaration. With the death of the character who embodies the love that "seeketh not her own," the narrator sardonically observes that "The Bishop," who embodies the stern law that is more willing to condemn than to forgive, "was avenged" (281). This grim observation foreshadows the more famous conclusion of *Tess of the d'Urbervilles*. Swithin, meanwhile, seems to be attracted to the youthful energy of Tabitha Lark, thus showing how easily he will recover from the experience, and further underlining the tragedy of Viviette's fate. Both High Passion and High Church have failed her. In Hardy's fiction, the ladder of love is a dangerous structure with broken rungs that does not provide reliable access to the divine.

"ALAS, POOR THEOLOGY!": *TESS OF THE D'URBERVILLES*

The standard reading of *Tess* suggests that the "pure" sexual love between Angel and Tess is destroyed by the hypocritical moral double standard supported by the Church, with the forces of the modern world and differences in social class variously factored in. In Shirley Stave's words, in a recent version of this interpretation, "The old Pagan world view has been defeated by a new Christian way of perceiving" (*Decline*, 109). However, Nature and Christianity alike fail Tess in her moments of need.[6] In his treatment of Nature, Hardy rejects both the optimistic Romanticism that viewed Nature as a source of solace in the modern world, and the kind of sacramentalism that combined the Romantic view of Nature with a Christian belief in revelation. The latter is something that one can find in poetry from John Keble to Gerard Manley Hopkins, and we have seen examples of it in Charlotte Mary Yonge's *The Heir of Redclyffe*, grounded on the Tractarian doctrine of analogy. The narrator of *Tess* as well as various characters distance themselves from what M.H. Abrams has called "natural supernaturalism." In commenting on the conditions of life of Tess and her siblings, growing up in "the shiftless house of Durbeyfield," the narrator digresses: "Some people would like to know whence the poet whose philosophy is in these days deemed as profound and trustworthy as his song is breezy and pure, gets his authority for speaking of 'Nature's holy plan'" (*Tess*, 28). This phrase, which comes at the end of Wordsworth's "Lines Written in Early Spring," typifies a benevolent Romantic view of nature.

When Angel leaves Tess after their disastrous honeymoon, he thinks of a line from Pippa's first song in Browning's *Pippa Passes* (1841), "with peculiar emendations of his own: – 'God's *not* in his heaven: all's *wrong* with the world!'" (248). One would not expect Hardy to endorse the complacent natural theology of Pippa's song – which is not exactly endorsed by *Pippa Passes* as a whole – for he once commented of Browning in a letter to Edmund Gosse: "The longer I live the more does B.'s character seem *the* literary puzzle of the 19th century. How could smug Christian optimism worthy of a dissenting grocer find a place inside a man who was so vast a seer & feeler when on neutral ground?" (*Letters* 2:216, 6 March 1899). Wordsworth is quoted a second time in a critical manner. Tess hears her brothers and sisters singing a children's hymn about heaven and reflects that because she doesn't believe in a divine Providence, she must be their providence: "for to Tess, as to not a few millions of others, there was ghastly satire in the poet's lines: 'Not in utter nakedness / But trailing clouds of glory do we come'" (*Tess*, 344). In all of these passages, then, the narrator and the main characters agree that Nature is either indifferent or hostile to the endeavours of human beings; there is clearly no sense of a Romantic "correspondent breeze." Other passages might be adduced to suggest the contrary, but I think that Charlotte Bonica's treatment of those passages in her article on *Tess* is the correct view. Bonica notes that many of the passages dealing with nature in *Tess* use sexual metaphors, which "are particularly significant in view of Hardy's conviction that natural forces and human life converge only in the human sexual impulse" ("Nature," 859). Both from his own observation and from Darwin, Hardy was aware that this impulse led to suffering as often as to happiness. Nature is simply indifferent to the projects of human consciousness.

As a final example, I will look at what could be called a parody of a Romantic nature epiphany. Significantly, this passage occurs immediately after Alec d'Urberville has rescued Tess from the hostile Trantridge workfolk, whose crude humour and violence are another argument against sentimentalizing and romanticizing Hardy's "paganism." Tess is carried away by Alec, to suffer a worse fate than any she would have suffered at the hands of the working people; the narrator describes those latter, as they make their way home:

> Then these children of the open air, whom even excess of alcohol could scarce injure permanently, betook themselves to the field-path; and as they went there moved onward with them, around the shadow of each one's head, a circle of opalized light, formed by the moon's rays upon the glistening sheet of dew. Each pedestrian could see no halo but his or her own, which never deserted the head-shadow whatever its vulgar unsteadiness might be; but adhered to it, and persistently beautified it; till the erratic motions seemed an inherent part of the irradiation and the fumes of their breathing a component of the night's mist: and the spirit of the scene, and of the moonlight, and of Nature, seemed harmoniously to mingle with the spirit of wine. (*Tess*, 71–2)

This wonderful passage comically reduces the mystical halo of natural supernaturalism to an optical effect that is the result of a combination of the mist of the night and the alcoholic mist of the characters; a combination of the spirit of nature and the spirit of wine. Hardy often parodies a supernatural effect in this way, by reducing it to a carnivalesque material cause (the miracle that prevents Henchard's suicide is another example).[7] The fact that each pedestrian can only see his or her own halo perhaps also indicates the narcissistic subjectivity inherent in Romantic nature mysticism. Hardy's passage comments ironically on poem 67 of Tennyson's *In Memoriam*, in which the speaker contemplates the grave of Hallam at night and seems to see it transfigured by an intimation of divine presence:[8]

> When on my bed the moonlight falls,
>   I know that in thy place of rest
>   By that broad water of the west,
> There comes a glory on the walls:
>
> Thy marble bright in dark appears,
>   As slowly steals a silver flame
>   Along the letters of thy name,
> And o'er the number of thy years. (Lines 1–8)

The violation scene immediately follows the passage I have just quoted from *Tess*, and the novel shifts from a comic, parodic epiphany to a tragedy that occurs because Nature is unable to come to Tess's aid: "Above them rose the primeval yews and oaks of The Chase, in which were poised gentle roosting birds in their last nap; and about them stole the hopping rabbits and hares. But, might some say, where was Tess's guardian angel? where was the Providence of her simple faith?" (*Tess*, 77). Clearly Nature is not that guardian angel, for the timid creatures are not going to be able to help her. Nor is there a Christian guardian angel; neither, later in the novel, will Angel Clare be Tess's guardian.

It is easy to overlook the similarities between *Tess of the d'Urbervilles* and *Jude the Obscure*, for one tends to remember the images of rural plenitude of the former and the scenes of urban angst in the latter. However, in spite of the tendency of critics to see Tess as a pagan figure or a Nature goddess, which is how Hardy himself sees her some of the time, she is at other points in the novel a distinctly modern young woman: "Between the mother, with her fast-perishing lumber of superstitions, folk-lore, dialect, and orally transmitted ballads, and the daughter, with her trained National teachings and Standard knowledge under an infinitely Revised Code, there was a gap of two hundred years as ordinarily understood. When they were together the Jacobean and the Victorian ages were juxtaposed" (28). Tess had hoped to be a teacher at the school (50), but her mother's plan for her interferes with that ambition, and when she meets Angel, she is described as "expressing in her own native phrases – assisted a little by her sixth-standard training – feelings which might almost have been called those of the age – the ache of modernism" (129). Tess has more in common with *Jude the Obscure*'s Sue Bridehead than one might think.

Appropriately, in a novel that is concerned with "the ache of modernism," Hardy represents orthodox Christianity in *Tess* as at best irrelevant and at worst a malevolent force. His criticism of Christianity is more pointed than in his earlier novels. Tess has a naturally religious sensibility and often uses Christian imagery and analogies in expressing herself. She is reminded of a confirmation when Mrs d'Urberville places her hands on the poultry; she baptizes her dying child herself; she sings the Benedicite when she leaves home for the second time (109). Each of these incidents is in some way ironical. The analogy between the chickens and young people being confirmed speaks for itself. The baby is baptized Sorrow, and in spite of the fact that his baptism is certainly valid by the strictest teaching on the subject, Sorrow is refused a proper Christian burial. After Tess sings the Benedicite, the narrator comments, "Probably the half-unconscious rhapsody was a Fetichistic utterance in a Monotheistic setting" (109). Eventually Tess takes on Angel Clare's beliefs, which constitute a kind of religion of humanity, telling Alec d'Urberville that it is possible to have "the religion of loving-kindness and purity" without dogma (319). It must have been this aspect of *Tess* that gave Frederic Harrison the impression that the novel was "like a Positivist allegory or sermon" (Hardy, *Letters* 1:251n). However, though Hardy would have agreed with the Positivists' critique of Christianity, he was not as sanguine about the utopian possibilities inherent in Positive knowledge. Ultimately Angel's beliefs are at least as harmful as those of his father. Furthermore, Hardy has not totally abandoned Christianity; for his critique of Evangelical religion is made in the name of Christian values. In the preface to *Tess*, Hardy defends the adjective "pure," as applied to the heroine in the subtitle, by saying that readers who object to his novel "ignore the meaning of the word in Nature, together with all aesthetic claims upon it, not to mention the spiritual interpretation afforded by the finest side of their own Christianity" (*Tess*, 4–5). There is an interesting passage on Positivism in Hardy's *Life and Work*, dated 1880: "George Eliot died during the winter in which he lay ill and this set him thinking about Positivism,

on which he remarks: 'If Comte had introduced Christ among the wor-
thies in his calendar it would have made Positivism tolerable to thousands
who, from position, family connection, or early education, now decry
what in their heart of hearts they hold to contain the germs of a true system'" (150–1). Characteristically, Hardy wants to have things both ways:
Positivism seems to him to be the beginning of a "true system," but for
reasons of policy it should incorporate aspects of what it seeks to replace.
There are some similarities with Arnold's argument in *Literature and
Dogma*.

   In the character of Mr Clare, Thomas Hardy provides his fullest portrait of an Evangelical clergyman. He is described as "an Evangelical of
the Evangelicals, a conversionist," and as a man who "was regarded even
by those of his own date and school of thinking as extreme" (*Tess*, 160–
1). Hardy's critique of Mr Clare may usefully be related to a passage in a
letter to his friend Edward Clodd: "The older one gets, the more deplorable
seems the effect of that terrible, dogmatic ecclesiasticism – Christianity
so called (but really Paulinism *plus* idolatry) – on morals & true religion:
a dogma with which the real teaching of Christ has hardly anything in
common" (*Letters* 2:143, 17 January 1897). In his presentation of the effects
of Mr Clare's beliefs, Hardy is suggesting the effects of "dogma-tic ecclesiasticism"; the issue is complicated, however, by the fact that Mr Clare
is more truly charitable than his son Angel, whose intellectual questioning
prevents him from accepting the theology of his father, which he terms
"an untenable redemptive theolatry" (*Tess*, 120). When Mr and Mrs Clare
are introduced, Hardy is careful to show their practice of charity, in spite
of their antinomian theology. This virtue is singularly lacking in their
two older sons and in the family friend Mercy Chant, who are responsible
for the failure of Tess's attempt to reach out to her in-laws. The only result
of Tess's journey is that her boots are appropriated on the assumption
that they belonged to an imposter, and she meets Alec d'Urberville once
more on her return.

   Angel's father tells him about his effort to bring Alec d'Urberville to
repentance, hoping that "one of those poor words of mine may spring
up in his heart as a good seed, some day" (169). At this point, however,
the reader has already seen one example of the plants that grow from Mr
Clare's seeds, and it is not encouraging. After her parting from Alec
d'Urberville at the beginning of Phase the Second, Tess returns home,
and Hardy's imagery suggests that this will be a failed attempt to return

to the Edenic state she enjoyed before she met him. She is haunted by a sense of guilt, and "she had learnt that the serpent hisses where the sweet birds sing" (81). As she walks she meets a sign-painter, whose mission to paint biblical texts across the countryside was inspired by Mr Clare. These texts appeal for a conversion, but Tess denies their validity. The narrator seems to judge them from an educated perspective as being out of step with the *Zeitgeist*: "Some people might have cried 'Alas, poor Theology!' at the hideous defacement – the last grotesque phase of a creed which had served mankind well in its time" (85). This passage clearly expresses Hardy's sense that Christianity as a dogmatic religion belonged to a past age, and here again we can see why the Positivist Frederic Harrison responded so positively to *Tess*. The epithet "poor Theology," like the "poor Newman" of Hardy's *Life and Work*, expresses the narrator's condescending pity for the descent of theology from the age of faith to the semiliterate sign-painter's fanatical zeal as he paints the words, each separated from the next by a comma as though to emphasize that his is a religion of the letter. Even though they were inspired by "a very earnest good man" (86), the texts do not address Tess's spiritual need.

Like the work of the sign-painter, Alec's preaching is the result of the "poor words" of Mr Clare. Hardy's description makes it clear that this is not a transformation that the reader is meant to accept. To Tess, there is "a ghastly *bizarrerie*, a grim incongruity," in hearing the words of Scripture from Alec's mouth (297). The narrator describes it as a "transfiguration" in which "sensuousness" becomes "devotional passion" and "riotousness" becomes "pious rhetoric" (297). However, the doctrine that conversion can transform the nature of a person is denied in Alec's case. His features have been "diverted from their hereditary connotation to signify impressions for which nature did not intend them" (298). The effect of this meeting is to reinforce in Tess the feeling that her past and her present are intextricably linked. She will never be free of d'Urberville, and he realizes that he still desires her. His religious conversion proves as short-lived as Angel's love. Hardy's description here suggests that Alec's fervent preaching originates in the same passionately violent temperament that determined his treatment of Tess; thus it is no surprise that when she reappears by chance, he is unable to resist the force of his desire, in spite of his supposed change of heart. Tess cannot believe in Alec's "conversion to a new spirit" (301), and he blames her attractiveness for tempting him from the way he has chosen. Alec is here linked to Angel, in spite of their very different doctrines; neither is capable of accepting Tess in her physical being as an embodiment of human goodness. Both the evangelical and the New Christian project onto Tess their own conflicted sexual feelings, blaming her for them: "And there was revived in her the wretched sentiment which had often come to her before, that in inhabiting the fleshly tabernacle with which Nature had endowed her, she was somehow doing wrong" (301). Thus Tess ends up self-condemned, having internalized a Gnostic heresy posing as Christianity.

In Angel Clare, as David DeLaura has shown, Hardy attacks liberal Christianity. In fact, the publication of Mary Ward's *Robert Elsmere* in February 1888 may have been a determining influence on the character-ization of Angel (DeLaura, "'Modernism,'" 385–6). In the Talbothays sec-tion of the novel, "The Rally," a religion of love begins to replace the "untenable redemptive theolatry" of Evangelical Christianity. In the scene where Angel declares his love, Tess is, as Simon Gatrell notes, "pure wo-man" in the sense of "wholly woman" ("Introduction," xvi). Angel responds to her as a loveable person whose attractiveness is bodily: "How very lov-able her face was to him. Yet there was nothing ethereal about it: all was real vitality, real warmth, real incarnation" (*Tess*, 152). Hardy presents this as a moment of revelation, of conversion: "Something had occurred which changed the pivot of the universe for their two natures ... A veil had been whisked aside; the tract of each one's outlook was to have a new horizon thenceforward – for a short time or for a long" (154). Much later, when Angel has abandoned Tess and she writes to him in despair, she presents their love most explicitly in terms of a religious conversion, in which the old self dies and a "new life" begins: "What was the past to me as soon as I met you? It was a dead thing altogether. I became another woman, filled full of new life from you" (325). Similarly, Angel and Tess's early-morning meetings are represented in explicitly religious imagery. Angel, who did not enter the Church because of his doubts about Article 4, "Of the Resurrection of Christ," often thinks of the resurrection-hour during these mornings, though he forgets that St Mary Magdalen is an integral part of the resurrection story (134).

The religion of love as laid out in the novel results in the virtual deifi-cation of the beloved in one another's eyes, especially Angel in Tess's eyes. Both his name and his superior social status contribute to the suggestion of inequality between them, and on several occasions Hardy uses the language of religious devotion to represent Tess's feelings for Angel (see for example 199, 212, 266). Angel's own erotic feelings are entangled with a liberal Christianity that, while claiming to be liberated from dogma, retains aspects of the moral teaching of orthodox Christianity without its compassion and ability to forgive. Thus, when Tess inevitably fails to measure up to Angel's exalted view of her, he is totally disillusioned. His parents, for all their evangelical sternness, would have been kinder towards Tess than he was: "Their hearts went out of them at a bound towards extreme cases, when the subtle mental troubles of the less desperate among mankind failed to win their interest or regard" (291). Angel, on the other hand, is "becoming ill with thinking" (238) and can only condemn Tess; his feelings do not overflow into loving-kindness towards her and forgiveness of her "sins." This is Hardy's most damning indictment of the Schleiermachian piety based on feelings alone. Hardy's language emphasizes the spiritual nature of Angel's love, suggesting that he can no longer respond to the "real incarnation" of Tess's actual presence. His love is described as "ethereal to a fault" (240), and Tess is appalled by "the determination revealed in the depths of this gentle being she had married – the will to subdue the grosser to the subtler emotion, the substance to the conception, the flesh to the spirit" (241). It is as though he had discovered an ascetic vocation, or, in fact, as though he were the Gnostic compared to his Christian parents. In Tess's case, as in Viviette Constantine's, sexual feeling is the source of self-denying charity: "She sought not her own; was not provoked; thought no evil of his treatment of her. She might just now have been Apostolic Charity herself returned to a self-seeking modern world" (237). Hardy at this point uses his touchstone reference to St Paul to show authentic Christian self-giving. Angel's intellectualism blinds him to this virtue in Tess and also renders his ethical response inferior to hers. Yet even in this coldly logical asceticism he is not consistent; shortly thereafter he is asking Izz Huett to accompany him to Brazil.

   Tess is something of a heretic gospel, a negative version of a biblical narrative that represents the failure of Christian charity and ends with Tess waiting for her death on a stone altar, like a pagan sacrificial victim. J. Hillis Miller notes that the novel is full of instances of false interpretation (*Fiction*, 143), many of which are given religious overtones, either by the character's statements or by the narrator's commentary: a bull thinks it is Christmas Eve because he hears the Nativity Hymn; the narrator suggests repeatedly that Tess's love for Angel leads her to deify him;

Alec blames Tess for his inability to master his desire for her, casting her as a temptress, a "dear damned witch of Babylon" (313). These examples are connected to the fact that Hardy is parodying typological narrative. In Miller's phrase, *Tess* contains repetitive structures without points of origin, which give to Tess's actions "a meaning alienated from her intention" (*Fiction*, 141). Such repetition is the opposite of the meaningful repetitions of typology in the interpretive tradition that was given new life by the Tractarians. Hardy's typological parody can be illustrated by a discussion of some of the many biblical references in the novel, in particular references to the story of the Fall and to the life of Jesus Christ.

There are a number of references to Adam and Eve and Eden in *Tess of the d'Urbervilles*, and their effect is to emphasize that Tess inhabits a fallen world. Whenever she seems to have attained some kind of redemption, she is cast out again, so that the Fall becomes an endlessly repeated experience rather than a condition from which deliverance is possible. As she tells her brother Abraham immediately before the death of their horse Prince, they live in a "blighted" world (*Tess*, 35). Her journey to the d'Urberville estate takes her out of the world she has known all her life to the false paradise of the Chase. In Phase the Second her departure from home is repeated, with an allusion to the Fall; for "she had learnt that the serpent hisses where the sweet birds sing, and her views of life had been totally changed for her by the lesson" (81). Talbothays is described as a world of Edenic innocence,[9] but Tess once more must leave in order to confront for a second time the demonic Alec d'Urberville. Jesus Christ is of course typologically the second Adam, and in several places Tess is presented as a Christ figure, in addition to the allusions to the Fall. At one point she is described as wearing a metaphorical "thorny crown" (150), and her departure from Talbothays is preceded by the ill omen of an afternoon cock crow, linking Angel's betrayal of her to Peter's betrayal of Christ. Like Christ, Hardy constantly insists, Tess is virtuous; for she is pure according to what he calls in the preface "the spiritual interpretation afforded by the finest side of … Christianity" (4–5). If Tess is a Christ figure, however, her sacrificial death occurs in a pagan context during the scene at Stonehenge, on the way to which she and Angel pass by Melchester cathedral in the dark, so that it is "lost upon them" (378). Thus, like Viviette's, Tess's end is more a sardonic twist than a redemptive sacrifice. There is no hint of a resurrection for her; as we have seen, the only resurrection is of Alec d'Urberville's old passionate nature in a passage that links Tess with Eve. He tells her, "I was firm as a man could be till I saw those eyes and that mouth again – surely there never was such a maddening mouth since Eve's" (313). For Angel, there is a kind of resurrection of Tess in the repetition of desire, as he walks away with Liza-Lu, but here too there is an ironic twist. Tess had wanted him to marry her sister, telling him that "people marry sister-laws constantly about Marlott" (380), but presumably the better-informed Angel knows that such a marriage is not permitted.[10]

Another central typological figure for the life of Christ is the story of the exodus from Egypt, which is also alluded to in *Tess* as part of a more general pattern of images of wandering. Once again, the typology is parodic, for none of the pilgrimages in Tess's life lead her to a true promised land. There are a number of references to the early narratives of the Bible. Tess's brother is named Abraham; when Angel carries the milkmaids across the puddle, Izz Huett applies a passage from Ecclesiastes, but Angel prefers one from Genesis, saying that he carries "three Leahs to get one Rachel" (147). Tess's various wanderings can be seen as a forlorn version of a pilgrimage, and at one of her lowest points, when the family with all their belongings are trying to find a new home, Hardy compares the annual migrations that occur on the eve of Old Lady-Day to the exodus narrative: "The Egypt of one family was the land of promise to the family who saw it from a distance; till by residence there it became in turn their Egypt also; and so they changed and changed" (339). As this passage suggests, all is purposeless change; Egypt and the promised land are reversible terms, just as Angel turns from beloved into betrayer, and Alec is transfigured from seducer to preacher. Tess is once again typologically a Christ figure, trying to deliver her family from slavery, but she can only do so by selling herself to the devil. There is no going back to the home from which she has been cast out, nor is there a heavenly city, only the distant prospect of Wintoncester and the black flag at the Wintoncester jail; instead of the Heavenly Father, there is only the President of the Immortals, whose actions are described "in Æschylean phrase" (384), a last touch of sardonic Hellenism.

In *Tess of the d'Urbervilles*, Hardy seems to suggest that only Christ can save us, but Hardy portrays a world empty of Christ's presence, a typological wilderness. Mr Clare's attempt to plant the seed of the evangelical good news leads only to the demonic parody of Christ in the reappearance of Alec d'Urberville. As an alternative to Christianity, Angel

Clare's Arnoldian Hellenism and new Christianity destroy the possibility of redemption by human love for Tess; and it is not possible to remain in the Edenic pastoral world of the Valley of the Great Dairies if you have been touched by the ache of modernism. Hardy's attack on various distorted versions of Christianity assumes as a point of reference the existence of an authentic gospel truth, but that evangel is only present in the novel as a negation, as though its incarnation in the modern world were an impossibility. Even as a point of reference, the gospel will be radically interrogated in Hardy's next novel.

"A DEADLY WAR WAGED BETWEEN FLESH AND SPIRIT": *JUDE THE OBSCURE*

In the Shaston section of *Jude the Obscure*, Jude is visiting Sue, who is now married to Phillotson, and in his typically unworldly way he asks if she knows of "any good readable edition of the uncanonical books of the New Testament" (213). She recommends one and tells him that "the Gospel of Nicodemus is very nice ... It is quite like the genuine article. All cut up into verses, too; so that it is like one of the other evangelists read in a dream, when things are the same, yet not the same" (213).[11] In *Tess* and *Jude*, Hardy's biblical parallels, especially his allusions to the life of Christ, make his fiction on one level a heretical counternarrative to the canonical gospels. If my contention is correct, Hardy is not so much the village atheist as a Victorian Marcion, producing a canon of his own like that second-century heretic in order to set out his radically sceptical version of Christianity. Paradoxically, as we have just seen in *Tess*, this sometimes results in a critique of the Church and of official Christianity that is far more compatible with orthodoxy than Hardy may have intended, because the gospel remains the standard by which the shortcomings of the Church are to be measured. (It is worth noting that Hardy feared that readers might find the conclusion to *Jude* "High-Churchy."[12]) Marcion thought that the Christian Gospel was wholly a Gospel of Love, to the absolute exclusion of law, and it was in fact his establishing of a canon of scripture – ten Pauline epistles and a redaction of Luke's gospel – that prompted the Catholic church to create the orthodox canon.

Hardy might be said to have shared Marcion's view about the Gospel of Love. He refers to St Paul's great hymn to love (1 Corinthians 13) in significant contexts in *Two on a Tower*, *Tess of the d'Urbervilles*, and *Jude the Obscure*. Comparing Hardy with George Eliot, Matthew Arnold, and Mary Augusta Ward, Lance Butler comments that Hardy, like the others, does seem to want to salvage some religious "truth" from the wreckage of the nineteenth-century church: "This religion of Hardy's boils down to not much more than 1 Corinthians 13, and an obsessive orientation towards Christ but it is not *nothing at all*" ("'Unless,'" 203). The epigraph to *Jude*, "The letter killeth" (2 Corinthians 3:6), suggests something of that novel's implacable opposition to the law, whether it be the Church's teachings or the laws of the state concerning marriage; as several critics have pointed out, however, by leaving out the end of the verse, "but the spirit giveth life," Hardy also suggests that the world of *Jude* is a world of the letter, a world in which the spirit is an illusion. As a final example of the heretical nature of *Jude*, one can instance Sue's "*new* New Testament," cut into its component books, rearranged according to the "chronological order as written," and rebound (*Jude*, 157). Although not as radical as Marcion's canon, Sue's Bible clearly places the authority of human reason, of the higher criticism that historicizes the biblical text, above any notion of revelation, or the authority of the Church in establishing the canonical order of the books.

In the preface to the first edition of *Jude the Obscure*, Hardy says that the subject of his novel is "a deadly war waged between flesh and spirit" (xxxv).[13] It is a war that the flesh is predestined to win, given the illusory nature of the spirit. At one pole is the materialist self-interest of Arabella Donn, who amply represents the flesh, both in her robust sexuality and in the way that she is associated with pigs, butchery, and alcohol. At the other pole, the spirit is represented by the intellectual Sue Bridehead, who in spite of her theoretical paganism is never comfortable with her sexuality, and who is last seen embracing a self-denying and joyless Christianity. Caught in between, the alternative to these two poles seems to be a bleak and despairing existentialism that offers neither comfort nor certainty. Christianity, as represented throughout *Jude the Obscure*, has few redeeming qualities. If it is not ascetic and destructive, it is the passionate but short-lived Methodism of Arabella, another version of Alec d'Urberville's "transfiguration," or the hypocrisy of the hymn writer who, disillusioned with the material rewards of devotional writing, contemplates switching to the wine business. The Arnoldian visions of an undogmatic religion and the life of culture are shown to be hollow alternatives. Whatever beliefs one holds, it seems that the flesh and the spirit are at odds, unless one merely pursues one's own material self-interest, like the other animals in a Darwinian universe. Central to the theology of *Jude the Obscure* are Hardy's critique of the Oxford Movement and the dogmatic church, and his presentation of the alternatives of Arnoldian culture. I shall look at these before coming to some conclusions about this most powerful of Hardy's apocryphal gospels, which is in many ways the culmination of, and perhaps the epitaph for, the Anglican theological novel of the nineteenth century.

As Raymond Chapman has demonstrated, Hardy's attitude towards the second phase of the Oxford Movement (often called Puseyism after its de facto leader) was not complimentary. Chapman suggests that Hardy saw the Anglo-Catholic revival "as a false antiquarianism, destroying the familiar without rediscovering the hidden roots of the past" ("'Arguing,'" 280). It is not difficult to document Hardy's animosity towards Christianity in *Jude the Obscure*, and in particular towards the Church of England. Early in the novel, in describing the village of Marygreen, the narrator comments that "the original church, hump-backed, wood-turreted, and quaintly hipped, had been taken down and either cracked up into heaps of road-metal in the lane, or utilized as pig-sty walls, garden seats, guard-stones to fences, and rockeries in the flower-beds of the neighbourhood. In place of it a tall new building of modern Gothic design, unfamiliar to English eyes, had been erected on a new piece of ground by a certain obliterator of historic records who had run down from London and back in a day" (*Jude*, 6). Shortly thereafter we learn that Farmer Troutham, the farmer who beats Jude for neglecting to scare the birds, has been a liberal subscriber to this new church "to testify his love for God and man" (11). Thus the medievalizing revival has been responsible for breaking the link with the past that the old church constituted, without notably contributing to an increase of Christian charity in the rather stern environment of Marygreen. (Hardy confessed that he had himself been responsible for the destruction of some ancient church architecture in the name of the Gothic revival.) What little we are told about the rector of Marygreen suggests that he does not provide much pastoral care. Instead of being on hand for the departure of Phillotson, he departs for the day himself, "being a man who disliked the sight of changes" (3).

The Church is either absent or represented as being totally incapable of dealing with all of the major crises and difficulties experienced by Jude and the other characters through the novel. In one of Hardy's most savage pieces of irony, Jude and Sue, immediately after the murder-suicide of their children, hear the organ of the college chapel adjacent to their lodg-ings playing the anthem from Psalm 73, "Truly God is loving unto Israel" (356). In the incident that follows, the Church's inutility in the face of Jude and Sue's despair is specifically related to Anglo-Catholic ritualism, for they hear two people in conversation whom Jude identifies as "two clergymen of different views, arguing about the eastward position" (356). Christianity, it seems, is a matter of rules and ritual and is unaware or impotent in the face of the Schopenhauerian gloom that has engulfed Jude and Sue. This is meant to make Sue's final conversion to Christianity all the more inexplicable and unsympathetic.

In *Jude the Obscure*, Hardy uses a form of parodic typology that both depends upon, yet denies the validity of, Christian modes of reading. The name of the protagonist is an obvious place to start. St Jude is a euphemism for Judas, not the disciple who betrayed Christ but the other Judas, the "Judas ... not Iscariot" of John 14:22, who perhaps because of his name came to be identified as the patron saint of hopeless causes.[14] Jude's name, along with the hereditary marital misfortunes of his family, seems to mark him out for tragedy. His career can be seen as a negative recapitulation of some of the central narratives of the Bible, and, like *Tess*, *Jude* can be seen as a novel organized by a principle of negative typology.[15] Jude moves backwards rather than forwards, gaining and then losing his heavenly Jerusalem and ending the novel as he began it, as a Job figure lamenting his misfortunes. At the beginning of the novel, after the depar-ture of Phillotson and his dismissal by Farmer Troutham, Jude re-enacts the position of Job after his first misfortunes: "he lay down upon his back on a heap of litter near the pig-sty" (13). This is one of many images of pigs in *Jude*, and the story comes full circle when, married to Arabella, the pig-breeder's daughter, for a second time, Jude laments the fact that Sue is "defiled" and recites the passage where Job curses the day of his birth (Job 3) as he hears the cheers from the Remembrance games (*Jude*, 426–7). In between, he has twice entered Christminster, his holy city, whose "beloved son" he had hoped to be, "in whom she shall be well pleased" (35).[16] In a tableau suggestive of Calvary, however, he ends up seeing his children hanging dead, and his heavenly city turns out to be the city of his destruction. Jerusalem turns out to be nothing more than a pedagogical model, "made after the best conjectural maps" (108), while a map of Palestine becomes a weapon used to beat a church warden in the riot that follows Phillotson's dismissal from the school in Shaston. Christminster itself is similarly reduced to a commodity, first in the model of Cardinal College, made by Jude and Sue, and then in the form of the Christminster cakes that Jude makes to try to earn some money when he is confined indoors.

Jude has his first vision of Christminster after climbing a ladder, from which perspective the city is "either directly seen, or miraged in the peculiar atmosphere" (17). It is then "veiled in mist," while "the foreground of the scene had grown funereally dark, and near objects put on the hues and shapes of chimaeras" (17). He envisions Christminster as New Jerusalem and the narrator suggests that there is "more of the painter's imagination, and less of the diamond merchant's" in Jude's dreams than in those of St John the Divine (18). The next vision of the city is at night:

> No individual light was visible, only a halo or glow-fog over-arching the place against the black heavens behind it, making the light and the city seem distant but a mile or so.
>
> He set himself to wonder on the exact point in the glow where the schoolmaster might be; he who never communicated with anybody at Marygreen now, who was as if dead to them here. In the glow he seemed to see Phillotson promenading at ease, like one of the forms in Nebuchadnezzar's furnace.
>
> He had heard that breezes travelled at the rate of ten miles an hour, and the fact now came into his mind. He parted his lips as he faced the north-east, and drew in the wind as if it were a sweet liquor.
>
> "You," he said, addressing the breeze caressingly, "were in Christminster city between one and two hours ago: floating along the streets, pulling round the weather-cocks, touching Mr Phillotson's face, being breathed by him; and now you are here, breathed by me; you, the very same."
>
> Suddenly there came along this wind something towards him; a message from the place – from some soul residing there, it seemed. Surely it was the sound of bells, the voice of the city; faint and musical, calling to him, "We are happy here." (18–19)

The vision of Phillotson "promenading at ease, like one of the forms in Nebuchadnezzar's furnace" is comically inappropriate to the prosaic schoolmaster, but it effectively conveys Jude's imaginative vision of Christminster, which here takes on a Blakean cast, expressed in a biblical image and suggesting a powerful creative energy. There is something similarly comical and yet visionary in the kiss from the breeze that might have touched Phillotson's face. Hardy's language here is erotic, and there is initially something almost sexual in the intensity of Jude's desire to get to Christminster.[17] When he is talking about the city to the carter, "like a young lover alluding to his mistress, he felt bashful at mentioning its name again" (19). The breeze additionally has the quality of the visionary breeze of Romantic inspiration, the "gentle breeze" of the opening of Wordsworth's *Prelude* (1850), which for Tractarians would be an image of the action of the Holy Spirit in the world. Here, it is the voice of a siren, constructing a dream of the city of learning and culture that will never come true, but that will be a tormenting memory for the dying Jude.

Another significant aspect of Hardy's critique of the Church in *Jude* is his attack on its teaching on marriage and sex. In this novel, erotic desire is not a source of religious feeling but is locked in a deadly struggle with it. It is Jude's sexual desire that first interrupts his plans to become a scholar, and when he is entrapped by Arabella he marries her out of a sense of honour: "For his own soothing he kept up a factitious belief in her. His idea of her was the thing of most consequence, not Arabella herself, he sometimes said laconically" (56). Hardy notes with mordant irony that the couple swear in their marriage vows that "they would assuredly believe, feel, and desire precisely as they had believed, felt, and desired during the few preceding weeks" (56). After the initial setback of his brief married life, Jude does manage to get to Christminster, where he enters the cathedral like Christ entering the temple. But now a Romantic version of erotic love intervenes, and once again Jude mistakes what is happening to him, for he confuses erotic attraction and spiritual affinity. Sue is transfigured not so much by her own piety as by his feelings towards her:

The girl for whom he was beginning to nourish an extraordinary tenderness, was at this time ensphered by the same harmonies as those which floated into his ears; and the thought was a delight to him. She was probably a frequenter of this place and, steeped body and soul in church sentiment as she must be by occupation and habit, had, no doubt, much in common with him. To an impressionable and lonely young man the consciousness of having at last found anchorage for his thoughts which promised to supply both social and spiritual possibilities, was like a dew of Hermon, and he remained throughout the service in a sustaining atmosphere of ecstasy. Though he was loth to suspect it, some people might have said to him that the atmosphere blew as distinctly from Cyprus as from Galilee. (93)

Sue has thus become Jude's divinity, as Angel was for Tess. At the end of the second part, Sue has a spiritual role for Jude as his consoler in affliction, but a consoler whose continuing presence is denied him. The epigraph to Part Third, however, is from a poem by Sappho: "For there was no other girl, O bridegroom, like her!" (132). This piece of classical eroticism belies the spiritualization of her in the previous chapter. Jude has not heeded his Aunt Drusilla's warnings; in fact, from the moment he sees her photograph, Sue becomes mixed up with his dream of Christminster. When Sue comes to his rooms at Melchester, Jude sees in her "almost a divinity" (150). He thinks of her in terms that contrast her spiritual nature to Arabella's physical one:

Looking at his loved one as she appeared to him now, in his tender thought the sweetest and most disinterested comrade that he had ever had, living largely in vivid imaginings, so ethereal a creature that her spirit could be seen trembling through her limbs, he felt heartily ashamed of his earthliness in spending the hours he had spent in Arabella's company. There was something rude and immoral in thrusting these recent facts of his life upon the mind of one who, to him, was so uncarnate as to seem at times impossible as a human wife to any average man. (195)

Whereas Tess Durbeyfield is incarnate, physical, and, at various points in the novel, made to feel ashamed of it, Sue is "uncarnate," not of this world, and it is Jude who feels ashamed. Sue aspires to be a kind of Comtean *schöne Seele*, for her goal is "to ennoble some man to high aims" (158). In a sense, Sue does achieve that goal with Jude, as she inspires him to adopt her own beliefs, but in a mirroring of his conversion to Hellenism she begins to practise ritualist Christianity. Once again, Hardy alludes to 1 Corinthians 13. When Sue decides to go back to Phillotson, she says: "Your generous devotion to me is unparalleled, Jude! Your worldly failure, if you have failed, is to your credit rather than to your blame. Remember that the best and greatest among mankind are those who do themselves no worldly good. Every successful man is more or less a selfish man. The devoted fail. 'Charity seeketh not her own'" (382). Sue's statement is certainly true by the theology that she has adopted. Worldly success is not always, or even usually, the result of charity. Nevertheless, the positioning of the passage, and the bleakness of the conclusion of the novel, which Goetz characterizes as "a sort of grotesque parody of the conventionally happy ending of the earlier English novel" ("Felicity," 191), suggests that evangelical charity is not a very practical guide to living in a world devoid of spirit. For if there is no spirit, there is only the letter, and as Jude tells Sue in their last meeting, "the letter killeth" (410).

In the character of Angel Clare, Hardy represented a character who accepted Matthew Arnold's views of religion; in *Jude*, Hardy is more concerned with Arnoldian culture. As a "tragedy of unfulfilled aims," as he characterizes the novel in his preface (xxxv), *Jude the Obscure* is the tragedy of the failure of culture to live up to the promises Arnold made on its behalf. In part this is because Jude Fawley is a poor reader of Arnold, but it is clear that there are problems with Arnold's prescription as well. For Arnold, the operation of culture was in some general sense religious. *Culture and Anarchy* draws on the thought of some of the leading figures of the Oxford of the preceding generation: Arnold's godfather John Keble, his father Thomas Arnold and the regimen of Rugby School, and especially John Henry Newman, whose memory is conjured up in Arnold's essay on Emerson. Matthew Arnold saw culture as taking on the role of self-perfection in a manner that is analogous to the idea of sanctification: "By our *best self* we are united, impersonal, at harmony ... Well, and this is the very self which culture, or the study of perfection, seeks to develop in us; at the expense of our old untransformed self, taking pleasure only in doing what it likes or is used to do, and exposing us to the risk of clashing with every one else who is doing the same!" (*Complete Prose* 5:134–5; Arnold's emphasis). It is language like this that enables J. Dover Wilson, in his 1932 introduction to *Culture and Anarchy*, to call it "a profoundly religious book" (xii). For Newman, of course, culture was secondary, and in *The Idea of a University*, even in the context of a defence of liberal education, he argued that it is a dangerous error to confuse culture and religion. Arnold, on the other hand, in a manner that can be seen as illogical, superficial, or optimistic, depending on one's point of view, thought that culture could provide an inner life and spiritual discipline that would be sufficiently rich to do the work of religion and combat social anarchy.

For Arnold in *Culture and Anarchy* and Newman in *The Idea of a University*, the main foe was utilitarianism, which stressed the immediate practical utility of education rather than the idea of cultivation of the self inherent in the gentlemanly ideal of liberal education. Jude Fawley shares their belief in the value of classical learning and seeks through his intellectual discipline and study to develop the best self that Arnold speaks of, the self that enables a member of any particular social class to overcome the characteristic defects of that class. Jude is a member of the Populace, that vast working class whose tendency to do as it liked Arnold feared as conducing to anarchy; Jude also shares the characteristic tastes of the "lighter side" of the working class, which in Arnold's analysis amounts to an excessive fondness for beer (*Complete Prose* 5:145). Jude seeks to develop his best self with an application that is heartbreaking in its pathos, but he is continually frustrated in the pursuit of perfection, and on numerous occasions he is betrayed by his ordinary self.

Jude's view of Christminster as a heavenly city provides a religious dimension to his love of learning and desire for culture. But the pilgrim Jude receives an ambiguous welcome when he actually visits the city of his dreams. The epigraph to Part Second underscores the delusive nature of Jude's sense of having reached the place where he truly belongs: "Save his own soul he hath no star" (76). The reality of Christminster is more like a maze than the heavenly city of St John the Divine or the beautiful city of Matthew Arnold's famous apostrophe in the preface to *Essays in Criticism* (1865). Even though he is surrounded by the spirits of the past, Jude feels "the isolation of his own personality" (79), as though his quest for harmony had only cut him off from others. Although Jude hears Arnold among the various voices, he does not take in the significance of the fact that Oxford is "serene" because "unravaged by the fierce intellectual life of our century" (82), nor, as the narrator points out, does he remember that Arnold "afterwards mourned Christminster as 'the home of lost causes'" (82). In his quest for self-betterment, Jude will have to be ravaged in his own person by all the intellectual strife of the century, and his pilgrimage will take him in a purposeless circle away from Christminster and back to his death.

Among the voices that Jude hears in his reverie on the first night in Christminster are those of Gibbon and two of the Tractarian leaders. The stage is thus set for the inconclusive battle that he will wage throughout the remainder of his life. Gibbon is "the sly author of the immortal chapter

on Christianity" (82) whose account of Julian the Apostate forms Sue's
bedtime reading while she lodges with Miss Fontover (96), and he is
quoted ironically by the narrator with reference to Jude's efforts to emulate
the chastity of the early Christians (201). On the other side, Jude hears
the voice of "poor Newman," and Hardy quotes the same passage about
converging probabilities that inspired his comments on Newman in the
Life and Work. He follows it with a quotation from Keble's *Christian Year*:
"Why should we faint, and fear to live alone, / Since all alone, so Heaven
has will'd, we die?" (in *Jude*, 83). This passage, which opens the poem for
the "Twenty-Fourth Sunday after Trinity," reinforces the sense of Jude's
isolation that, for Hardy as for Arnold, is a characteristic part of "the
ache of modernism." For Keble, however, this fact of one's ultimate isolation is what allows us to communicate with God:

> For if one heart in perfect sympathy
>   Beat with another, answering love for love,
> Weak mortals, all entranc'd, on earth would lie,
>   Nor listen for those purer strains above.
>   (*Christian Year*, 144, lines 13–16)

Jude's sense of isolation in Christminster is proleptic, for he will always
be shut out by the walls of the colleges. In "the constant internal warfare
between flesh and spirit" (*Jude*, 201) he rarely gets a sense of the presence
of the spirit; he seeks the "perfect sympathy" with another that Keble
refers to, yet that other's heart too is internally divided, so that he finds
fulfillment neither in divine nor human love.

Sue tells Jude after his disillusionment with Christminster: "You are
one of the very men Christminster was intended for when the colleges
were founded; a man with a passion for learning, but no money, or oppor-
tunities, or friends" (156). Social inequities, it is clear, ensure that Arnold's
vision of culture is not as accessible to the poor as to the rich. An interesting irony that Hardy was most likely not aware of is that John Keble,
one of the shades of Christminster, had a more socially radical vision of
Oxford than his godson Matthew Arnold did. During his Crewian oration to the university on the occasion of the awarding of an honorary
degree to William Wordsworth, Keble remarked that "the medieval idea
of a university, centering on poverty and learning, was fatally undermined
by the materialism of the Reformation" (Prickett, "Social Conscience,"

88).[18] A true Christianity might have opened up the university, but the Christminster that Jude inhabits is dominated by those who want to preserve the social status quo. It is only with social change – of the kind that Keble had supported – that individuals like Jude can have a chance to better themselves through education. Arnold's vision of the inward operation of culture is thus fatally flawed, because it emphasizes the individual self in a manner that might be appropriate to religious writing but that is not as effective in the context of social institutions (it should be remembered that the subtitle of *Culture and Anarchy* is "An Essay in Political and Social Criticism").

The return to Christminster in Part Sixth of *Jude the Obscure* emphasizes the impossibility of the ideal of culture for the working man in the existing social system. In his speech to the crowd on Encaenia Day, Jude describes himself as being "in a chaos of principles – groping in the dark – acting by instinct and not after example" (*Jude*, 345). Christminster becomes positively sinister in this final part of the book, as Jude and his family, a parodic Holy Family, have difficulty finding lodgings. The walls of the colleges make Father Time think that they are jails (348), and they mock the failure of Jude's aspirations, the impossible dream of culture, the failure of Keble's vision of a more socially inclusive university. Sue sits in the bleak room she has rented and "the outer walls of Sarcophagus College – silent, black and windowless – threw their four centuries of gloom, bigotry, and decay into the little room she occupied" (351). As he waits for death, Jude can only hope that others may succeed where he has failed, leaving a glimmer of hope that social change will make the precise form of Jude's tragedy impossible to repeat: "I felt I could do one thing if I had the opportunity. I could accumulate ideas, and impart them to others. I wonder if the Founders had such as I in their minds – a fellow good for nothing else but that particular thing ... I hear that soon there is going to be a better chance for such helpless students as I was" (421). Whether that chance will enable others to overcome the deadly opposition between flesh and spirit, however, is another question.

The critical reception of *Jude the Obscure* varied according to whether it was seen primarily as a tragedy of frustrated ambition, or as an outspoken, if not obscene, novel about sex and marriage. R.Y. Tyrrell claimed in the *Fortnightly Review* that "the book is steeped in sex" (quoted in Cox, *Critical Heritage*, 293). Writing in the *Westminster Review*, D.F. Hannigan saw the novel in more spiritual terms: "This story of crushed aspirations can only be appreciated by those who have the power of true sympathy. Unfortunately, we live in an age when nearly all human beings are concerned only with their material success in life" (in Cox, ibid., 272–3). The review in the *Illustrated London News* also took a philosophical perspective: "Such is the spaciousness which his grasp of elemental things imparts to the story that a tragedy of three lives seems to fill the world with sorrow, and invite irony from the heavens" (in Cox, ibid., 274). Christminster is neither Athens nor Jerusalem for Jude: both his dream of culture and his dream of serving God fail. Arabella survives, but she does so by living in an amoral, materialistic manner that makes her well adapted to the atomistic and material world she inhabits. Sue survives, but she does not seem very well, looking "years and years older" (*Jude*, 431), and in spite of Mrs Edlin's pious hopes it doesn't seem likely that she will find peace. Jude is dead, having failed in all of his aspirations. If the world is as truly devoid of spirit as much of the novel suggests, then Sue's actions are totally misguided, and Arabella and Physician Vilbert are the types one ought to emulate. There is nothing in *Jude* to suggest that it will do you any good to attempt to live by the gospel, but the gospel remains the standard by which Hardy can critique a world that is ruled only by the letter, and devoid of any trace of divinity.

SEVEN

‛LITERATURE AND DOGMA:
MARY AUGUSTA WARD'S
ROBERT ELSMERE AND WALTER PATER'S
MARIUS THE EPICUREAN

The Christian problem, as the world is now beginning to understand,
is first and foremost a literary problem.

Mary Augusta Ward, "Sin and Unbelief"

And who will deny that to trace the influence of religion upon human
character is one of the legitimate functions of the novel? In truth,
the modern "novel of character" needs some such interest, to lift it
sufficiently above the humdrum of life.

Walter Pater, "Review" of *Robert Elsmere*

"*LITERATURE AND DOGMA* WITH THE LITERATURE
LEFT OUT": MARY WARD'S NEW REFORMATION

IN THE 1880S TWO WRITERS who were well known to each other – Mary
Augusta Ward and Walter Pater[1] – each published novels of enduring
critical interest, and each reviewed the other's book. Pater's *Marius the
Epicurean* is a highly sophisticated and skilful example of the popular
Victorian genre of the early church novel, and it was praised by Mary
Ward as "a wonderfully delicate and faithful reflection of the workings

of a real mind" ("Review," 131). Ward's *Robert Elsmere* is an example of another popular genre, the novel of religious controversy, which I discussed earlier as part of the background to Brontë's *Shirley*.[2] In his review Pater described *Robert Elsmere* as a "*chef d'œuvre* of that kind of quiet evolution of character through circumstance, introduced into English literature by Miss Austen, and carried to perfection in France by George Sand" (55) Pater added, "We should say that the author's special ethical gift lay in a delicately intuitive sympathy, not, perhaps, with all phases of character, but certainly with the very varied class of persons represented in these volumes" (57). What is distinctive about *Robert Elsmere*, according to Pater, is that the author's gift for writing social fiction coexists "with a very sincerely felt religious interest" (56).

In earlier chapters, I concentrated on works that raise theological questions implicitly. Even in *The Bertrams*, theological controversy is primarily the means by which Trollope explores the psychological and social differences among his main characters. I have been exploring the religious horizons of novels by writers who are of continuing critical interest, and largely for reasons other than their theological concerns. Charlotte Yonge is a partial exception, and in her case I sought to suggest that *The Heir of Redclyffe* is of both literary and religious interest. As I noted at the outset of the book, novels of religious controversy and early church novels have for the most part been left undisturbed by the recent reprinting of Victorian novels that had long been inaccessible. *Robert Elsmere* and *Marius the Epicurean*, on the other hand, have consistently been the objects of scholarly attention, although at the time of writing neither is in print with a major publisher.[3] It may be helpful to begin by considering the reasons for the enduring interest of these two novels, in contrast to most of their predecessors in the same subgenres.

In the last fifteen years or so of the nineteenth century, the novel became even more important as a vehicle for religious discussion than it had been earlier in the century, perhaps because the tract and the sermon were losing their authority, while theology and ecclesiastical matters retained a level of public interest that they would soon lose. To cite the most famous example of this public interest, William Gladstone was so absorbed by the issues raised in *Robert Elsmere* that he met Mary Ward to discuss the book and then wrote a long review of it in the journal *Nineteenth Century*. As a leader in the *Pall Mall Gazette* put it on 7 April 1888, "Mrs Humphry Ward deserves the hearty congratulations of the whole Liberal party. For her new novel has done that which all other books and all other events have failed to effect. From December 1885, to March 1888, Mr Gladstone has been able to think of nothing but Ireland and Home Rule. But Mrs Ward has changed all that" (quoted in W. Peterson, "Gladstone's Review," 442). The increased role of the novel in public discussion of religion at this time has been documented and analyzed by Lynne Hapgood, who quotes one clerical writer as saying, "It sometimes seems as though the man who has fresh light to throw upon the problems of theology will be compelled to write a novel to get himself listened to" ("Reconceiving," 332).[4] In her autobiography, *A Writer's Recollections* (1918), Mary Ward provided her own explanation of the role of fiction in religious discussion: "The root difficulty was of course the dealing with such a subject in a novel at all. Yet I was determined to deal with it so, in order to reach the public. There were great precedents – Froude's *Nemesis of Faith*, Newman's *Loss and Gain*, Kingsley's *Alton Locke* – for the novel of religious or social propaganda. And it seemed to me that the novel was capable of holding and shaping real experience of any kind, as it affects the lives of men and women" (2:66).

Commercially *Robert Elsmere* was phenomenally successful. It was one of the best-sellers of the nineteenth century, both in England and the United States.[5] Critics have often speculated about the reasons for the great success of such an earnest book, which to a later generation embodied everything that was stuffy and ridiculous about the Victorians, and which may seem to be a *roman à thèse*, concerned with the religious controversies of a bygone era. Oscar Wilde's witticisms at Mary Ward's expense are the best example of this reaction. A speech by Vivian in the critical dialogue "The Decay of Lying" (1889) describes *Robert Elsmere* as "a masterpiece of the 'genre ennuyeux,' the one form of literature that the English people seem to thoroughly enjoy." Replying to Vivian, Cyril says that *Elsmere* "is simply Arnold's *Literature and Dogma* with the literature left out" (Wilde, *Critical Writings*, 295–6, 298). Nevertheless, Wilde seems to allude to *Robert Elsmere* in his 1891 novel *The Picture of Dorian Gray*, and it is likely that he was himself the object of caricature as the egotistical poet Mr Wood in chapter 31 of *Elsmere* (Schroeder, "A Quotation," 327, 328). Although Ward refers to "novels of religious or social propaganda" as precedents for *Robert Elsmere*, the novel may also be related to the genre of confessional literature. In his book-length study of *Elsmere*, William Peterson writes that "if Carlyle's *Sartor Resartus* may be regarded as the most important spiritual autobiography (fictionalized and concealed, but autobiography nevertheless) of the early Victorian age, and Tennyson's *In Memoriam* and Newman's *Apologia* those of the mid-Victorian age, then certainly no literary work can lay stronger claims to that position in the century's closing decades than *Robert Elsmere*" (*Heretic*, 14). It is relevant in this context to quote a well-known passage from Ward's review of *Marius*:

> As a nation we are not fond of direct "confessions". All our autobiographical literature, compared to the French or German, has a touch of dryness and reserve. It is in books like "Sartor Resartus", or "The Nemesis of Faith", "Alton Locke", or "Marius", rather than in the avowed specimens of self-revelation which the time has produced, that the future student of the nineteenth century will have to look for what is deepest, most intimate, and most real in its personal experience. In the case of those natures whose spiritual experience is richest and most original, there is with us, coupled with the natural tendency to expression, a natural tendency to disguise. ("Review," 130–1)

Certainly Mary Ward's most popular novel has its share of "dryness and reserve": it is not without reason that Patricia Meyer Spacks used it as a test case in her investigation of boredom in literature. There is ample emotion in the novel, however, and like some of the writers I have already considered, Ward investigates the relationship between eros and religious belief. Her description of Pater's *Marius* can therefore be applied to her own book.

What is most valuable about *Robert Elsmere* is Ward's ability to dramatize the crisis of faith in a compelling human narrative that finds its centre in a detailed portrait of a late-Victorian marriage. While she sets out an explicit model for a new mode of religious practice, using typology to heighten the significance of her hero's endeavours, Ward is more important for her account of the autobiographical path and the emotional experiences of what were once called Modernist Christians. Modernism in its most restricted sense refers to a movement within the Roman Catholic church in the late nineteenth century to rethink Christian beliefs in the light of modern thought. It was condemned by Pope Pius X in 1907. In a more general sense, Modernism can refer to similar radical trends in the Church of England, exemplified in a figure such as W.R. Inge, who was

Dean of St Paul's from 1911–34. According to A.N. Wilson, one of the most acute contemporary commentators on religious matters in England, all Christians are now in some sense Modernists; hence Ward's analysis is still of considerable significance for people of faith.[6] When contrasted with Ward's self-consciously "modern" story, Pater's slightly earlier *Marius* might seem, on a superficial reading, something of an antiquarian exercise. More than a century later, however, it is Pater's novel, with its scepticism towards all forms of knowledge and belief combined with an aestheticized yearning towards spirituality, that seems the more modern work, and *Marius* is thus an appropriate concluding point for this study, speaking eloquently as it does to the condition of postmodernity at the beginning of the twenty-first century.

Ward's analysis of the nineteenth-century crisis of faith is in some ways very similar to that of her uncle, Matthew Arnold, as Lionel Trilling pointed out (Trilling, *Matthew Arnold*, 303–16). The remark Arnold made in 1880 at the beginning of "The Study of Poetry" bears repeating: "There is not a creed which is not shaken, not an accredited dogma which is not shown to be questionable, not a received tradition which does not threaten to dissolve. Our religion has materialised itself in the fact, in the supposed fact; it has attached its emotion to the fact, and now the fact is failing it" (*Complete Prose* 9:161). Arnold's emphasis on the "fact" shows how the crisis of faith was precipitated by scientific inquiry, which in many areas – geology, biology, history – seemed to question the facts on which the Christian religion was based. The cause of Robert Elsmere's doubt is positivist historiography: under the light of historical science the miraculous element of the New Testament vanishes. As a result, like Renan, Elsmere comes to accept a merely human account of Jesus, and he thus finds himself in conflict with the articles of faith of his church. Like his creator Mary Ward at that point in her life, he regards those articles in a literal-minded way. They are either true according to the understanding of truth of positivist science, or they are false and must be superseded. Arnold's language, however, allows for the possibility of Christianity's being seen differently, without any changes in liturgy or statements of doctrine; it is rather the way those things are experienced and understood that should change.

Unlike Arnold, who thought that the language of scripture and liturgy could be viewed poetically, Elsmere considers a liberal position within the established church to be hypocritical. By implication, he regards the

Church of England as fixed forever in a particular understanding of its faith, unable to evolve or develop. At the turning point in his career he catechizes himself and finds that he believes in Christ as teacher, martyr, and symbol, but not as God incarnate. Echoing Arnold, he concludes that "*miracles do not happen!*" (*Elsmere*, 332; Ward's italics). Elsmere can continue to believe in God because theism as a position can never be disproved, whereas because the grounds for Christianity are "literary and historical" it will always pose problems of "*documents and testimony*" (394; Ward's italics). Faith is thus subordinate to reason for Elsmere, whose understanding of literary truth also seems rather utilitarian, and he is convinced by his own logic that he must resign his living and give up his Anglican orders.

Both Elsmere and Mary Ward resemble Ward's uncle, Matthew Arnold, in regarding Christian morality as separable from dogma. Thus Nietzsche's caustic description of George Eliot in *The Twilight of the Idols* (1888) could also apply to Ward: "They are rid of the Christian God and therefore think it all the more incumbent upon them to hold tight to Christian morality: this is an English way of reasoning, but let us not take it ill in moral females *à la* Eliot. In England, every man who indulges in any trifling emancipation from theology must retrieve his honor in the most terrifying manner by becoming a moral fanatic" (in Clive, ed., *Philosophy*, 324). William Peterson notes that the combination of "conservative morality and revolutionary theology" was not unusual among Victorians (*Heretic*, 6); he says of Ward, "Conduct was for her not simply three-fourths of life, as Matthew Arnold had said, but rather very nearly the whole of it" (199–200). The incident where Mme de Netteville tempts Elsmere sexually and is refused with a vigour worthy of a Spenserian knight is particularly important for refuting the connection between unbelief and immorality that was part of the rhetoric of orthodox literature and, indeed, formed a prominent part of the plot of Froude's *Nemesis of Faith*. Early in Ward's career, she published an attack on the Bampton Lectures of John Wordsworth, a champion of the High Church party, who had connected sinful behaviour and doctrinal unorthodoxy.[7]

Ward was not content to write a novel of doubt; her ambitious task was to describe how faith might be reconstructed in a form that would be intellectually unassailable. A number of commentators on the novel, both in Ward's time and more recently, have regarded Elsmere's ethical theism as a species of Unitarianism, an impression encouraged by the fact that Elsmere works with a Unitarian clergyman in the east end of London.[8] Ward, however, seeks somewhat confusingly to dissociate the New Brotherhood from existing forms of Unitarianism. She comments in a passage of authorial narration that "Unitarianism of the old sort is perhaps the most illogical creed that exists, and certainly it has never been the creed of the poor" (*Elsmere*, 401). The most improbable piece of romance in the novel is the way that Elsmere's New Brotherhood is able to evangelize the workers of the East End in a way that the Church of England is not. Ward tries to make this possible by mythologizing Elsmere, who by the end of the novel, and the end of his life, has changed status from a realistic character who does not believe in miracles to a romance character who works them.

Catherine's response to Robert's neo-Christianity anticipates the arguments of C.S. Lewis: "Your historical Christ, Robert, will never win souls. If he was God, every word you speak will insult him. If he was man, he was not a good man!" (461).[9] Reviewers of the book often agreed with Catherine; for example, Henry Wace, who had earlier commissioned articles from Ward for the *Dictionary of Christian Biography* (Sutherland, *Mrs Humphry*, 71), commented that there was not one object promoted by the New Brotherhood that was not already attained by the Christian church (Wace, "*Robert Elsmere*," 299). Gladstone expressed himself in a striking metaphor, saying of the demythologized faith presented in the novel, "From my antiquated point of view, this is simply to bark the tree, and then, as the death which ensues is not immediate, to point out with satisfaction on the instant that it still waves living branches in the wind" ("Battle," 783). It is interesting that Ward's liberal optimism still persists in theologians and clergy such as Don Cupitt and Bishop John Spong, who seem to believe that the main cause of the decline in church attendance is that their radical theological ideas have not been adopted wholesale. In fact, there is an uncanny similarity between the simple creed and rites of the New Brotherhood and the vision of the church of the future in Cupitt's *Radicals and the Future of the Church*.[10]

In *The Case of Richard Meynell* (1911), her sequel to *Robert Elsmere*, Ward modified her position, allowing for the possibility of evolution in the Church's understanding of the faith, but she retained a literal-minded view of creeds and formularies, which she still believed should be altered, not reinterpreted. She explained her difference from Arnold, and eventual shift towards agreement, in a passage in her autobiography:

> My uncle was a Modernist long before the time. In *Literature and Dogma* he threw out in detail much of the argument suggested in *Robert Elsmere*, but to the end of his life he was a contented member of the Anglican Church, so far as attendance at her services was concerned, and belief in her mission of "edification" to the English people. He had little sympathy with people who "went out." Like Mr Jowett, he would have liked to see the Church slowly reformed and "modernized" from within. So that with the main theme of my book – that a priest who doubts must depart – he could never have had full sympathy. And in the course of years – as I showed in a later novel written twenty-four years after *Robert Elsmere* – I feel that I have very much come to agree with him! (*Writer's Recollections* 2:74)

If Arnold's religious thought was quite similar to that of the Catholic Modernists, Ward's indicated a more Protestant sensibility.[11]

As a third-generation member of the famous Arnold family, Mary Ward grew up with a strong connection to the Lake District, and Wordsworthian descriptions of the Lakeland scenery figure prominently in each of her "theological fictions," *Robert Elsmere*, *Helbeck of Bannisdale* (1898), and *The Case of Richard Meynell*. Walter Pater recognized Wordsworth's influence on her work in his discussion of *Elsmere* ("Review," 63). However, as with *Jude the Obscure*, there are hints from the beginning of *Robert Elsmere* that the Wordsworthian bond with nature is part of a vanishing way of life. The novel moves from "the lonely Westmoreland valley of Long Whindale" (*Elsmere*, 5) to the gentler countryside, readily accessible to the metropolis, of Surrey, then to London itself, and finally within London to the East End. At the beginning, modernity is as far away as it can be in an English setting: the road in the valley is described as "the only link between the farmhouses sheltered by the crags at the head of the valley and those far-away regions of town and civilisation suggested by the smoke wreaths of Whinborough on the southern horizon" (5). Catherine's first bond with Robert is their love of Wordsworth, which in her case arises from a "mountain life" amidst the very settings in which Wordsworth lived: "Clearly she was the daughter of a primitive unexhausted race" (39); the "religious genius" (152) that Langham later recognizes in her is the product of this mountain life. In her eyes, Robert sees "a beautiful, mystical light – responsive, lofty, full of soul" (40). Catherine represents Anglican orthodoxy – indeed to Langham's unsympathetic eyes "She is the Thirty-nine Articles in the flesh!" (162) – but her piety seems to derive from the same Romantic emotional source as Robert's. Their different spiritual paths are determined by their gender and education. Robert Elsmere's eventual crisis is the result of his pursuit of intellectual truth, as he follows to their logical conclusion the implications of his academic training at Oxford.

Mary Ward, who would later put her celebrity to notorious use as an anti-suffrage campaigner, shows a keen awareness of the way that theological questions interacted with those of gender in the late nineteenth century. In *Robert Elsmere*, Catherine dutifully supports her husband to his death even though she disagrees with his new creed, and after his death she continues to attend the services of the Brotherhood. She is unable to share in his intellectual journey, which might imply a critique of her lack of higher education and her subservience to her dead father's ways, but the emancipated women in the novel are not portrayed favourably, and in the subplot involving Catherine's sister Rose, Ward provides an interesting contrast to Catherine's career. Unlike Catherine, Rose has no attachment to their remote home in the Lake District; she is presented as an aesthete and New Woman, someone longing for an artistic life in the cosmopolitan world of the sort that George Eliot depicts in *Daniel Deronda*. Drawing a contrast between the pious woman and the New Woman was common in the art and literature of the late nineteenth century.[12] Ward uses Catherine, the image of domestic sanctity, as a counterpoint to the more adventurous Rose, who also manages in the end to find a man whom she can respect and obey.

In contrast with the orthdox belief and piety of Catherine, Robert Elsmere's final position is a radical break from traditional Christianity in that it undermines the uniqueness of Christ. He is afraid that his loss of faith will be a terrible blow to the woman whose piety he once shared, and after his moment of renunciation his immediate thought is *"O God! My wife – my work!"* (333; Ward's italics). However, the integrity of his family and the love that binds it together are affirmed in the tableau of Elsmere's death, in which he recalls the birth of his daughter and then calls out his wife's name (576). Instead of an incarnate God who is the personal saviour of all humankind, Ward offers a demythologized theism in which a chain of charismatic individuals can play the role of saviour for others and inspire disciples who will be future leaders. The chapter describing the death and funeral of Henry Grey makes it clear that he has played this role for Robert Elsmere, and his significance to his disciple is described thus: "At a time when a religion which can no longer be believed clashes with a scepticism full of danger to conduct, every such witness as Grey to the power of a new and coming truth holds a special place in the hearts of men who can neither accept fairy tales, nor reconcile themselves to a world without faith. The saintly life grows to be a beacon, a witness" (513). At the end of the chapter Elsmere meets MacNiell, another disciple who came up for the funeral; Elsmere says to him, "At a dark moment in my own life I owed him everything. There is nothing we can do for him in return but – to remember him! Write to me, if you can or will, from New Zealand, for his sake" (518). The biblical echo suggests that communication between the two men will be a kind of sacrament of their lost saviour; similarly, in a passage mocked by orthodox Christian reviewers, Elsmere reflects that in the absence of faith in the resurrection, "Grey's trust" will answer for him (516). It is interesting that Robert returns to Oxford, like Jude Fawley, during Commemoration week, and Hardy's bitter parodies of the life of Christ in *Jude* might also be parodies of the demythologizing typology of *Elsmere*. The pattern is completed in the last section of the novel when Elsmere inspires his own group of disciples, imparting his teachings to them in the form of letters, and, when he dies, leaving behind him a new religious organization that, the last paragraph tells us, "still exists, and grows" (576).

Ward's analysis of the sources of religious feeling and the changes that can take place beneath the apparent continuity of religious practice gives rise to some of the profoundest insights of *Robert Elsmere*. Elsmere's initial vocation is seen as part of a "fresh wave of religious romanticism," a reaction to the liberalism of the mid-century (65). In spite of the fellow feeling between Robert and Catherine, however, there are already signs of their future divergence. Robert, who in some respects resembles Charles Kingsley, has none of Catherine's asceticism: "For his more modern sense, deeply Christianised as it is, assumes almost without argument the sacredness of passion and its claim" (112). As a perceptive American reviewer wrote, "Robert Elsmere's faith is founded upon emotion; his unfaith has root in reason" (Harland, "Mental Struggles," 103). As he belatedly applies the scientific spirit to his religious faith under the tuition of Roger Wendover, the scholarly squire of his parish, Elsmere finds that the faith he had adopted without serious questioning has become simply an incredible fairy tale. What happens is that Elsmere's belief in the intellectual side of

Christianity becomes totally separated from his spiritual life; the former disappears when he loses his faith, while the latter, "the religion of the heart" (*Elsmere*, 320), persists and endures: "With Elsmere, as with all men of religious temperament, belief in Christianity and faith in God had not at the outset been a matter of reasoning at all, but of sympathy, feeling, association, daily experience. Then the intellect had broken in, and destroyed or transformed the belief in Christianity. But after the crash, *faith* emerged as strong as ever, only craving and eager to make a fresh peace, a fresh compact with the reason" (393; Ward's emphasis).

Perhaps the most interesting insight of all is the way that Ward presents the change in Catherine's understanding of her religious position. Although, as noted above, she rebukes her husband for trying to undertake the task of Christianity without the support of its supernatural dimension, she comes to accept his work in the New Brotherhood to the extent of attending its meetings along with the worship of the Church of England: "Love, and her husband, and the thousand subtle forces of a changing world had conquered. She would live and die steadfast to the old faiths. But her present mind and its outlook was no more the mind of her early married life than the Christian philosophy of to-day is the Christian philosophy of the Middle Ages. She was not conscious of change, but change there was. She had, in fact, undergone that dissociation of the moral judgment from a special series of religious formulae which is the crucial, the epoch-making fact of our day" (534). Catherine believes herself to be unchanged, an orthodox Christian; but in a world where belief has been relativized, where there is no longer an authoritative set of shared assumptions, orthodoxy becomes one set of opinions alongside all of the others. No matter how sincere the believer is, Christianity cannot function the same way in a postmodern world as it did in the era of Christendom. Catherine's beliefs have become a personal choice, perhaps the expression of an emotional need to remain faithful to the memory of her father, who is fused with her love of God the Father. The change Ward identifies is that there is a new commonality of *feeling* between husband and wife, even though they have lost a commonality of intellectual belief. The final tableau of the novel suggests that this community of feeling is the most important thing, linking *Elsmere*'s treatment of marriage to the Romantic tradition of affective piety. The subtlety with which Ward presents Catherine's position and, indeed, analyzes the dynamics of the Elsmeres' marriage is one of the great achievements of *Robert Elsmere*. Catherine is at once a dutiful late-Victorian wife, bound to support her husband, and a profoundly sincere Church of England Christian, and Ward makes us share her anguish when these two parts of her life come into conflict. Ward also shows us, again very convincingly, Robert's anguish as he is torn between his intellectual convictions and his love of his wife. Undoubtedly Mary Ward's observation of the tensions in her own family caused by her father's various changes of religious allegiance went into the making of her portrait of a marriage.[13]

In a sense, Catherine may be said to have become a Modernist Christian without realizing it. As we have seen, Ward later became more sympathetic to her uncle's position and, in *The Case of Richard Meynell*, told the story of a clergyman who stays within the Church and argues his modern understanding of the faith there. *Richard Meynell*, however, is more melodramatic and less subtle than *Elsmere*. In the place of a hero who becomes a new type of Christ (rather like Arthur Henry Hallam in *In Memoriam*) and dies exhausted from his evangelical labours, Richard Meynell is presented as a military-style leader of the age of imperialism, fighting for his place in the national church.[14] Similarly, the love plot is simpler: Catherine Elsmere's daughter Mary becomes convinced of the truth of Meynell's Modernist creed, so that her love is simply an affirmation of the rightness of his position (aided at one point by Catherine's having a vision of her dead husband). Even here, however, Ward is not a whole hearted Modernist; for Meynell wants to change the liturgy and the statements of faith, not simply to claim the right to a new way of understanding them.[15] The dogmatism that survives in this novel is the legacy of Ward's very Victorian liberalism. It is what most dates her religious thought, what makes her older friend, Walter Pater, appear today as the more modern figure.

A "RELIGIOUS PHASE POSSIBLE FOR THE MODERN MIND": PATER'S AESTHETIC MODERNISM

Robert Elsmere's faith was emotional in its origin, while his loss of faith came from intellectual questioning of the historical grounds that he had supposed that faith to have. In Arnold's terms, Elsmere came to believe that the fact had failed Christianity. Walter Pater's attraction to Christianity was similarly emotional, with a predominance of aesthetic emotion. But unlike Ward, Pater was willing to allow for the possibility of mystery, of something beyond the ability of the rational intellect to ascertain. He did not regard the intellect as the final court in questions of faith, something that Ward criticized him for, identifying in him an escapist aestheticism that sacrificed truth: "All existing religions have issued from the sense of reality, from a perception of some truth; certain facts or supposed facts of sense or spirit have lain at the root of them" (Ward, "Review," 136). She contrasted Pater with Clough, whom she praised for his determination "to put no fairy tales knowingly into the place which belongs to realities" (136). Pater's own position was more complex, however, than Mary Ward was willing or able to acknowledge. Her late-Victorian liberal earnestness makes her book and her reflections on faith and doubt very much documents of her time, whereas Pater's Christianity, which could be characterized as aesthetic Modernism, has more in common with postmodern theology. Pater's views may be similar to the position towards which Mary Ward was herself groping in *The Case of Richard Meynell*. Whereas Ward was a liberal Protestant in tendency, Pater's sympathies were with Catholicism, and his approach to religious belief has affinities with that of John Henry Newman.

Once again, as with Matthew Arnold, one might well apply Newman's question about Thomas Arnold to Walter Pater: Was he a Christian? Inevitably, the answer reflects the values and beliefs of the writer who seeks to describe Pater's faith, both because of the subjectivity of the question and because of the enigmatic nature of the evidence we have. Michael Levey constructs a radically Nietzschean Pater out of that evidence[16] and dismisses as "unpardonable exaggeration" the statement of Pater's friend F.W. Bussell that "the entire interest of his later years was religious" (*Case*, 22). From an opposing perspective, Nathan Scott treats Pater as a religious writer whom he compares to Hopkins, Buber, Simone Weil, and T.S. Eliot, and he asserts that *Marius* "surely deserves to be accounted amongst the few great religious classics of the modern period" ("Imperative," 115); Scott also observes, "In his 'reserve' how much like Keble he is!" (ibid.). There is a much-cited incident recorded by Mary Ward in *A Writer's Recollections* in which Pater scandalized an Oxford professor and his wife by making an agnostic remark;[17] Scott comments that "such badinage is not unknown even amongst professional theologians, particularly when they may feel it appropriate to administer a shock to some kind of smug and unthinking orthodoxy" (117n33). The most judicious approach to the question of Pater's beliefs is that of Ellis Hanson. "In defining Pater," he writes, "it is important to preserve the sensuous mobility of his mind, his eternal tenuousness, his perennial ambivalence, and what he would have called the Heraclitean flux of his impressions and his ideas. Only with numerous qualifications do I claim Pater as a decadent, a homosexual, and an Anglo-Catholic" (*Decadence*, 170).

The evidence for Pater's religious beliefs can be briefly summarized. He was a pious schoolboy who was attracted to Anglo-Catholic ritual, but who intellectually rejected Christian dogma as an undergraduate. He was nevertheless planning to put himself forward for ordination when a friend wrote to the bishop of London saying that his agnosticism made him an unsuitable candidate. After his election to Brasenose College, Pater enjoyed shocking the members of a discussion society called "Old Mortality" with his heterodox views (Levey, *Case*, 100–1). In the Trinity term of 1866, Pater was the tutor of Gerard Manley Hopkins, who recorded in his journal on 31 May, "A little rain and at evening and night hard rain. – Pater talking two hours against Xtianity" (138). Pater's early essays are not sympathetic to Christianity, and because of its philosophical materialism, the conclusion to *The Renaissance* (1873) was widely thought to recommend an amoral pursuit of pleasure. It was condemned by the bishop of Oxford in an episcopal charge and by George Eliot in one of her less-enlightened utterances.[18] Pater himself regretted the notoriety of the conclusion and briefly suppressed it, though he never disavowed the sentiments it expresses. His footnote to the third edition of *The Renaissance* directs the reader to *Marius* as a commentary on the views expressed in the conclusion: "This brief 'Conclusion' was omitted in the second edition of this book, as I conceived it might possibly mislead some of those young men into whose hands it might fall. On the whole, I have thought it best to reprint it here, with some slight changes which bring it closer to my original meaning. I have dealt more fully in *Marius the Epicurean* with the thoughts suggested by it" (*Renaissance*, 150).

Somewhere between the first publication of *The Renaissance* and that of *Marius the Epicurean* twelve years later, Pater began what Mary Ward calls his "hesitating and wistful return toward Christianity, and Christianity of the Catholic type" (*Recollections* 1:161). She adds, "It may be said, I think, that he never returned to Christianity in the orthodox or intellectual sense. But his heart returned to it" (1:162). This return can be traced in several key texts, one of which, of course, is *Marius*, as Ward acknowledges, calling it "the most beautiful of the spiritual romances of

Europe since the *Confessions*" (1:161). The earliest of these texts is a letter to Violet Paget, who published under the name of Vernon Lee. Paget had published a dialogue entitled "The Responsibilities of Unbelief," a conversation between three different types of unbelievers: Rheinhardt, an "optimistic Voltairean"; Vere, an aesthete and pessimist; and Baldwin, a militantly atheist Postivist. Primarily they were discussing whether truth is for all, or for an educated elite, and whether it is relative. Pater wrote one of his more revealing and interesting letters to Paget (usually his letters are remarkable for their reserve), relating *Marius* to this dialogue:

> I have hopes of completing one half of my present chief work – an Imaginary Portrait of a peculiar type of mind in the time of Marcus Aurelius – by the end of this Vacation, and meant to have asked you to look at some of the MS. perhaps. I am wishing to get the whole completed, as I have visions of many smaller pieces of work the composition of which would be actually pleasanter to me. However, I regard this present matter as a sort of duty. For, you know, I think that there is a fourth sort of religious phase possible for the modern mind, over and above those presented in your late admirable paper in the Contemporary, the conditions of which phase it is the main object of my design to convey. (*Letters*, 52, 22 July 1883)

It is important to emphasize the word "modern" in this passage. Pater agreed with Arnold and Ward that it was no longer possible to believe in Christianity in the same way one could believe before biblical criticism, geology, Darwin, and other solvents of pre-Victorian orthodoxy transformed the *Zeitgeist*. Nevertheless, Pater regarded the modern mind as capable of a "religious phase," a notion that he explained most extensively in *Marius*. Ian Fletcher suggests that here Pater may have been thinking of something like the Broad Church doctrine of accommodation (*Pater*, 23). Pater's view of history is certainly Hegelian in the manner of the liberal Anglican historians, and by the "religious phase possible for the modern mind" he may have meant a form of revelation of the divine that conformed to the rational and scientific world view that prevailed in late-Victorian intellectual circles. Pater's achievement in *Marius*, from a theological perspective, was to fuse the liberalism of Stanley and the Broad Church with an idea of the Church and of religious assent derived from Newman, and to add his own aesthetic stamp that was neverthless only a radical development of the idea of the poetic qualities of religion to be found in the Tractarians.[19]

In 1885, the year that *Marius* came out, Mary Ward published her translation of selections of Henri-Frédéric Amiel's *Journal intime*. Pater's responses to this work continued the debate that had opened with Ward's review of *Marius*. In a letter to Ward Pater issued one of the most revealing statements about his attitude to Christianity:

> To my mind, the beliefs, and the function in the world, of the historic church, form just one of those obscure but all-important possibilities, which the human mind is powerless effectively to dismiss from itself; and might wisely accept, in the first place, as a workable hypothesis. The supposed facts on which Christianity rests, utterly incapable as they have become of any ordinary test, seem to me matters of very much the same sort of assent we give to any assumption, in the strict and ultimate sense, moral. The question whether those facts were real will, I think, always continue to be what I should call one of the *natural* questions of the human mind. (*Letters*, 64–5, 23 December 1885)

Pater's idea that the human mind cannot dismiss the possibility of faith, even if it cannot be scientifically proven, echoes Newman's idea of religious assent arising from the accumulation of probabilities. David DeLaura has demonstrated the extent of the affinities between Pater and Newman (*Hebrew*, 305–44), and he goes so far as to say that "the central argument of Marius's 'conversion' is taken almost bodily from the *Grammar of Assent* (1870) and other writings of Newman" (316). Among Pater's still-unpublished manuscript essays are a paper on Newman and a fragmentary essay on "Art and Religion," which make much of John Stuart Mill's acknowledgment that the hypothesis of religious belief "cannot be known to be false."[20]

Pater added to the points made in his letter to Ward in a review of her translation of Amiel in which he contrasted Amiel with Pascal. To Amiel's question "When will the Church to which I belong in heart rise into being?" Pater replied, "To many at least of those who can detect the ideal through the disturbing circumstances which belong to all actual institutions in the world, it was already there" ("Amiel's 'Journal,'" 34). Two years later Ward published *Robert Elsmere*, and in his review of that work Pater might be thought to be replying to her earlier review of *Marius*. As already noted, he identified Elsmere's New Brotherhood as "a kind of Unitarian-ism" ("Review," 65), and in the penultimate paragraph his aesthetic censure of Ward's vision of a newly reformed Christianity echoes, ironically enough, Matthew Arnold's comments on dissenting churches: "At his death Elsmere has started what to us would be a most unattractive place of worship" (69). Pater thought there could be little of interest to say in a church that believed in a purely human Christ; for "it is the infinite nature of Christ which has led to such diversities of genius in preaching as St Francis, and Taylor, and Wesley" (69). Pater tactfully suggested that Ward had oversimplified matters, and that Elsmere's sudden onset of doubt was not very convincing: "It strikes us as a blot on his philo-sophical pretensions that he should have been both so late in perceiving the difficulty, and then so sudden and trenchant in dealing with so great and complex a question" (67). In the key passage in the review, Pater wrote:

> Robert Elsmere was a type of a large class of minds which cannot be sure that the sacred story is true. It is philosophical, doubtless, and a duty to the intellect to recognize our doubts, to locate them, perhaps to give them practical effect. It may also be a moral duty to do this. But then there is also a large class of minds which cannot be sure it is false – minds of very various degrees of conscientiousness and intel-lectual power, up to the highest. They will think those who are quite sure it is false unphilosophical through lack of doubt. For their part, they make allowance in their scheme of life for a great possibility, and with some of them that bare concession of possibility (the subject of it being what it is) becomes the most important fact in the world. The recognition of it straightway opens wide the door to hope and love; and such persons are, as we fancy they always will be, the nucleus of a Church. (67–8)

In the last essay he wrote, his study of Pascal, Pater was still wrestling with these questions. While he was unsympathetic to the ascetic element in Pascal – indeed, he saw his attitudes "as precisely an inversion of what is called the aesthetic life" ("Pascal," 75) – Pater eloquently emphasized Pascal's faith amid doubt. There was an element of self-description when Pater said that for Pascal, "revelation is to be received on evidence, indeed, but an evidence conclusive only on a presupposition or series of presuppositions, evidence that is supplemented by an act of imagination, or by the grace of faith, shall we say?" (82–3).

Marius the Epicurean: His Sensations and Ideas has been described both as Pater's *Apologia* (McCraw, "Riddle," 247) and his *Grammar of Assent* (Vogeler, "Meaning," 291). According to James Eli Adams, "the novel enacts a familiar pattern of the Victorian *Bildungsroman*: a traditional childhood religious faith collapses under the force of contemporary scepticism, but the emotional rewards of that faith are subsequently recuperated in a secular devotion to the forces of 'intellectual light'" (*Dandies*, 149). The novel's interiority, accurately reflected in the subtitle, has given *Marius* a significant place in the history of Modernism as a literary movement. Like Joyce's *Portrait of the Artist as a Young Man* (1916), Pater's novel shifts to the "lyrical" mode of diary in the late chapter "*Sunt Lacrimae Rerum*." One of the most enduring questions about *Marius* is whether it is in fact a conversion narrative, whether Marius can be said to be a Christian at the end.[21] Reading the arguments for and against the idea that Marius dies a Christian, it is apparent that although he does not undergo a very definite personal conversion, he is absorbed by a Christian community and from an objective point of view might be said to have become a Christian. From a more subjective point of view, as the title implies, he always remains an Epicurean, just as Pater never renounced the views expressed in the conclusion to *The Renaissance*.[22] Given the genre Pater chose and his presentation of cultural history, I would argue that the novel as a whole can be called a Christian novel; indeed, that with the exception of *The Heir of Redclyffe*, it is the most clearly Christian of the works in this study.

The focus on cultural change rather than individual conversion can be related to the fact that *Marius* is not really a realistic novel, nor is it a typical romance of ancient times, though it certainly has a wealth of specific detail and it reproduces many of the generic features of the Victorian novel about early Christianity. The difference lies in the focus on ideas rather than on events or personal interaction. Marius is always the "curious spectator" (Pater, *Marius*, 217), the one who sets "seeing" above "having" or "doing" (293). Through him, and through the interpretive commentary of the nineteenth-century narrator, the cultural history of the west is re-experienced and reinterpreted for the reader. However, it is problematic cultural history. From one point of view, the novel is a Hegelian *Bildungsroman*, chronicling the dialectic between paganism and Christianity; thus Carolyn Williams can refer to *Marius* as "an auto-biography of the *Zeitgeist*" (*World*, 189). Paganism, even in the highly speculative version exemplified in the discourse of Apuleius, has reached its end, and it will be absorbed into the Christian civilization that will replace it. At the same time *Marius* is a historical romance that seeks to provide a mirror for the Victorian present,[23] just as Charles Kingsley's *Hypatia* presents, in the words of its subtitle, *New Foes with an Old Face*. By means of various forward-looking references Pater's narrator encourages the reader to look for parallels between past and present. He uses phrases such as "'aesthetic' education" (*Marius*, 117) words and phrases alluding to Arnold, Newman, and Tennyson, and references to St Augustine's future views (92) and to Mantegna's paintings of Roman pageantry (282), and he explicitly comments on his own practice: "That age and our own have much in common – many difficulties and hopes. Let the reader pardon me if here and there I seem to be passing from Marius to his modern representatives – from Rome, to Paris or London" (181).

In the late Victorian period, parallels with Antonine Rome were particularly popular, for the two societies were seen as "two summits of power and civilization sloping downward in decadence" (Bloom, *Ringers*, 188). In terms of such parallels, the pagan "religion of Numa" that is powerfully depicted in the opening chapter would be parallel to the Church of England. It most resembles the kind of village Anglicanism represented by George Eliot in *Adam Bede*, where the church year and the agricultural cycle of the community are intertwined. Dwight Culler observes that an allusion to Wordsworth serves to link the religion of Marius's childhood "with the traditional Anglicanism of the English countryside, also conservative and patriarchal, linked with festivals and domestic life, a religion of natural piety rather than dogmatic creeds" (*Mirror*, 264). The Christian church of the second century must then represent the form of religious life that Pater hopes will emerge, his own more attractive version of the New Brotherhood. Pater is no W.B. Yeats, imagining a rough beast slouching towards Bethlehem; he envisions a remade form of Christianity that gives primacy to aesthetic experience rather than to dogmatic theology, while remaining centred in the ritual and the life of the Church, and comprehending both charity and community. Pater is thus an Anglo-Catholic Modernist, and what is most polemical about *Marius* is the way that he locates his vision of the Modernist church in the Roman church of St Cecilia, in just the same way that Kingsley and Newman fought over the authentic nature of Christianity by writing their own historical novels of the early church, Kingsley with *Hypatia* and Newman with *Callista* (1856).

In writing a historical novel about Antonine Rome, Pater takes issue with Matthew Arnold's essay "Marcus Aurelius." While Arnold judges the emperor to be a failure in the end, he also sees him as "perhaps the most beautiful figure in history" (Arnold, *Complete Prose* 3:140). Pater, on the other hand, presents him as a tragic, flawed figure, a virtuous philosopher-king surrounded by his unappealing family and acquiescing in brutality and torture, his ineffectuality highlighted by the contrast with the figures of Cecilia and Cornelius. As Richard Dellamora has noted, Arnold's essay responds to John Stuart Mill's criticism of Marcus Aurelius in chapter 2 of *On Liberty* for persecuting Christians in the name of social coherence (*Masculine Desire*, 14). Arnold rationalizes the persecution of minority groups: "Who can doubt that among the professing Christians of the second century, as among the professing Christians of the nineteenth, there was plenty of folly, plenty of rabid nonsense, plenty of gross fanaticism? who will even venture to affirm that, separated in great measure from the intellect and civilisation of the world for one or two centuries, Christianity, wonderful as have been its fruits, had the development perfectly worthy of its inestimable germ?" (*Complete Prose* 3:145). In response Pater portray's the church in Cecilia's house as an exemplification of Arnoldian culture, as a fusion of Hellenism and Hebraism, and makes Marcus Aurelius's persecution of Christians the final stage in Marius's gradual disillusionment with him. For Arnold, St Louis, for all his admirable qualities, "inhabits an atmosphere of mediaeval Catholicism, which the man of the nineteenth century may admire, indeed, may even passionately wish to inhabit, but which, strive as he will, he cannot really inhabit" (*Complete Prose* 3:140). Marcus Aurelius, by contrast, is presented as virtually a contemporary: "He lived and acted in a state of society modern by its essential characteristics, in an epoch akin to our own, in a brilliant centre of civilisation" (3:140). Pater responds by suggesting that St Louis is a better example of Plato's philosopher-king than Plato's avowed disciple Marcus Aurelius was (*Marius*, 205).

Like a typical nineteenth-century *Bildungsroman*, *Marius* begins with its hero in a provincial world dominated by archaic customs and rituals. He may find more aesthetic and even religious meaning in these than most heroes of such novels, but his destiny is clearly to be one set apart;

this is confirmed by his visit to the temple of Aesculapius, where he is told that "he was of the number of those who, in the words of a poet who came long after, must be 'made perfect by the love of visible beauty'" (53). In order to educate his sensibility, he leaves home and eventually ends up – much like Pip in Dickens's *Great Expectations* – in the imperial capital; in fact, he enters the service of the emperor himself. The novel's end, however, is prefigured in its beginning, as the assembled community and the simple gifts offered in the pagan religious rite, including bread and wine, obviously foreshadow the Christian eucharist that is described in detail in Part the Fourth. The religion of Numa is closely linked to Marius's family and ancestral home; after the death of his parents he is without close family ties, and eventually he finds a new family in the Church. The urns of the family dead preserved at his home prefigure the underground tombs at Cecilia's house. The difference between pagan religion and Christianity is indicated by the suffering of the sacrificial animals in the former. From the beginning, Marius feels pity for the sacrificial victims. Pater's love of animals is well documented, and its prominent place in *Marius* can be regarded as a protest against a purely mechanical Darwinian universe.

At school in Pisa, Marius develops his Epicurean nature through literature. The literature of the time, notably Apuleius and the writing of the fictitious Flavian, parallels the decadent literature of the later nineteenth century (see D. Culler, *Mirror*, 264–5). Marius's reading, like the religious rites of his ancestral home, develops his longing for an ideal. His beloved story of Cupid and Psyche, framed by the bawdy and violent adventures that surround it in Lucius Apuleius's *Golden Ass*, represents "the ideal of a perfect imaginative love, centered upon a type of beauty entirely flawless and clean" (*Marius*, 87). Marius's sensibility, and his sense of "the *hiddenness* of perfect things" (87), has strong affinities with the tradition of Tractarian poetics; at times he resembles John Keble, at times Gerard Manley Hopkins. The following passage, for example, comes from the description of Marius's early days in Pisa:

> And as, in that gray monastic tranquillity of the villa, inward voices from the reality of unseen things had come abundantly; so here, with the sounds and aspects of the shore, and amid the urbanities, the graceful follies, of a bathing-place, it was the reality, the tyrannous reality, of things visible that was borne in upon him. The real world around –

a present humanity not less comely, it might seem, than that of the old heroic days – endowing everything it touched upon, however remotely, down to its little passing tricks of fashion even, with a kind of fleeting beauty, exercised over him just then a great fascination. (62)

The passage echoes Romans 1:20, the epigraph to Keble's poem "Septuagesima Sunday": "For the invisible things of him from the creation of the world are clearly seen, being understood by the things that are made." Throughout the book, especially after being inspired by Psyche's quest for Cupid, Marius seeks spiritual truth or revelation through the medium of the material world. He strives to connect the sense of the world of unseen things he had in his days at the villa called White-nights with his sensitivity to the beauty of the appearances of the visible world. In so doing, he remains true to the materialism of his epicurean philosophy and rejects the Platonic doctrines of Apuleius. This is one of the reasons why he is attracted to Christianity; for the sacramental world view makes visible beauty the sign of divine truth, as we see most vividly in the poetry of Pater's pupil Hopkins.

Juxtaposed with Marius's visions of beauty and his sense of the presence of divinity is his awareness of mortality; from the beginning, the novel is full of images of funeral urns, graves, sudden death, the death of children, and the presence of the dead. The treatment of the death of Flavian as "a Pagan End" marks an important transition in the book in that it represents the finality of death in the pagan view of it, and also the dead-end of paganism itself. Having witnessed his friend's death, and feeling powerless to share in and thereby relieve his suffering, Marius adopts a position of philosophical materialism and scepticism, in which his religious sensibility becomes dedicated to intellectual scrupulousness. In the design of the novel, however, Flavian's life has already provided a forward-looking image, linking an older paganism through the art of the present to the religious expression of the future. For Jules Lubbock, the incident in which the fictional Flavian writes the real poem "Pervigilium Veneris" is an example and a central demonstration of "Pater's conception of the way in which a civilization renews itself" ("Portrait," 184). The refrain of the poem comes from an ancient folk song that is itself a remnant from the Greek colony that once occupied the region around Pisa. A poet at a time when literature was highly self-conscious, and overwhelmed with the weight of the past achievements of ancient literature, Flavian succeeds in projecting a fragment from the more naive literature of the past into something proleptic of a future Christian civilization: "The peculiar resultant note, associating itself with certain other experiences of his, was to Marius like the foretaste of an entirely novel world of poetic beauty to come. Flavian had caught, indeed, something of the rhyming cadence, the sonorous organ-music of the medieval Latin, and therewithal something of its unction and mysticity of spirit" (*Marius*, 98). What is subjectively a pagan end, a life extinguished and unfulfilled, is in terms of the cultural paradigms of the novel an early sign of the renewing, or, in Hegelian terms, the sublation, of paganism in Christianity. The description of Cecilia's house repeats this pattern, as the pagan art and architecture are put to the service of the Christian community: "It was the old way of true *Renaissance* ... conceiving the new organism by no sudden and abrupt creation, but rather by the action of a new principle upon elements, all of which had in truth already lived and died many times" (228).

In Part the Second, Marius follows the teachings of Aristippus, founder of the Cyrenaic school. He is described in Arnoldian terms, for in contrast to other philosophers of his time Pater suggests that there is a "modern" element in his thought and expression (111). As Marius develops his own epicurean philosophy, or "new Cyrenaicism," the echoes of Arnold continue: he seeks "culture ... a wide, a complete, education" (117), a life that in its quest for perfection becomes "a kind of religion – an inward, visionary, mystic piety, or religion" (118). Pater thus presents the views of his notorious conclusion in the language of Arnoldian humanism and explains that the quest for such a life may sometimes lead to a conflict with "the received morality" (119). This position, however, even on its own terms, is not ultimately satisfactory. The admired emperor acquiesces in the unlovely spectacle of the slaughter in the amphitheatre, while in contrast Marius realizes that beneath the reserve of his friend Cornelius there is "some inward standard ... of distinction, selection, refusal, amid the various elements of the fervid and corrupt life across which they were moving together: – some secret, constraining motive" (165). The rhetorician Marcus Cornelius Fronto's stoic discourse suggests to Marius the possibility of considering morality as possessing an aesthetic beauty. Remaining in his purely epicurean position would rob him of certain experiences that epicureanism itself would encourage him to explore. The attitude to the old religion and morality indicated here parallels the view of Christianity that should be taken by the Victorian intellectual, and indeed in some ways it resembles Arnold's, but Pater views the old morality aesthetically in a way that Arnold does not.

In presenting Christianity as the new alternative, Pater emphasizes two things about the new faith. First, charity and community are emphasized as the loving bonds that potentially unite all human beings, in contrast to the hostile and sometimes literally poisonous relations between members of the imperial family. Second, both Christian worship and the whole way of life of the Christian community are seen to have a profound aesthetic appeal. In chapter 19 Marius has a revelatory experience that prepares him, and the reader, for the final stage of his pilgrimage. Pater carefully presents it as a purely natural experience that nevertheless contains intimations of something supernatural: "*as if* by favour of an invisible power withdrawing some unknown cause of dejection from around him, he enjoyed a quite unusual sense of self-possession – the possession of his own best and happiest self" (208; Pater's emphasis). He considers the possibility that if one makes a conscious decision to assent to the doctrine of "the hypothesis of an eternal friend to man, just hidden behind the veil of a mechanical and material order" one might be led "at last into the region of a corresponding certitude of the intellect" (208). This is Newman's understanding of assent as the certitude arising from converging probabilities. Sitting in an olive garden, he seems to become aware of "an unfailing companion, ever at his side" in addition to his sometime companions Flavian and then Cornelius (210). Cornelius in particular becomes for Marius an image of the ideal, with his splendid armour, his "new song" (180), and his secret inner standard. He thus becomes an image of the divine eternal companion, and a type of Christ, that companion made man. Marius is led to Christianity by male friendship, a fraternal relationship with erotic overtones that is a type of the love of God. In the final phase of his exploration, Marius thus has an intimation of the Christian community's sense of the continuing presence of Christ in their midst.

Pater's aesthetic Christianity finds its fullest expression in the description of Cecilia's house, which can be contrasted not only with the first "curious house" in the preceding chapter but with his family home of White-nights and with the temple of Aesculapius, as well as with the austere residence of Marcus Aurelius. The narrator tells us that "it was still, indeed, according to the unchangeable law of his temperament, to the eye, to the visual faculty of mind, that those experiences appealed ... But, in his case, what was thus visible constituted a moral or spiritual influence" (233–4). Marius admired the new uses to which the fragments of the pagan world are put, "the old way of true *Renaissance*" (228). He is also impressed with the reverent burial of the dead, reviving an ancient Roman practice. The Church thus draws on ancient traditions, yet at the same time it is characterized by the new music that is referred to several times, representing the novel element in Christianity. As Pater presents it, the early Church lacks what Graham Hough calls the "Augustinian element," leading him to suggest that "we cannot fit Pater into the pattern of even the broadest of Broad Churchmanship. The Augustinian element is not the whole of Christianity, but there is no Christianity without it" (*Romantics*, 156).

It is certainly true that Pater presents the second-century church in terms of Arnoldian Hellenism rather than Hebraism: "for its constant outward token, its significant manner or index, it issued in a certain debonair grace, and a certain mystic attractiveness, a courtesy, which made Marius doubt whether that famed Greek 'blitheness', or gaiety, or grace, in the handling of life, had been, after all, an unrivalled success" (*Marius*, 236). Asceticism is seen as one of two distinct Christian ideals, the other deriving from the image of the Good Shepherd. The latter, as an "ideal of culture," represents moral effort "as a harmonious development of all the parts of human nature, in just proportion to each other" (241). The "aesthetic charm" (242) of the Church lies not only in its strictly artistic productions but in the beauty of the way of life it fosters. This looks back to Cornelius Fronto's praise of the ancient morality for its aesthetic qualities. Pater speaks, in a phrase that has sometimes been ridiculed, of "'the beauty of holiness', nay! the elegance of sanctity" (242). Ellis Hanson says of this passage that "religious and aesthetic experience are deeply intertwined here, if not wholly indistinguishable. Moreover, Pater reasserts his notion of Christianity as a practice in flux, a practice that reforms itself with history rather than a doctrine that remains steadfast and static" (*Decadence*, 202). Chapter 22 ends on a note of Catholic triumphalism, and the presentation of aesthetic Christianity continues in the next chapter with the description of the Christmas mass in Cecilia's church. In a passage that seems to be addressed to Arnold, Marius is presented as responding to the Christian narrative as well as to the beauty of the liturgy: "In the old pagan worship there had been little to call the understanding into play. Here, on the other hand, the utterance, the eloquence, the music of worship conveyed, as Marius readily understood, a fact or series of facts, for intellectual reception" (*Marius*, 248). The facts are the various parts of the Christian narrative, as glimpsed in fragmentary form in the mass. Pater is not so concerned with the historical truth of the narrative as with the "fact" of its "intellectual reception." Christianity is more like a work of art, he implies, than like postive knowledge. The emphasis on the young men involved in the liturgy leads into what Marius "dimly" discerns through his experience of the rite, "the most touching image truly that had ever come within the scope of his mental or physical gaze. It was the image of a young man giving up voluntarily, one by one, for the greatest of ends, the greatest gifts" (250). We recall that Marius had wished he could make some sacrifice of himself and share in the suffering of Flavian; we also recall his friendship with Cornelius, who has brought him to Cecilia's house. These friendships, with their homoerotic overtones, are fused with the image of the loving Christ and lie behind Marius's decision to sacrifice himself for Cornelius when they are arrested at the end of the novel. It is also worth noting that the passage I have just quoted culminates in the naming of Jesus (251), briefly setting aside the veil of reserve that has been maintained throughout the novel, as Marius discovers the source of the difference he has always been aware of in his friend Cornelius and discovers the identity of the companion whose presence he has felt intimations of. It is through the mass supremely that he draws near to that companion: "So deep is the emotion that at moments it seems to Marius as if some there present apprehend that prayer prevails, that the very object of this pathetic crying himself draws near" (250). Pater's theology is Catholic in its emphasis on the eucharist as the central means through which Christ is present in the world.

It is important to add that although Pater presents Christianity foremost in aesthetic terms, the Church is also seen as a community bound together by charity. The narrator describes the faith of the period of "the minor peace of the Church" as "Christianity in its humanity, or even its humanism, in its generous hopes for man, its common sense and alacrity of cheerful service, its sympathy with all creatures" (238). Even Hough, who criticizes the absence from Pater's vision of what Arnold calls "Hebraism" and what he himself calls "the Augustinian element," acknowledges that "experience of a Christian society is not a disreputable motive for being attracted to Christianity" (154). Marius's experience of the Church makes the persecution that Marcus Aurelius institutes seem all the more reprehensible, and the chapter in which we hear Marius's own voice (chapter 25, "Sunt Lacrimae Rerum"), as a result of his "modern" habit of keeping a journal, emphasizes the pageant of human suffering he sees in the streets of Rome. The poetic evocation of Christianity in the chapter "Divine Service" is followed by a shift in tone to the ironic philosophical dialogue in "A Conversation Not Imaginary" (chapter 24), which presents the impossibility of attaining truth through the exercise of human reason and concludes with Marius reflecting on "a certain Christian legend he had heard" (258) and longing for a revelation from the gods.

One must recognize that Marius does not himself view the end of his life as the heroic death of a martyr. Yet he acknowledges that something new has come into the world, and he sees Cornelius as the son who will inherit it: "Identifying himself with Cornelius in so dear a friendship, through him, Marius seemed to touch, to ally himself to, actually to become a possessor of the coming world" (289). In looking forward to the future of the Christian church, which Marius has not fully embraced, but which has embraced him as he dies, Pater is commenting on the position of the doubting or humanist Christian at the end of the nineteenth century. Pater's acknowledgment of the possiblity of a divine presence beyond "the flaming ramparts of the world" (116) is the radical element in Christian orthodoxy that postmodern theology reasserts against the materialist systems of thought of modernity: "There had been a permanent protest established in the world, a plea, a perpetual after-thought, which humanity henceforth would ever possess in reserve, against any wholly mechanical and disheartening theory of itself and its conditions" (295).

More than one hundred years after Pater wrote these words, his view of Christianity is still attractive and challenging. He offers no dogmatic claims, and yet he makes use of Newman's doctrines of assent and of the Church; the Christianity he presents seems radically humanist in its use of the natural world and artistic creation to express its meaning, and yet it is always on the threshold of communion with unseen presences. He depicts the central act of Christian worship as an experience that, while both aesthetic and communal, is also a making present of the unseen God. Pater's vision of Christianity makes it far more appealing than Robert Elsmere's Brotherhood, yet like Arnold and Ward, Pater seeks an accommodation between Christianity and modernity. In its use of history, its sense of Christianity remaking a previous culture, its philosophical scepticism, and its use of multiple voices and sources, Pater's novel represents a version of Christianity that is possible for postmodernity. Thus, it is not only a fitting point of conclusion, articulating and synthesizing what had been hints and intimations in the other works I have discussed; *Marius* remains, in the twenty-first century, a novel with a claim to be taken seriously as a *religious* classic.

NOTES

———◄○►———

INTRODUCTION

1 For general surveys of the novel of religious controversy see Maison, *Search*, and Wolff, *Gains and Losses*; the novel and the Oxford Movement is discussed by Baker (*Novel*) and Chapman (*Faith*); poetry and the Oxford Movement by G.B. Tennyson, *Devotional Poetry*; for the Victorian historical novel about early Christianity see Rhodes, *The Lion*.

2 For Booth's ethical concerns see *The Company We Keep*; for Nussbaum's, *Love's Knowledge*; Bloom is less concerned with ethics than with literature's revelation of the human condition and contribution to the development of the self. See his *Western Canon* and *How to Read and Why*.

3 Bakhtin himself may well have been a Russian Orthodox believer, but he resists any form of closure in fiction, censuring Dostoevsky for his use of *"conventionally literary, conventionally monologic"* endings (*Problems*, 39; Bakhtin's italics) and suggesting that the ending of *Crime and Punishment* is "especially characteristic in this respect" (40). Clark and Holquist note the difficulty of establishing Bakhtin's relationship to the Orthodox church (see *Bakhtin*, especially 343). Coates surveys the "Christian motifs" in Bakhtin's work, which she argues have been unduly neglected; however, she writes, "I am not convinced that Bakhtin's unorthodox Christianity is of an Orthodox persuasion" (*Christianity*, 22).

4 For the Hampden controversy, see Chadwick, *Victorian* 1:112–21; for the controversy over Pusey's sermon and his suspension from preaching see ibid., 1:205, and H.P. Liddon, *Life of Pusey* 2:306–69; for Ambassador Everett's honorary degree see Chadwick, *Victorian* 1:205–6.

5 For the Lewes riot see Chandler, *Life and Work*, 88–90, and Neale, *Lewes*.

6 For an account of the *Essays and Reviews* controversy see Chadwick, *Victorian* 2:75–90. A wealth of documentation can be found in Shea and Whitla's scholarly edition of *Essays and Reviews*.

7 Said's comments come in a brief conclusion to *The World, the Text, and the Critic*. See also his comments in Salusinszky, "Interview," 140–1. Culler's comments occur in two short pieces ("Critic" and "Comparative"), and in a longer article based on them ("Political Criticism").

8 Such work requires a long immersion in the writing of the period, an immersion that my experience as a scholar and teacher tells me is no longer encouraged by an academy that emphasizes quantity of scholarly output over quality of scholarship. W. David Shaw laments that, where once an array of disciplines was represented in the field of Victorian scholarship at the University of Toronto, all that remains is "one small band of cultural historians" (*Babel*, 64).

9 I have been influenced by the reception theory of Hans Robert Jauss, although I have not followed his terminology or methodology closely. His concept – derived from Hans-Georg Gadamer – of the "fusion of horizons," the meeting point of the horizon of expectations of the text and of the reader, describes one of the key theoretical assumptions informing my approach. See Jauss, "Literary History," particularly 29–30.

10 See Altick's discussion of religious movements, with numerous examples, in *The Presence of the Present*, 95–106.

11 By surveying religious fiction according to categories such as these, Wolff gives a most helpful overview of the subject.

12 See James, "Mrs Humphrey Ward," and his review of Yonge's *Life of John Coleridge Patterson*.

13 "There are many who would laugh at the idea of a novelist teaching either virtue or nobility, – those, for instance, who regard the reading of novels as a sin, and those also who think it to be simply an idle pastime ... I have regarded my art from so different a point of view that I have ever thought of myself as a preacher of sermons, and my pulpit as one which I could make both salutary and agreeable to my audience" (Trollope, *Autobiography*, 146).

14 See Haight, *George Eliot*, 490–9.

15 I am thinking here of Frank Kermode's use of this term in *The Genesis of Secrecy*, where he discusses both the gospel narratives and works of fiction by writers such as Franz Kafka, James Joyce, and Henry Green. For Kermode's explanation of the term see *Genesis*, ix–xi and 81–3.

16 See Houghton's opening chapter, "Character of the Age" (*Victorian Frame of Mind*, 1–23) for many representative quotations.

17 In his earlier *Romanticism and Religion*, Prickett had already written about "Coleridge and Wordsworth as religious thinkers" in relation to a "minority tradition" of Victorian writers and theologians (4). Prickett has made several important contributions to the rethinking of the relationship between literature and religion in the nineteenth century, and I am greatly indebted to his work.

18 The term is described as "vague" by Chadwick (*Victorian* 1:545). It was first used by Arthur Hugh Clough and A.P. Stanley (ibid., 1:544n2) but was popularized by an article in the *Edinburgh Review* on church parties by W.J. Conybeare.

19 The most comprehensive discussion of Tractarianism and Victorian literature in general is Raymond Chapman's *Faith and Revolt*.

20 For a thorough discussion of Tractarian poetry see G.B. Tennyson, *Devotional Poetry*.

21 See Baker, *Novel*, for an old but still useful account of the novel and the Oxford Movement. Wolff has an extensive discussion of Tractarian and anti-Tractarian fiction in chapter 2 of *Gains and Losses*, 111–200.

22 Quoted in Prickett, *Romanticism*, 119.

23 See *Apologia*, 33–5 for Newman's account of Hurrell Froude's character and influence.

24 See Gilley, "Ecclesiology," for an argument that makes use of a similar assumption, though from a point of view that is less sympathetic to the Church of England.

25 Coleridge's influence on a group of Anglican historians is discussed in Forbes, *Anglican Idea*.

26 As we shall see, this anticipates Benjamin Jowett's contribution to *Essays and Reviews*. See David Jasper's introduction to the Fortress Press edition of Coleridge's *Confessions* (7–16) for a discussion of its relationship to *Essays and Reviews*. In *Victorian Interpretation*, Suzy Anger discusses the cultural impact of the mode of scriptural hermeneutics exemplified in *Essays and Reviews*; see especially chapter 1, 22–48.

27 Williamson, *Liberalism*, provides a detailed account of Thomas Arnold's religious thought and his influence. For the latter see especially the section entitled "Arnoldism and the Later Nineteenth Century," 95–111. A more recent discussion of the senior Arnold may be found in Zemka, *Testaments*, 68–99.

28 Here I am drastically summarizing Prickett's argument in his commentary on Kingsley's *Hypatia* (1853) and Newman's *Callista* (1855) in *Origins*, 222–47.

29 See the two works by Alter, *Biblical Narrative* and *Biblical Poetry*; Bal's *Anti-Covenant*, *Death*, and *Lethal Love*; Frye's *Great Code* and *Words*; Kermode's *Genesis*; Kermode and Alter's *Literary Guide*; and Bloom's *Book of J*. In his Bucknell Lecture, "New Ways with Bible Stories," Kermode explains the value of reading biblical narratives with the techniques of secular literary criticism and gives some background and context for this critical development.

30 Rowell et al., *Love's Redeeming Work*, indicates the extent of this tradition.

31 Fiddes has also edited *The Novel, Spirituality and Modern Culture: Eight Novelists Write about Their Craft and Their Context*. See Hodgson for a theologian's reading of the fiction of George Eliot.

32 Since the late 1980s, the journal *Literature and Theology* has provided a forum for this kind of interdisciplinary work. David Jasper served for a number of years as the journal's editor, and T.R. Wright as an associate editor.

33 See for example his *Grace and Necessity*, theological reflections on literature, and *Lost Icons*, in which he reflects on contemporary culture. During a study leave in 2007, Rowan Williams wrote *Dostoevsky: Language, Faith and Fiction*. I regret that this book appeared too late to have an impact on my own study; I

am very sympathetic to the approach taken by Dr Williams in his important and fascinating book.

34 Another useful account of the position of radical orthodoxy is provided by Catherine Pickstock, who writes that it "insists that the secular postmodern is only the logical outcome of the rationalism of modernity, and in no sense its inversion. And whereas the postmodern indulges in 'playful' recuperation of the premodern cultural inheritance, radical orthodoxy rediscovers certain pre-modern themes as once again viable, by showing how they were not so trammelled by a dogmatic 'metaphysics' as both modernists and postmodernists have tended to assume" (*After Writing*, xii–xiii).

35 Janet Larson's *Dickens and the Broken Scripture* is a valuable book on Dickens and the Bible.

CHAPTER ONE

1 See Qualls, *Secular Pilgrims*, 6–7, 190–3.

2 In "*Vanity Fair* and the Celestial City," Baker reads *Vanity Fair* from an Augustinian perspective but does not devote much critical attention to the complexities of Thackeray's text.

3 See Ray, *Thackeray* 1:131–2, 2:121–3.

4 I am quoting from the more reliable text of this letter in Harden, ed., *Letters* 1:228.

5 See, for example, *Thackeray, Letters* 1:467.

6 This is an allusion to Ephesians 2:12, and, as Gordon Ray notes, the same biblical phrase forms the basis of a well-known passage in Newman's *Apologia* (see Thackeray, *Letters* 2:309n80).

7 Also relevant here are the comments on Thackeray's morality in the reviews of *Vanity Fair* by Bell and Forster. More comments by Charlotte Brontë can be found in her letters to W.S. Williams, reprinted in Tillotson and Hawes, eds., 51–2.

8 It is not clear what this word means, or whether it is a proper name. For a summary of scholarly conjecture on this topic, see Crenshaw, "Ecclesiastes," 271–2.

9 The Jerusalem Bible translates the word as "futility" and the New English Bible as "emptiness." My own biblical quotations are from the King James Bible.

10 See Finley, "Bunyan," for an excellent discussion of the Victorian reception of Bunyan. Finley's analysis of J.A. Froude's view of Bunyan as the representative of a lost world of theological wholeness (78–9) accords with my sense of Thackeray's use of *Pilgrim's Progress*.

11 For *Vanity Fair* as satire, see Burch, "'The World.'"

12 The article on "world" in Rahner and Vorgrimler, *Theological Dictionary*, is the main source for my discussion of the theological significance of this word.

13 The *Oxford English Dictionary* (OED) cites *Bleak House* under "world," 17a: "The

world is before you; and it is most probable that as you enter it, so it will receive you."

14 The quotations from novelists that illustrate the phrase "man of the world" in the OED make it clear that for Thackeray it would have more pejorative implications than it does today.

15 Although his focus in reading *Vanity Fair* is very different from mine, Iser makes a similar point about the role of gaps or absences in the novel. He comments that "the reader is given only as much information as will keep him oriented and interested, but the narrator deliberately leaves open the inferences that are to be drawn from this information" (*Implied Reader*, 106). I am grateful to Michael Lund for drawing my attention to this passage.

6 These points are noted in Shillingsburg's edition of *Vanity Fair*; see also his useful discussion in "Reading the Boring Bits: The Crawley Genealogy."

17 For a discussion of this aspect of Broad Church moral thinking, see Cockshut, *Anglican Attitudes*, 64–5.

18 Among the many analyses of nineteenth-century liberal Protestant theology, Karl Barth's essay on Schleiermacher stands out. For discussions of ethnocentrism and racism in liberal theology, see Almog, "The Racial Motif"; Alan T. Davies, "The Aryan Christ"; and Heschel, "Image of Judaism."

CHAPTER TWO

1 For useful overviews of the topic from quite different perspectives, see Marianne Thormählen's *The Brontës* and John Maynard's "Brontës and Religion."

2 Recent discussions of Brontë and anti-Catholicism may be found in Schiefelbein, "Baptism"; Griffin, *Anti-Catholicism*; Wheeler, *Enemies*; and Peschier, *Discourses*. Peterson discusses *Jane Eyre* in the context of the autobiographies of missionary women.

3 Since human attention is finite, any expansion of the canon in one direction is usually accompanied by a contraction in a different direction. Novels of religious controversy are less accessible now than they were a generation ago, when affordable annotated editions of works such as Newman's *Loss and Gain*, Ward's *Robert Elsmere*, and Pater's *Marius the Epicurean* were available in the Oxford World's Classics or Penguin Classics series.

4 Jauss sees the individual literary work as existing "within the objectifiable system of expectations that arises for each work in the historical moment of its appearance, from a pre-understanding of the genre, from the form and themes of already familiar works, and from the opposition between poetic and practical language" ("Literary History," 22).

5 Kathleen Tillotson provides an excellent discussions of the "novel with a purpose" in the 1840s (*Novels*, 115–25) and the religious novel of ideas (125–37).

6 My sample includes the following novels: Charles Maurice Davies, *Philip Pater-*

noster (1858); J.A. Froude, *Shadows of the Clouds* (1847), and *The Nemesis of Faith* (1849); William Gresley, *Charles Lever* (1841); Anne Howard, *Mary Spencer* (1844); Geraldine Jewsbury, *Zoe* (1845); Charles Kingsley, *Yeast* (1848 serial; 1851), and *Alton Locke* (1850); John Mason Neale, *Ayton Priory* (1843); John Henry Newman, *Loss and Gain* (1848); Francis E. Paget, *St Antholin's* (1841), and *Milford Malvoisin* (1842); Elizabeth Missing Sewell, *Margaret Percival* (1847); William Sewell, *Hawkstone* (1845); Charlotte Elizabeth Tonna, *Conformity* (1841), and *Falsehood and Truth* (1841); Charlotte Mary Yonge, *Abbeychurch* (1844), and *The Castle Builders* (1854).

7   See Colby, *Woman*, chapter 4 (145–209); Jay, *Religion*; Kelly, "Evangelicalism."

8   For contemporary commentary on the religious novel of the 1840s see "Religious Stories" (1848) and the review by William Francis Wilkinson of *The Rector in Search of a Curate* (1843).

9   The first recorded use of both "Anglo-Catholicism" and "Anglo-Catholic" was in 1838. Brontë's references to the Oxford Movement are of course anachronistic in a novel set in 1812; the novel thus historically displaces its treatment of religious controversy as well as industrial conflict.

10 More evidence of Brontë's dislike of the Anglo-Catholic movement can be found in her condemnation of two sermons against dissent, in the course of which she declares, "My conscience will not let me be either a Puseyite or a Hookist" (in Smith, ed., *Letters* 1:214). See also the satirical reference in Brontë's letter to Hartley Coleridge (ibid., 1:240) and, later in her career, her comment to George Smith about the "Puseyite priesthood" (ibid., 2:583). In a letter of 1853 she imagines the response to *Villette* of a "clever, hard headed high-church ecclesiastic of sinewy bigotry and genuine talent" (ibid., 3:152).

11 Brontë expresses her admiration for and support of Maurice in a letter to Elizabeth Gaskell written after hearing of his dismissal from his King's professorship. She writes, "When Men – calling themselves Churchmen condemn teaching like Maurice's, what are their own tenets? Such as for my part – it would seem to me equivalent to raving madness to hold" (Smith, ed., *Letters* 3:215).

12 Chadwick discusses the Athanasian Creed several times in the second volume of *The Victorian Church*. See especially 2:150.

13 Brontë's affinities with Kingsley are pointed out in Smith's note to her comments on Elizabeth of Hungary in a letter of 1852 (see Smith, ed., *Letters* 3:33 and 3:34n4).

14 See Dolin, "Territory," 203–4, for a discussion of Brontë's attempt to use, and resistance to, the Thackerayan narrative voice in *Shirley*.

15 There is a striking similarity between this passage and the imagery in the "Finale" of George Eliot's *Middlemarch*: "Her full nature, like that river of which Cyrus broke the strength, spent itself in channels which had no great name on the earth" (822).

16 Southey made the suggestion in his *Colloquies on the Progress and Prospects of Society*. See Anson, *The Call*, 26-7; Allchin, *Rebellion*, 40-3.

17 See Reed for a detailed discussion of women and Victorian Anglo-Catholicism.

18 For the Lewes riot see Chandler, *Life and Work,* 88-90, and Neale, *Lewes Riot.*

19 See also Griffin, *Anti-Catholisism*, chapter 1, 27-61.

20 See Vicinus, *Independent Women,* chapter 2, 46-84.

21 See Rogal, "Methodist Connection," 11-12, for an analysis of this incident in relation to Brontë's treatment of Methodism in *Shirley.*

22 Keble, "Septuagesima Sunday," in *The Christian Year*, 42, lines 1-4.

23 A similar reworking of scripture occurs much later in the novel, in Shirley's youthful essay on Eve as the first bluestocking (vol. 3, chapter 4). These passages are discussed in some detail in Lawson, "Imagining Eve."

24 See my "Locking George Sand in the Attic" for a discussion of Sand's influence on Victorian women novelists.

25 Glen contrasts Brontë's conclusion with the "muted optimism" of such social-problem novels as *Mary Barton* and *Dombey and Son* ("*Shirley*," 132).

26 Noting Charlotte Brontë's admiration for Carlyle's "manly love of truth" (Smith, ed., *Letters* 2:202), Pam Morris suggests that in *Shirley* Brontë is presenting herself as a "hero as ... woman of letters" ("Heroes," 307).

CHAPTER THREE

1 It is difficult to verify the exact scope of Yonge's oeuvre in the absence of a definitive bibliography. The best available is that compiled by Marghanita Laski and Kathleen Tillotson.

2 Kingsley wrote to John Parker, Yonge's publisher, that *Heartsease* was "the most delightful and wholesome novel I ever read." The letter is reproduced in C. Coleridge, *Yonge*, 348. For Tennyson's enthusiastic reading of Yonge, see Battiscombe, *Charlotte Mary Yonge*, 118-19. George Eliot mentions her desire to read Yonge's *Book of Golden Deeds* in Eliot, *Letters* 5:444, 10 October 1875.

3 *The Heir of Redclyffe* was briefly in print in the late twentieth century in two editions, the Oxford World's Classics and Wordsworth Classics series. All quotations from *The Heir* are from Barbara Dennis's Oxford edition. Virago published both *The Clever Woman of the Family* (1985) and *The Daisy Chain* (1988) but they have been allowed to go out of print. In 2001 Broadview brought out a new edition of *The Clever Woman.*

4 Charles Dickens wrote part of this article, but it is clear from Harry Stone's headnote that Collins wrote the passages I have quoted.

5 For a discussion of Hutton as a literary critic see Woodfield, *R.H. Hutton.* He discusses Hutton's response to George Eliot in chapter 6, 152-84.

6 Gavin Budge discusses *The Heir of Redclyffe* in the context of an argument about

the philosophical underpinnings of both typology and realistic fiction. In rejecting George Levine's "rigid opposition" between romance and realism in the nineteenth century (Budge, "Realism," 197), he reads *the Heir of Redclyffe* in a manner analogous my own.

7 See the preface to Mare and Percival, *Best-Seller*, 5–6.

8 "The Second Spring" was preached on 13 July 1852 in St Mary's, Oscott.

9 See Sandbach-Dahlström, *Be Good*; Sturrock, "*Heaven*"; Wheatley, "Death."

10 Charlotte Yonge told Ethel Romanes that she could not feel much sympathy for "the *Lux Mundi* school of thought" (Romanes, *Charlotte*, 190).

11 For a discussion of some of the reasons for this, see Archer, "Review."

12 In the first lecture, Keble uses a version of the doctrine of reserve to defend the use of Latin. Like Wordsworth in the preface to *Lyrical Ballads*, he laments the nature of popular periodical literature and continues, "Amid such circumstances, I think it a happy chance that, in this important task, we should be governed, paramountly, by statutes framed to protect your reputation, and the serious study of a serious subject, rather than to produce a short-lived pleasure of the ear, or satisfy the expectations of clever men" (*Lectures* 1:17–18).

13 See Prickett, "Church," 109–19; Tennyson, *Devotional Poetry*, 56–71; Rowell, "John Keble," 42–66. Keble's poetry has all but disappeared from view. It is remarkable that while Victorian poetry anthologies grow in size, as more and more neglected poets are rediscovered, the works of the most popular poet of the century are not included and remain largely neglected by scholars. Prickett points out that *The Christian Year* sold an average of ten thousand copies a year for fifty years (*Romanticism*, 104).

14 The Oxford edition of Keble's poems does not reprint the Advertisement.

15 Engel (*Heir*, 133–4) makes some comments about the importance of the calendar, but he does not take account of all of the examples, and he makes some connections between dates in the novel and the proper readings for that day that are to my mind far-fetched. As I have suggested, the important point about Guy's birthday is that it occurs in Holy Week, not that there is a lesson from Ruth appointed for 28 March.

16 See Yonge, *The Heir*, 212; *Musings*, lvi. The phrase is a quotation from John 5:35.

17 For more details about Yonge's responses to Byron see Tillotson, "Charlotte Yonge as a Critic of Literature."

18 This epigraph on the title page does not appear in Barbara Dennis's Oxford edition of *The Heir of Redclyffe*; I am here citing the fifteenth edition published by Macmillan in 1864. The entire epigraph reads as follows:

> None of all the wreaths ye prize,
> But was nurst by weeping skies;
> Keen March winds, soft April showers,

> Braced the roots, embalmed the flowers.
> So, if e'er that second spring
> Her green robe o'er you shall fling,
> Stern self-mastery, tearful prayer,
> Must the way of bliss prepare.
> How should else earth's flowerets prove
> Meet for those pure crowns above.
>   LYRA INNOCENTIUM

The lines are the conclusion to the poem "May Garlands" in Keble's *Christian Year*, 308, lines 33–42.

CHAPTER FOUR

1 There is a thorough treatment of Thomas Arnold's thought, including his doctrine of the Church, in Williamson, *Liberalism*.
2 For a study of Renan and Judaism see Almog, "Racial Motif."
3 A lively exchange on the VICTORIA listserv in May 1994 indicates the passions aroused by the issue of Arnold and anti-Semitism. This discussion is accessible by searching the topic "'Hebraic'/'Hellenic' faiths" in the archive of VICTORIA: 19th-Century British Culture & Society, <http://listserv.indiana.edu/archives/victoria.html>. There is a significant body of scholarship on Christian theology and anti-Semitism in the nineteenth and early twentieth centuries. See Almog, "Racial Motif"; Alan T. Davies, "Aryan Christ," "Aryan Myth," "Racism"; and Heschel, "Image of Judaism." By the standards of some of the theologians discussed by these scholars, Arnold seems fairly innocuous.
4 The bibliography of scholarship and commentary on Arnold's religious writings is substantial. The main critical issue could be expressed as a repetition of John Henry Newman's famous question in *Apologia Pro Vita Sua* about Matthew Arnold's father, "But is *he* a Christian?" (see Scott, "Arnold's Vision," 262). Scott's article and the books by James Livingston (*Matthew Arnold*) and Ruth apRoberts (*Arnold and God*) represent the most important of the defences of Arnold's religious thought from the more negative views of commentators such as T.S. Eliot (see the discussion in *The Use of Poetry*, 103–19, and the essays "Arnold and Pater" and "Francis Herbert Bradley") and F.H. Bradley. A.O.J. Cockshut (*Unbelievers*, 59–72) provides an insightful discussion that is ultimately unsympathetic to Arnold. Livingston argues persuasively – like Cockshut – for regarding Arnold as a religious modernist. Both Livingston and apRoberts place Arnold's religious writings at the centre rather than on the margins of his critical project. This approach convincingly recovers a Victorian Matthew Arnold who has often been obscured by our preoccupation with the literary-humanist Arnold.

5 For Arnold's mockery of Anglo-Catholic ritual, see DeLaura, *Hebrew*, 59–61. DeLaura quotes the same passage from *Literature and Dogma* that I quote below in the text.

6 Arnold is no doubt referring in part to John Henry Newman, with whom he wrestled all through his career. See DeLaura, *Hebrew*, 130.

7 For example, see Cockshut, *Unbelievers*, 70.

8 "More and more mankind will discover that we have to turn to poetry to interpret life for us, to console us, to sustain us. Without poetry, our science will appear incomplete; and most of what now passes with us for religion and philosophy will be replaced by poetry" (in *Complete Prose* 9:161–2).

9 See, for example, lines 39–42 in M. Arnold, *Poems*, 287:

> With penitential cries they kneel
> And wrestle; rising then, with bare
> And white uplifted faces stand,
> Passing the Host from hand to hand.

10 See Nardin's discussion of apRoberts's *The Moral Trollope* and Letwin's *The Gentleman in Trollope* (Nardin, *Trollope*, 138–48).

11 See Shaw's discussion of *Barchester Towers* in *Victorians and Mystery*, 122–32.

12 Cf. Matthew 25:29.

13 For details of the trip see Super, *Chronicler*, 88–94.

14 The statement occurs in the preface to the Popular Edition of *Literature and Dogma*. Renan is somewhat more cautious in the *Life of Jesus*, noting that "up to this time a miracle has never been proved" (59), but in practice his "historical criticism" operates according to the same principle as Arnold's; for Renan operates on the assumption "that a supernatural account cannot be admitted as such, that it always implies credulity or imposture, that the duty of the historian is to explain it" (60).

15 "This was the third blow, which finally shattered my faith in the Anglican Church" (Newman, *Apologia*, 133). For Newman's discussion of the Jerusalem bishopric see 131–6.

16 For Newman's explanation of the branch theory, see *Apologia*, 72–3. Newman condemns the Jerusalem bishopric with characteristic wit: "If England could be in Palestine, Rome might be in England" (139).

17 For a useful summary of the history of the Jerusalem bishopric see Chadwick, *Victorian Church* 1:189–93.

18 Some of them are documented in Williamson, *Liberalism*: see chapter 1, 25–66.

19 Arnold was not entirely comfortable with Renan's book, though he preferred it to the rationalistic criticism of Bishop Colenso. In "The Function of Criticism," he wrote that "M. Renan's attempt is, for criticism, of the most real interest and

importance, since, with all its difficulty, a fresh synthesis of the New Testament *data* ... is the very essence of the religious problem, as now presented; and only by efforts in this direction can it receive a solution" (in *Complete Prose* 3:279).

20 Like its nine predecessors, "The Clergyman Who Subscribes to Colenso" was first published in *The Pall Mall Gazette* (25 January 1866).

21 For a discussion of the doctrine of accommodation in relation to historiography, see Forbes, *Liberal Anglican*. For the intellectual background to Arnold's theology, see Christensen, "Arnold's Debt."

CHAPTER FIVE

1 Richard Altick cites an illustration from the *Evangelical Magazine* (1800) of a "spiritual barometer" in which novel reading is represented as minus 40 on a scale that descended to "perdition" at minus 70. For the compiler of this barometer, reading fiction was ten degrees worse than attending the theatre, and ten degrees higher than such things as "masquerades; drunkenness; adultery" (*Common Reader*, 114).

2 I am quoting from the copy of the second edition of Hennell's *Inquiry* (1841), signed Mary Ann Evans and dated 1 January 1842, which is held by the Dr Williams Library, London, as part of a bequest by George Henry Lewes's son. According to Ashton, there is evidence that Mary Ann had read the book earlier than this date (36).

3 See for example Willey, *Studies* 214–60; Knoepflmacher, *Humanism*; Prickett, "Romantics." Shaffer provides an excellent analysis of *Daniel Deronda* in the context of "the mythological school in biblical criticism" ("*Kubla Khan*," 225–91). Carpenter discusses Eliot's fiction in relation to Protestant apocalyptic exegesis (see *George Eliot*). I find her numerological points and her use of the Anglican lectionary to comment on *Adam Bede* unconvincing. Many other critical discussions of particular works make reference to the history of ideas, and Rosemary Ashton's *Life* offers a lucid summary of Eliot's intellectual career, relating it suggestively to her fiction. Two anthologies of Eliot's prose edited by Ashton (*Writings*) and Byatt (*Selected Essays*) offer helpful commentary and notes.

4 See Ashton, *A Life*, 171 for a discussion of what she calls the "androgynous" narrator of *Scenes of Clerical Life*. Some Victorian readers, notably Charles Dickens, realized that "George Eliot" was probably a woman, so the gender of the narrator is not a straightforward matter; my point is simply that Mary Ann Evans, in assuming the pseudonym George Eliot, sought to impersonate a male narrative voice. See also the discussion of the narrator's voice in the early fiction in Beer, *George Eliot*, 52–81.

5 Notable feminist discussions of *Adam Bede* include Gilbert and Gubar, *Mad-*

woman (1979), 491–9; Sedgwick, *Between Men* (1985), 134–46; Brady, *George Eliot* (1992), 84–93. The term "camouflage" is used by Gilbert and Gubar (491).

6 Hodgson is not attentive to this use of historical distance in Eliot's fiction. For the narrator of the novel, the events of sixty years earlier are already part of an earlier phase of historical development.

7 Although it may have been well known in intellectual circles that Mary Ann Evans was the translator of the *Life of Jesus*, the translation was in fact published anonymously. Her translation of *The Essence of Christianity* was the only work to appear under the name "Marian Evans."

8 Hetty's reference, in her confession to Dinah, to her child as being "like a heavy weight hanging round my neck" (*Bede*, 453) seems to allude to Coleridge's "The Rime of the Ancient Mariner." Arthur finds this poem to be "a strange, striking thing," though he "can hardly make head or tail of it as a story" (65), which is perhaps because he has trouble accepting the fact that some actions have inevitable and irreversible consequences. As for Wordsworth's contributions to *Lyrical Ballads*, Arthur pronounces them "twaddling stuff" (65).

9 Notably W.J. Harvey. See *The Art of George Eliot*, 115–21, 248n.

10 The Thirty-Nine Articles are a set of doctrinal statements that define the Church of England's position in relation to a variety of contentious theological questions such as the nature of the eucharist and predestination. They took their final form in 1571, and are printed in the *Book of Common Prayer*.

11 It may be relevant to note here that in *Origins of Narrative*, Stephen Prickett discusses what might be called the "novelization" of the Bible in the Romantic period. He draws two significant conclusions: first, that the Bible ceased to be read "as though it spoke with a single omniscient dogmatic voice" (108), and second, *pace* Hans Frei's argument in *The Eclipse of Biblical Narrative*, "it was the English novel tradition that was influenced by the rise of biblical criticism rather than *vice versa*" (109).

12 This was the view of Henry James, who said of the marriage of "the nun-like Dinah" that the reader of the novel "sees in it a base concession" ("Life," 1,005).

13 Hodgson, who describes Dinah as "the mediatrix of a divine redemptive presence" (*Mystery*, 52), misses the fact that she has her own limitations and blindnesses. Charlotte Mary Yonge uses a similar description of Laura to indicate her self-absorption after she has agreed to a secret engagement to Philip: "On coming home, she ran up to her own room, and sitting by the open window, gave herself up to that delicious dream of new-found joy" (*Heir*, 122).

14 See also the repetition of the phrase "a great gulf" at the end of chapter 43 (436). In the parable of Lazarus and the rich man, Abraham tells the rich man, who is in hell, "Between us and you there is a great gulf fixed: so that they which would pass from hence to you cannot" (Luke 16:26).

15 Hodgson argues that George Eliot "was actually closer to Schleiermacher's than to Feuerbach's understanding of religious feeling" (*Mystery*, 197n15).

16 Strauss describes Schleiermacher's view as follows:

> As a member of the church, he could have no satisfaction but in perfect equality, in the consciousness that all receive alike, both in kind and manner, from the same source. And as a teacher and spokesman to the church, he could not possibly attempt the task of elevating old and young, without distinction, to the idea of God and of man: he must rather attack their faith as a groundless one, or else endeavour to strengthen and confirm it while knowing it to be groundless. As thus in the matter of religion an impassable gulf would be fixed between two parties in the church, the speculative theology threatens us with the distinction of an esoteric and exoteric doctrine, which ill accords with the declaration of Christ, that all shall be taught of God. The scientific alone have the foundation of the faith: the unscientific have only the faith, and receive it only by means of tradition. (*Life*, 781–2)

17 For a more detailed discussion of the reception of *Daniel Deronda* see my *Reception-History of George Eliot's Fiction*, 59–84.
18 Ashton asks, "Why does an agnostic, one who respects the need for religious belief in others but repudiates it for herself, set out, without irony, a religious ideal? Moreover, is the history of Judaism any less fraught with superstition, narrowness, exclusiveness than that of Christianity?" (*A Life*, 347). Hodgson notes in response that "Jews for the most part have been the victims of history, not victimizers, and conditions of persecution and oppression have given their religion a distinctive ethical and communal intensity that appealed to George Eliot" (*Mystery*, 147).
19 See Henry, *George Eliot*, 113–23.

CHAPTER SIX

1 Another important book on this topic is Jan Jedrzejewski's *Thomas Hardy and the Church*. Other studies of Hardy's religious attitudes as they manifest themselves in his works include David DeLaura's classic article "The 'Ache of Modernism'"; Chapman, "Arguing"; Holland, "Indictment"; McNees, "Typology"; Nemesvari, "Word"; Deborah Collins, *Thomas Hardy*; and Stave, *Decline*.
2 The controversy takes its name from the Reverend G.C. Gorham, whom Bishop Phillpotts of Exeter refused to institute to a living due to Gorham's views on the doctrine of baptismal regeneration. The case was appealed to the Judicial Committee of the Privy Council, which found in Gorham's favour. As a result, a number of High Church clergy became Roman Catholics. See the discussion in Cockshut, *Attitudes*, 39–61.
3 For documentation of the use of Arnold's ideas in *A Laodicean* see Taylor, *Neglected*, 97, 108–9, and 191–2n.

4 Several critics, including Moynahan (*Casterbridge*, 128) have drawn attention to a passage in *The Life and Work* dated Easter Sunday, 1885, in which Hardy discusses the literary qualities of the biblical narratives, commenting that "their so-called simplicity is, in fact, the simplicity of the highest cunning" (177). Hardy uses their narrative realism as an argument *against* their authenticity: "Is not the fact of their being so convincing, an argument, not for their actuality, but for the actuality of a consummate artist who was no more content with what Nature offered than Sophocles and Pheidias were content?" (177).

5 For example from *Tower*, chapter 40: "To speak of their doings on this pilgrimage, of ingress and egress, of tangent and parallax, of external and internal contact, would avail nothing. Is it not all written in the Chronicles of the Astronomical Society?" (263). The passage parodies a recurring formula in 1 and 2 Kings. See, e.g., 1 Kings 14:19.

6 This has been demonstrated in J. Hillis Miller's analysis of chapter 11 of the novel (*Fiction*, 128–40).

7 There is in fact a recurrent identification in Hardy's work of religion and alcohol, two things that the Victorian temperance movement tried to keep far apart. For an interesting discussion see Hands, *Preacher*, 93–6.

8 Elsewhere in *Tess*, Hardy quotes from poem 33 of *In Memoriam* (174).

9 In one passage, a just-awakened Tess regards Angel "as Eve at her second waking might have regarded Adam" (172). It is interesting that Tess is compared with a snake in this same passage, as though she carries within her the cause of her expulsion from Paradise.

10 See Barrineau's note, *Tess* 410.

11 Nemesvari's article ("Word") is a valuable discussion of Hardy's use of deutero-canonical biblical materials in *Jude the Obscure*, and it suggested to me the title for this chapter. The epigraphs to two of the parts of *Jude* are from apocryphal books: 1 Esdras (Part One) and the Additions to the Book of Esther (Part Six).

12 See the letters to Lady Jeune (17 November 1895); Sir George Douglas (20 November 1895); Edmund Gosse (20 November 1895), *Letters* 2:97–9. Hardy writes to Douglas, "I fancied that, having made Sue become a Christian, & recant all her 'views' at the end, I shd be deemed High-Churchy in tone: you can imagine my surprise at the *Guardian* saying that everything sacred is brought into contempt, &c. in the novel!" (2:98).

13 Cf. Galatians 5:17. "For the flesh lusteth against the Spirit, and the Spirit against the flesh; and these are contrary the one to the other: so that ye cannot do the things that ye would."

14 Norman Holland rather unconvincingly bases an argument on the fact that "Jude" is German for Jew ("Indictment," 51), although it is certainly true that the abundance of biblical allusion associates Hardy's hero with many aspects of Jewish history and culture.

15 I am indebted to Eleanor McNees's valuable article on "Reverse Typology in *Jude the Obscure.*"

16 Patricia Ingham's notes to *Jude the Obscure* identify four comparisons of Jude to Job and eight of Jude to Jesus Christ.

17 Richard Dellamora briefly discusses the erotic aspect of this passage, noting that in Hardy's earliest draft it referred to Sue rather than Phillotson (see "Male," 153–5).

18 Considering the university in relation to the attributes of the Christian church, Keble finds it lacking in catholicity: "For by the mere judgement of the eyes, this Athens of ours belongs not so much to the poor, as to those who were born to some position in the world" (Keble's speech has been translated by Paul Jeffreys-Powell but is unpublished; this passage is quoted in Prickett, "Church and University," 204, and it is thanks to Stephen Prickett that we know the actual contents of Keble's speech; see "Social Conscience").

CHAPTER SEVEN

1 Pater had been the tutor of Mary's husband Humphry Ward, who then became his colleague at Brasenose College. Pater is generally regarded as one of the models for the character of Edward Langham in *Elsmere* (Sutherland, *Mrs Humphry*, 121). I should note here that I refer to Ward by her own given name of Mary throughout, although I cite her works as written by "Mrs Humphry Ward," since this was the name under which she published.

2 Wolff classifies *Robert Elsmere* as a "novel of doubt," like works such as Geraldine Jewsbury's *Zoe* and J.A. Froude's *The Nemesis of Faith*. However, in view of the emphasis on reconstruction in the concluding part of *Elsmere*, it might be better to call it a novel of "neo-Christianity," borrowing Frederic Harrison's term for the writers of *Essays and Reviews*.

3 *Robert Elsmere* is still discussed regularly by critics. See Hapgood, "Reconceiving"; Loesberg, "Deconstruction"; Spacks, "A Dull Book"; Towheed, "Gladsonte's Reception"; and Wilt, "Romance." Pater has often been considered as a precursor to postmodernism, and he is often discussed in terms of masculinity, but my impression is that *Marius* is no longer very widely taught. Perhaps it makes too many demands on the present-day reader, with its lack of action and dialogue and its frequent Latin words and phrases. In 2007 the small reprint press Valancourt Books brought out an edition of *Marius* edited by Gerald Monsman. My quotations from *Marius* are all from Michael Levey's Penguin edition.

4 Hapgood is quoting Thomas G. Selby, *The Theology of Modern Fiction* (1890), 191.

5 For details see Sutherland's chapter entitled "*Elsmere* Mania: 1888" (*Mrs Humphry*, 125–31). The critical reception of *Elsmere* is also discussed by W. Peterson in *Heretic*, 159–84.

6 "With ideas about private morality and about doctrine which would probably have scandalized Pius X, most church-goers today are in some respects Modernists" (A.N. Wilson, *God's Funeral*, 354).

7 See Sutherland, *Mrs Humphry*, 79–80 for an account of Ward's pamphlet "Unbelief and Sin: A Protest addressed to those who attended the Bampton Lecture of Sunday, March 6ᵗʰ." Sutherland suggests that "Pater's cult of homosexuality was alluded to in a veiled way" (*Mrs Humphry*, 79). The pamphlet was suppressed because a "well-known High Church clergyman" noted it bore no printer's name and was therefore illegal (Ward, "Sin," 161); after the publicity surrounding *Robert Elsmere*, it was published in the *North American Review* with an introduction by Ward.

8 E.g., "We find Mrs Ward herself describing the old Unitarian scheme as one wholly destitute of logic; but in what respect she improves upon it I have not yet perceived" (Gladstone, "Battle," 781); Elsmere "carries his learning, his fine intellect, his goodness, nay, his saintliness, into a kind of Unitarianism" (Pater, "Review," 65).

9 Cf. Lewis: "A man who was merely a man and said the sort of things Jesus said would not be a great moral teacher. He would either be a lunatic – on a level with the man who says he is a poached egg – or else he would be the Devil of Hell" (*Mere Christianity*, 52).

10 See Cupitt, 169–73.

11 A.O.J. Cockshut contrasts Arnold with Dean Inge as an example of a Protestant Modernist: "Dean Inge was trying to get back to the hard core of historical truth. For Arnold, the only essential core was in the mind of man – certain moral truths which Jesus had discovered" (*Unbelievers*, 72).

12 For some examples, including Ward's own *Helbeck of Bannisdale*, see Hogan, "Angel or Eve?"; and for some parallel examples from the visual arts see Casteras, "Domestic Threat."

13 Bergonzi's *Victorian Wanderer* is an excellent account of the life of Mary Ward's father Thomas Arnold, and it is a useful complement to Sutherland's biography of Mary.

14 See Wilt for a comparison of the two novels and their heroes. Wilt's article gives one of the few extended analyses of *Richard Meynell*; she notes the pervasive imagery of war and violence in the novel ("Romance," 38–9).

15 In the introduction to *Richard Meynell* in the Westmoreland Edition, Ward wrote: "Religion, as most of us believe, is imperishable, and the churches, so far as they are religious, share in religion's immortality. Something, indeed, must change; either the outward symbolism of dogma and rite, or the inner spirit which gives them life. Protestantism represents the one process; modern Catholicism presents the most striking example of the second" (viii).

16 J. Hillis Miller suggests that Pater is "the nearest thing to Nietzsche" in English literature ("Walter Pater," 97).

17 "I can remember a dinner-party at his house, where a great tumult arose over some abrupt statement of his made to the High Church wife of a well-known

Professor. Pater had been in some way pressed controversially beyond the point of wisdom, and had said suddenly that no reasonable person could govern his life by the opinions or actions of a man who died eighteen centuries ago. The Professor and his wife – I look back to them both with the warmest affection – departed hurriedly, in agitation; and the rest of us only gradually found out what had happened" (Ward, *Recollections* 1:161–2).

18 See "Bishop of Oxford on Scepticism," in Seiler, *Critical Heritage*, 94–7. George Eliot wrote in a letter to John Blackwood, responding to Margaret Oliphant's review of Pater's *Renaissance* in *Blackwood's*, "I agreed very warmly with the remarks made by your contributor this month on Mr Pater's book, which seems to me quite poisonous in its false principles of criticism and false conceptions of life" (Eliot, *Letters* 5:455, 5 November 1873).

19 A.P. Stanley was a canon of Canterbury Cathedral when Pater was a schoolboy in Canterbury, and Pater would thus have heard his preaching during the most religious phase of his youth. See Levey, *Case*, 51–5.

20 Quoted in Shuter, *Rereading*, 43. Shuter provides a fairly detailed account of the unpublished manuscripts.

21 Iser (*Walter Pater*, 191n91) and Loesberg (*Aestheticism*, 215n6) have lists of critics who take one or other side in this debate. See also Rhodes, *The Lion*, 66–7. Wolff believes that Marius dies a Christian, and he includes the novel in his chapter on High Church novels, though with the caveat that Marius is "a most peculiar kind of Tractarian novel indeed" (*Gains and Losses*, 189).

22 Shuter writes, "Pater never recanted, and whatever it is that Marius experiences, it can hardly be called a conversion" (*Rereading*, 50). According to Harold Bloom, "Though Epicureanism … is supposedly the dominant element of only the second part of the novel, its presence in the book's title is no accident, as in the broad sense Marius, like Pater, lives and dies an Epicurean" ("Introduction," xvii).

23 See Dwight Culler for the Victorian habit of using analogies with the past in controversial writing; Culler discusses *Marius* in *Mirror*, 258–70.

WORKS CITED

———◄○►———

Abrams, M.H. *The Mirror and the Lamp: Romantic Theory and the Critical Tradition*. Oxford: Oxford University Press, 1953.
– *Natural Supernaturalism: Tradition and Revolution in Romantic Literature*. New York: Norton, 1971.
Adams, James Eli. *Dandies and Desert Saints: Styles of Victorian Masculinity*. Ithaca and London: Cornell University Press, 1995.
Ahmad, Suleiman M. Introduction. In Thomas Hardy, *Two on a Towerh*. Edited by Suleiman M. Ahmad, xi–xxiii.
Allchin, A.M. *The Silent Rebellion: Anglican Religious Communities 1845–1900*. London: SCM, 1958.
Allen, Walter. *The English Novel: A Short Critical History*. 1954. Harmondsworth: Penguin, 1958.
Allott, Miriam, ed. *The Brontës: The Critical Heritage*. London: Routledge, 1974.
Almog, Shmuel. "The Racial Motif in Renan's Attitude to Jews and Judaism." In *Antisemitism through the Ages*, edited by Shmuel Almog, 255–78. Translated by Nathan H. Reisner. Oxford: Pergamon, 1988.
Alter, Robert. *The Art of Biblical Narrative*. New York: Basic Books, 1981.
– *The Art of Biblical Poetry*. New York: Basic Books, 1985.
Altick, Richard D. *The English Common Reader: A Social History of the Mass Reading Public 1800–1900*. Chicago: University of Chicago Press, 1957.
– *The Presence of the Present: Topics of the Day in the Victorian Novel*. Columbus: Ohio State University Press, 1991.
– *Victorian People and Ideas*. New York: Norton, 1973.
Anchor Bible Dictionary. Edited by David Noel Freedman, et al. 6 vols. New York: Doubleday, 1992.
Anger, Suzy. *Victorian Interpretation*. Ithaca and London: Cornell University Press, 2005.
Anson, Peter F. *The Call of the Cloister: Religious Communities and Kindred Bodies in the Anglican Communion*. London: SPCK, 1955.
apRoberts, Ruth. *Arnold and God*. Berkeley and Los Angeles: University of California Press, 1983.

– *The Moral Trollope*. Athens: Ohio University Press, 1971.

Archer, Margaret S. Review of *Charlotte Yonge (1823–1901): Novelist of the Oxford Movement*. By Barbara Dennis. *Victorian Periodicals Review* 27 (1994): 362–5.

Argyle, Gisela. "Gender and Generic Mixing in Charlotte Brontë's *Shirley*." *Studies in English Literature* 35 (1995): 741–56.

Arnold, Matthew. *The Complete Prose Works of Matthew Arnold*. 11 vols. Edited by R.H. Super. Ann Arbor: University of Michigan Press, 1960–77.

– *The Letters of Matthew Arnold*. 6 vols. Edited by Cecil Y. Lang. Charlottesville and London: University Press of Virginia, 1996–2001.

– *The Poems of Matthew Arnold*. Edited by Kenneth Allott. New York: Barnes and Noble, 1965.

Arnold, Thomas. "On the Right Interpretation and Understanding of the Scriptures." In Thomas Arnold. *Sermons, with an Essay on the Right Interpretation and Understanding of the Scriptures*. 3^d ed. Vol. 2, 374–425. London: B. Fellowes, 1844.

Ashton, Rosemary. *George Eliot: A Life*. London: Penguin, 1996.

Auerbach, Erich. *Mimesis: The Representation of Reality in Western Literature*. Translated by Willard R. Trask. Princeton: Princeton University Press, 1953.

Baker, Joseph Ellis. *The Novel and the Oxford Movement*. Princeton: Princeton University Press, 1932. New York: Russell and Russell, 1965.

– "*Vanity Fair* and the Celestial City." *Nineteenth-Century Fiction* 10 (1955): 89–98.

Bakhtin, Mikhail Mikhailovich. *The Dialogic Imagination: Four Essays*. Translated by Caryl Emerson and Michael Holquist. Austin: University of Texas Press, 1981.

– *Problems of Dostoevsky's Poetics*. Edited and translated by Caryl Emerson. Minneapolis: University of Minnesota Press, 1984.

Bal, Mieke. *Anti-Covenant: Counter-Reading Women's Lives in the Hebrew Bible*. Sheffield: Almond, 1989.

– *Death and Disymmetry: The Politics of Coherence in the Book of Judges*. Chicago: University of Chicago Press, 1988.

– *Lethal Love: Feminist Literary Readings of Biblical Love Stories*. Bloomington: Indiana University Press, 1987.

Barth, Karl. "Schleiermacher." In Karl Barth. *Protestant Theology in the Nineteenth Century: Its Background and History*, 425–73. No trans. London: SCM, 1972.

Battiscombe, Georgina. *Charlotte Mary Yonge: The Story of an Uneventful Life*. London: Constable, 1943.

Battiscombe, Georgina, and Marghanita Laski, eds. *A Chaplet for Charlotte Yonge*. London: Cresset, 1965.

Beer, Gillian. *George Eliot*. Bloomington: Indiana University Press, 1986.

Bell, Robert. Review of *Vanity Fair*. By William Makepeace Thackeray. *Fraser's Magazine* (September 1848). In *Thackeray: The Critical Heritage*, edited by Geoffrey Tillotson and Donald Hawes, 62–7.

Bergonzi, Bernard. *A Victorian Wanderer: The Life of Thomas Arnold the Younger*. Oxford: Oxford University Press, 2003.

Bloom, Harold. *The Book of J*. New York: Grove Weidenfeld, 1990.

– *How to Read and Why*. New York: Scribner, 2000.

– Introduction. Walter Pater. *Marius the Epicurean: His Sensations and Ideas*, ix–xix. New York: New American Library, 1970.

– *The Ringers in the Tower: Studies in Romantic Tradition*. Chicago and London: University of Chicago Press, 1971.

– *The Western Canon: The Books and School of the Ages*. New York: Harcourt Brace, 1994.

Bonica, Charlotte. "Nature and Paganism in Hardy's *Tess of the d'Urbervilles*." ELH 49 (1982): 849–62.

Book of Common Prayer. Oxford: Oxford University Press, 1969.

Booth, Wayne. *The Company We Keep: An Ethics of Fiction*. Berkeley and Los Angeles: University of California Press, 1988.

Bradley, Ian, ed. *The Penguin Book of Hymns*. London: Viking, 1989.

Bradstock, Andrew, Sean Gill, Anne Hogan, and Sue Morgan, eds. *Masculinity and Spirituality in Victorian Culture*. Basingstoke: Macmillan, 2000.

Brady, Kristin. *George Eliot*. London: Macmillan, 1992.

Brontë, Charlotte. *Jane Eyre: An Autobiography*. [1847.] Edited by Jane Jack and Margaret Smith. Oxford: Clarendon, 1969.

– *Shirley: A Tale*. [1849.] Edited by Herbert Rosengarten and Margaret Smith. Oxford: Clarendon, 1979.

Brown, Dan. *The Da Vinci Code: A Novel*. New York: Doubleday, 2003.

Brownell, David. "The Two Worlds of Charlotte Yonge." In *The Worlds of Victorian Fiction*, edited by Jerome H. Buckley, 165–78. Cambridge, MA: Harvard University Press, 1975.

Browning, Robert. "A Death in the Desert." In Robert Browning. *Dramatis Personae*. [1864.] Edited by F.B. Pinion, 71–92. London: Collins, 1969.

Budge, Gavin. "Realism and Typology in Charlotte M. Yonge's *The Heir of Redclyffe*." *Victorian Literature and Culture* 31, no. 1 (2003): 193–223.

Bunyan, John. *The Pilgrim's Progress*. [1678.] Edited by Roger Sharrock. Harmondsworth: Penguin, 1965.

Burch, Mark H. "'The world is a looking-glass': *Vanity Fair* as Satire." *Genre* 15 (1982): 265–79.

Butler, Joseph. *The Analogy of Religion*. Introduced by Ernest C. Mossner. New York: Frederick Ungar, 1961.

Butler, Lance St John. "'Unless the World Is to Perish': Hardy and Christian Discourse." In Lance St John Butler. *Victorian Doubt: Literary and Cultural Discourses*, 190–218. Hemel Hempstead: Harvester, 1990.

Byatt, A.S. Introduction. *Selected Essays, Poems and Other Writings*. By George Eliot. Edited by A.S. Byatt and Nicholas Warren, ix–xxxiv. London: Penguin, 1990.

Carlyle, Thomas. *Past and Present*. [1843.] Edited by Richard D. Altick. New York: New York University Press, 1977.

– *Sartor Resartus*. [1833–34.] Edited by Kerry McSweeney and Peter Sabor. Oxford: Oxford University Press, 1987. .

Carpenter, Mary Wilson. *George Eliot and the Landscape of Time: Narrative Form and Protestant Apocalyptic History*. Chapel Hill and London: University of North Carolina Press, 1986.

Carroll, David. *George Eliot and the Conflict of Interpretations: A Reading of the Novels*. Cambridge: Cambridge University Press, 1992.

Casteras, Susan P. "The Victorian Lady's Domestic Threat: The Good, the Bad and the Indifferent Female Adversary in Contemporary Art." In *Women of Faith in Victorian Culture: Reassessing the Angel in the House*, edited by Anne Hogan and Andrew Bradstock, 186–208.

– "Virgin Vows: The Early Victorian Artists' Portrayal of Nuns and Novices." *Victorian Studies* 24 (1981): 157–84.

Chadwick, Owen. *The Spirit of the Oxford Movement: Tractarian Essays*. Cambridge: Cambridge University Press, 1990.

– *The Victorian Church*. 2 vols. *Part One 1829–1859. Part Two 1860–1901*. 3^d ed. London: SCM, 1971.

Chandler, Michael. *The Life and Work of John Mason Neale 1818–1866*. Leominster: Gracewing, 1995.

Chapman, Raymond. "'Arguing about the Eastward Position': Thomas Hardy and Puseyism." *Nineteenth-Century Literature* 42 (1987–88): 275–94.

– *Faith and Revolt: Studies in the Literary Influence of the Oxford Movement*. London: Weidenfeld and Nicolson, 1970.

Chesterton, G.K. *The Victorian Age in Literature*. London: Thornton Butterworth, 1913.

Christensen, Merton A. "Thomas Arnold's Debt to German Theologians: A Prelude to Matthew Arnold's *Literature and Dogma*." *Modern Philology* 55 (1957–58): 14–20.

Clark, Katerina, and Michael Holquist. *Mikhail Bakhtin*. Cambridge, MA: Harvard University Press, 1984.

Clive, Geoffrey, ed. *The Philosophy of Nietzsche*. New York: New American Library, 1965.

Coates, Ruth. *Christianity in Bakhtin: God and the Exiled Author*. Cambridge: Cambridge University Press, 1998.

Cockshut, A.O.J. *Anglican Attitudes: A Study of Victorian Religious Controversies.* London: Collins, 1959.

– *The Unbelievers: English Agnostic Thought 1840–1890.* London: Collins, 1964.

Colby, Vineta. *Yesterday's Woman: Domestic Realism in the English Novel.* Princeton: Princeton University Press, 1974.

Coleridge, Christabel. *Charlotte Mary Yonge: Her Life and Letters.* London: Macmillan, 1903.

Coleridge, Samuel Taylor. *Confessions of an Inquiring Spirit.* [1840.] Introduced by David Jasper. Philadelphia: Fortress, 1988.

Collins, Deborah. *Thomas Hardy and His God: A Liturgy of Unbelief.* New York: St Martin's, 1990.

Collins, Wilkie, and Charles Dickens. "Doctor Dulcamara, M.P." [*Household Words* (18 December 1858).] In Charles Dickens. *Charles Dickens' Uncollected Writings from* Household Words *1850–1859.* 2 vols. Edited by Harry Stone. Vol. 2, 619–26. Bloomington and London: Indiana University Press, 1968.

[Conybeare, W.J.] "Church Parties." *Edinburgh Review* 98 (October 1853): 273–342.

Cox, R.G. *Thomas Hardy: The Critical Heritage.* New York: Barnes and Noble, 1970.

Crenshaw, James L. "Ecclesiastes, Book of." *Anchor* 2: 271–80.

Cruse, Amy. *The Victorians and Their Books.* London: George Allen and Unwin, 1935.

Culler, A. Dwight. *The Victorian Mirror of History.* New Haven and London: Yale University Press, 1985.

Culler, Jonathan. "Comparative Literature and the Pieties." *Profession 1986* (1986): 30–2.

– "A Critic against the Christians." Review of *Using Biography.* By William Empson. *Times Literary Supplement* (23 November 1984): 1,327–8.

– "Political Criticism: Confronting Religion." In Jonathan Culler. *Framing the Sign: Criticism and Its Institutions,* 69–82. Norman and London: University of Oklahoma Press, 1988.

Cunningham, Valentine. *In the Reading Gaol: Postmodernity, Texts, and History.* Oxford: Blackwell, 1994.

Cupitt, Don. *Radicals and the Future of the Church.* London: SCM, 1989.

Davies, Alan T. "The Aryan Christ: A Motif in Christian Anti-Semitism." *Journal of Ecumenical Studies* 12 (1975): 569–79.

– "The Aryan Myth: Its Religious Significance." *Studies in Religion* 10 (1981): 287–98.

– "Racism and German Protestant Theology: A Prelude to the Holocaust." In *Reflections on the Holocaust: Historical, Philosophical, and Educational Dimensions.* Annals of the American Academy of Political and Social Science

450, edited by Irene G. Shur, Franklin H. Littell, and Marvin E. Wolfgang, 20–34. Philadelphia: American Academy of Political and Social Science, 1980.

Davies, Charles Maurice. *Philip Paternoster: A Tractarian Love Story. By an Ex-Puseyite.* [1858.] New York and London: Garland, 1975.

Dawkins, Richard. *The God Delusion.* Boston: Houghton Mifflin, 2006.

DeLaura, David J. "'The Ache of Modernism' in Hardy's Later Novels." ELH 34 (1967): 380–99.

– *Hebrew and Hellene in Victorian England: Newman, Arnold, and Pater.* Austin and London: University of Texas Press, 1969.

Dellamora, Richard. "Male Relations in Thomas Hardy's *Jude the Obscure.*" In *Jude the Obscure: Thomas Hardy,* edited by Penny Boumelha, 144–65. Basingstoke: Macmillan, 2000.

– *Masculine Desire: The Sexual Politics of Victorian Aestheticism.* Chapel Hill and London: University of North Carolina Press, 1990.

Dennett, Daniel C. *Breaking the Spell: Religion as a Natural Phenomenon.* New York: Viking, 2006.

Dennis, Barbara. *Charlotte Yonge (1823–1901): Novelist of the Oxford Movement: A Literature of Victorian Culture and Society.* Lewiston: Edwin Mellen, 1992.

Disraeli, Benjamin. *Tancred, or The New Crusade.* 1847. London: Longmans, 1878.

Dolin, Tim. "Fictional Territory and a Woman's Place: Regional and Sexual Differences in *Shirley.*" ELH 62 (1995): 197–215.

Dyson, A.E. "*Vanity Fair*: An Irony Against Heroes" *Critical Quarterly* 6 (1964): 11–31.

Eliot, George. *Adam Bede.* [1859.] Edited by Valentine Cunningham. Oxford: Oxford University Press, 1996.

– *Daniel Deronda.* [1874–76.] Edited by Graham Handley. Oxford: Oxford University Press, 1988.

– *Felix Holt, The Radical.* [1866.] Edited by Fred C. Thomson. Oxford: Oxford University Press, 1988.

– *The George Eliot Letters.* Edited by Gordon S. Haight. 9 vols. New Haven: Yale University Press, 1954–78.

– *Middlemarch: A Study of Provincial Life.* [1871–72.] Edited by David Carroll. Oxford: Oxford University Press, 1997.

– "The Modern Hep! Hep! Hep!" [1879.] In George Eliot. *The Impressions of Theophrastus Such.* Edited by D.J. Enright, 135–55. London: Dent, 1995.

– *Scenes of Clerical Life.* [1858.] Edited by Thomas A. Noble. Oxford: Oxford University Press, 1988.

– *Selected Critical Writings.* Edited by Rosemary Ashton. Oxford: Oxford University Press, 1992.

Eliot, T.S. "Arnold and Pater." In T.S. Eliot. *Selected Essays,* 431–43.

– *The Complete Poems and Plays of T.S. Eliot*. London: Faber and Faber, 1969.

– "Francis Herbert Bradley." In T.S. Eliot. *Selected Essays*, 444–55.

– *Selected Essays*. 3ᵈ ed. London: Faber and Faber, 1951.

– *The Use of Poetry and the Use of Criticism: Studies in the Relation of Criticism to Poetry in England*. London: Faber and Faber, 1933.

Engel, Elliot. "Heir of the Oxford Movement: Charlotte Mary Yonge's *The Heir of Redclyffe*." *Études anglaises* 33 (1980): 132–41.

Essays and Reviews: The 1860 Text and Its Reading. Edited by Victor Shea and William Whitla. Charlottesville and London: University Press of Virginia, 2000.

Faverty, Frederic E. *Matthew Arnold: The Ethnologist*. Evanston, IL: Northwestern University Press, 1951.

Feuerbach, Ludwig. *The Essence of Christianity*. [1841.] Translated by George Eliot. [1854.] New York: Harper and Row, 1957.

Fiddes, Paul S. *Freedom and Limit: A Dialogue Between Literature and Christian Doctrine*. New York: St Martin's, 1991.

Fiddes, Paul S., ed. *The Novel, Spirituality and Modern Culture: Eight Novelists Write about Their Craft and Their Context*. Cardiff: University of Wales Press, 2000.

Finley, C. Stephen. "Bunyan among the Victorians: Macaulay, Froude, Ruskin." *Literature and Theology* 3 (1989): 77–94.

Fish, Stanley. "One University Under God." *Chronicle of Higher Education* (7 January 2005): C1.

Fletcher, Iain. *Walter Pater*. London: Longmans, 1959.

[Fonblanque, Albany]. Unsigned review of *Shirley: A Tale*. By Charlotte Brontë. *Examiner* 3 (November 1849): 692–4. In *The Brontës: The Critical Heritage*, edited by Miriam Allott, 125–9.

Forbes, Duncan. *The Liberal Anglican Idea of History*. Cambridge: Cambridge University Press, 1952.

Forster, John. Review of *Vanity Fair*. By William Makepeace Thackeray. *Examiner* (22 July 1848). In *Thackeray: The Critical Heritage*, edited by Geoffrey Tillotson and Donald Hawes, 53–8.

Fouqué, Friedrich de la Motte. *Sintram and His Companions: A Romance*. Translated by Julius Charles Hare. London: C. and J. Ollier, and Edinburgh: William Blackwood, 1820.

Frei, Hans. *The Eclipse of Biblical Narrative: A Study in Eighteenth and Nineteenth Century Hermeneutics*. New Haven and London: Yale University Press, 1974.

Froude, James Anthony. *The Nemesis of Faith*. [1849.] New York and London: Garland, 1975.

[–] 'Zeta.' *Shadows of the Clouds*. London: Ollivier, 1847.

Frye, Northrop. *Anatomy of Criticism: Four Essays*. Princeton: Princeton University Press, 1957.

- *The Great Code: The Bible and Literature.* Toronto: Academic Press, 1981, 1982.
- *Myth and Metaphor: Selected Essays, 1974–1988.* Charlottesville and London: University of Virginia Press, 1990.
- *Words with Power: Being a Second Study of "The Bible and Literature."* Toronto: Penguin, 1990.

Garrett, Peter K. *The Victorian Multiplot Novel: Studies in Dialogical Form.* New Haven: Yale University Press, 1980.

Gatrell, Simon. Introduction. In Thomas Hardy. *Tess of the d'Urbervilles,* xiii–xxiv.

Gilbert, Sandra M., and Susan Gubar. *The Madwoman in the Attic: The Woman Writer and the Nineteenth-Century Literary Imagination.* New Haven and London: Yale University Press, 1979.

Gilley, Sheridan. "The Ecclesiology of the Oxford Movement: A Reconsideration." In *From Oxford to the People: Reconsidering Newman and the Oxford Movement,* edited by Paul Vaiss, 60–75.

Gladstone, William Ewart. "*Robert Elsmere* and the Battle of Belief." *The Nineteenth Century* 23 (May 1888): 766–88.

Glen, Heather, ed. *The Cambridge Companion to the Brontës.* Cambridge: Cambridge University Press, 2002.
- "Introduction." In *The Cambridge Companion to the Brontës,* edited by Heather Glen, 1–12.
- "*Shirley* and *Villette.*" In *The Cambridge Companion to the Brontës,* edited by Heather Glen, 122–47.

Goetz, William R. "The Felicity and Infelicity of Marriage in *Jude the Obscure.*" *Nineteenth-Century Fiction* 38 (1983–84): 189–213.

Greene, Sally. "Apocalypse When? *Shirley*'s Vision and the Politics of Reading." *Studies in the Novel* 26 (1994): 350–71.

[Greg, W.R.] "False Morality of Lady Novelists." *National Review* 8 (January 1859): 144–67.

Gresley, William. *Charles Lever; or, The Man of the Nineteenth Century.* [1841.] New York and London: Garland, 1975.

Griffin, Susan M. *Anti-Catholicism and Nineteenth-Century Fiction.* Cambridge: Cambridge University Press, 2004.

Haight, Gordon S. *George Eliot: A Biography.* New York and Oxford: Oxford University Press, 1968.

Hands, Timothy. *Thomas Hardy: Distracted Preacher? Hardy's Religious Biography and Its Influence on His Novels.* New York: St Martin's, 1989.

Hanson, Ellis. *Decadence and Catholicism.* Cambridge: Harvard University Press, 1997.

Hapgood, Lynne. "'The Reconceiving of Christianity': Secularisation, Realism and the Religious Novel: 1888–1900. *Literature and Theology* 10 (1996): 329–50.

Harden, Edgar F., ed. *The Letters and Private Papers of William Makepeace Thackeray: A Supplement to Gordon N. Ray, The Letters and Private Papers of William Makepeace Thackeray.* 2 vols. New York and London: Garland, 1994.

Hardy, Barbara. *The Exposure of Luxury: Radical Themes in Thackeray.* London: Peter Owen, 1972.

Hardy, Thomas. *The Collected Letters of Thomas Hardy.* Edited by Richard Little Purdy and Michael Millgate. 7 vols. Oxford: Clarendon, 1978–1988.

– *The Complete Poems of Thomas Hardy.* Edited by James Gibson. The New Wessex Edition. London: Macmillan, 1976.

– *Jude the Obscure.* [1895.] Edited by Patricia Ingham. Oxford: Oxford University Press, 1985.

– *A Laodicean; or, The Castle of the De Stancys: A Story of To-Day.* [1881.] Edited by Jane Gatewood. Oxford: Oxford University Press, 1991.

– *The Mayor of Casterbridge: A Story of a Man of Character.* [1886.] Edited by Dale Kramer. Oxford: Oxford University Press, 1987.

– *The Life and Work of Thomas Hardy.* [1878.] Edited by Michael Millgate. London: Macmillan, 1984.

– *The Return of the Native.* [1878.] Edited by Simon Gatrell. Oxford: Oxford University Press, 1990.

– *Tess of the d'Urbervilles: A Pure Woman.* [1891.] Edited by Juliet Grindle and Simon Gatrell. Explanatory Notes by Nancy Barrineau. Oxford: Oxford University Press, 1988.

– *Two on a Tower.* [1882.] Edited by Suleiman M. Ahmad. Oxford: Oxford University Press, 1993.

[Harrison, Frederic.] "Neo-Christianity." Review of *Essays and Reviews. Westminster Review* 18, new series; 74, old series (October 1860): 293–332.

Harvey, W.J. *The Art of George Eliot.* London: Chatto and Windus, 1963.

Heeney, Brian. *The Women's Movement in the Church of England 1850–1930.* Oxford: Clarendon, 1988.

Hennell, Charles C. *An Inquiry Concerning the Origin of Christianity.* 2^d ed. London: T. Allman, 1841.

Henry, Nancy. *George Eliot and the British Empire.* Cambridge: Cambridge University Press, 2002.

Heschel, Susannah. "The Image of Judaism in Nineteenth-Century Christian New Testament Scholarship in Germany." In *Jewish-Christian Encounters over the Centuries: Symbiosis, Prejudice, Holocaust, Dialogue,* edited by Marvin Perry and Frederick M. Schweitzer, 215–40. New York: Peter Lang, 1994.

Hitchens, Christopher. *God Is Not Great: How Religion Poisons Everything.* Toronto: McClelland and Stewart, 2007.

Hock, Ronald F. "Lazarus and Dives." *Anchor* 4: 266–7.

Hodgson, Peter C. *The Mystery beneath the Real: Theology in the Fiction of George Eliot*. Minneapolis: Fortress, 2000.

Hogan, Anne. "Angel or Eve? Victorian Catholicism and the Angel in the House." In *Women of Faith in Victorian Culture: Reassessing the Angel in the House*, edited by Anne Hogan and Andrew Bradstock, 91–100.

Hogan, Anne, and Andrew Bradstock, eds. *Women of Faith in Victorian Culture: Reassessing the Angel in the House*. Basingstoke: Macmillan, 1998.

Holland, Norman. "*Jude the Obscure*: Hardy's Symbolic Indictment of Christianity." *Nineteenth-Century Fiction* 9 (1954–55): 50–60.

Holloway, John. *The Victorian Sage: Studies in Argument*. London: Macmillan, 1953.

Honan, Park. *Matthew Arnold: A Life*. [1981.] Cambridge, MA: Harvard University Press, 1983.

Hopkins, Gerard Manley. *The Journals and Papers of Gerard Manley Hopkins*. Edited by Humphry House and Graham Storey. London: Oxford University Press, 1959.

Hough, Graham. *The Last Romantics*. [1947.] London: Methuen, 1961.

Houghton, Walter E. *The Victorian Frame of Mind, 1830–1870*. New Haven and London: Yale University Press, 1957.

Howard, Anne. *Mary Spencer: A Tale for the Times*. [1844.] New York and London: Garland, 1975.

[Hutton, Richard Holt]. "The Author of *Heartsease* and Modern Schools of Fiction." *Prospective Review* 10 (November 1854): 460–82.

– "Ethical and Dogmatic Fiction: Miss Yonge." *National Review* 12 (1861): 211–30.

Irvin, Glenn. "High Passion and High Church in Hardy's *Two on a Tower*." *English Literature in Transition* 3 (1985): 121–9.

Iser, Wolfgang. *The Implied Reader: Patterns of Communication in Prose Fiction from Bunyan to Beckett*. Baltimore: Johns Hopkins University Press, 1974.

– *Walter Pater: The Aesthetic Moment* (*Walter Pater: Die Autonomie des Ästhetischen*) [1960.] Translated by David Henry Wilson. Cambridge: Cambridge University Press, 1987.

James, Henry. "*Daniel Deronda*: A Conversation." In Henry James. *Essays on Literature*, 974–92.

– *Essays on Literature. American Writers. English Writers*. Vol. 1 of Henry James. *Literary Criticism*. New York: Library of America, 1984.

– "The Life of George Eliot." In Henry James. *Essays on Literature*, 994–1,010.

– "Mrs Humphry Ward." In Henry James. *Essays on Literature*, 1,371–4.

– Review of *Life of John Coleridge Patteson*. By Charlotte Mary Yonge. In Henry James. *Essays on Literature*, 1,382–6.

Jauss, Hans Robert. "Literary History as a Challenge to Literary Theory." *Toward an Aesthetic of Reception.* Translated by Timothy Bahti, 3–45. Minneapolis: University of Minnesota Press, 1982.

Jay, Elisabeth. *The Religion of the Heart: Anglican Evangelicalism and the Nineteenth-Century Novel.* Oxford: Clarendon, 1979.

Jedrzejewski, Jan. *Thomas Hardy and the Church.* Basingstoke: Macmillan, 1996.

Jenkins, Ruth Y. *Reclaiming Myths of Power: Women Writers and the Victorian Spiritual Crisis.* Lewisburg: Bucknell University Press, 1995.

Jewsbury, Geraldine. *Zoe: The History of Two Lives.* [1845.] London: Virago, 1989.

Keble, John. "Advertisement." In John Keble. *The Christian Year: Thoughts in Verse for the Sundays and Holydays Throughout the Year* [1827], v–vi. London: Frederick Warne, n.d.

– *The Christian Year, Lyra Innocentium, and Other Poems.* London: Oxford University Press, 1914.

– *Keble's Lectures on Poetry 1832–1841.* 2 vols. Translated by Edward Kershaw Francis. Oxford: Clarendon Press, 1912.

– *Letters of Spiritual Counsel and Guidance, by the Late Rev. J. Keble, M.A.* Edited by R.F. Wilson. Oxford and London: J. Parker, 1870.

Kelly, Gary. "Romantic Evangelicalism: Religion, Social Conflict, and Literary Form in Legh Richmond's *Annals of the Poor.*" *English Studies in Canada* 16 (1990): 165–86.

Kermode, Frank. *The Genesis of Secrecy: On the Interpretation of Narrative.* Cambridge, MA: Harvard University Press, 1979.

– "New Ways with Bible Stories." In Frank Kermode. *Poetry, Narrative, History,* 29–48. Oxford: Blackwell, 1990.

Kermode, Frank, and Robert Alter, eds. *The Literary Guide to the Bible.* Cambridge, MA: Harvard University Press, 1987.

Kingsley, Charles. *Alton Locke, Tailor and Poet.* [1850.] 2 vols. The Bideford Edition of the Works of Charles Kingsley. New York: Co-operative Publication Society, 1899.

– *Yeast: A Problem.* [Serialized 1848, 1851.] The Bideford Edition of the Works of Charles Kingsley. New York: Co-operative Publication Society, 1899.

Kirkham, Margaret. "Reading 'The Brontës.'" In *Women Reading Women's Writing,* edited by Sue Roe, 61–82. New York: St Martin's, 1987.

Knoepflmacher, U.C. *Religious Humanism and the Victorian Novel: George Eliot, Walter Pater, and Samuel Butler.* Princeton: Princeton University Press, 1965.

Korg, Jacob. "The Problem of Unity in *Shirley.*" *Nineteenth-Century Fiction* 12 (1957–58): 125–36.

Kundera, Milan. *The Art of the Novel.* Translated by Linda Asher. New York: Harper and Row, 1988.

Larson, Janet L. *Dickens and the Broken Scripture.* Athens: University of Georgia Press, 1985.

Laski, Marghanita, and Kathleen Tillotson. "Bibliography." In *A Chaplet for Charlotte Yonge*, edited by Georgina Battiscombe and Marghanita Laski, 204–16.

Lawrence, D.H. "Morality and the Novel." In D.H. Lawrence. *Selected Literary Criticism*. Edited by Anthony Beal, 108–13. New York: Viking, 1966.

– "Why the Novel Matters." In D.H. Lawrence. *Selected Literary Criticism*. Edited by Anthony Beal, 102–8. New York: Viking, 1966.

Lawson, Kate. "The Dissenting Voice: *Shirley's* Vision of Women and Christianity." *Studies in English Literature* 29 (1989): 729–43.

– "Imagining Eve: Charlotte Brontë, Kate Millett, Hélène Cixous." *Women's Studies* 24 (1995): 411–26.

Leavis, Q.D. "Charlotte Yonge and 'Christian Discrimination.'" In *The Novel of Religious Controversy*. Vol. 3 of Q.D. Leavis. *Collected Essays*. Edited by G. Singh, 234–44. Cambridge: Cambridge University Press, 1989.

Lee, Vernon. [Violet Paget]. "The Responsibilities of Unbelief: A Conversation of Three Rationalists." *Contemporary Review* 43 (May 1883): 685–710. In Vernon Lee. *Baldwin: Being Dialogues on Views and Aspirations*, 15–73. London: Unwin, 1886.

Letwin, Shirley Robin. *The Gentleman in Trollope: Individuality and Moral Conduct*. Cambridge: Harvard University Press, 1982.

Levey, Michael. *The Case of Walter Pater*. London: Thames and Hudson, 1978.

[Lewes, George Henry]. Unsigned review of *Shirley: A Tale*. By Charlotte Brontë. *Edinburgh Review* 91 (January 1850): 153–73. In *The Brontës: The Critical Heritage*, edited by Marion Allott, 160–70.

Lewis, C.S. *Mere Christianity*. [1952.] London: Fount, 1977.

Liddon, H.P. *Life of Edward Bouverie Pusey*. 4 vols. 3ᵈ ed. London: Longmans, Green, 1893–97.

Literary History and the Religious Turn. Edited by Bruce Holsinger. Special issue of *English Language Notes* 44, no. 1 (Spring 2006).

Livingston, James C. *Matthew Arnold and Christianity: His Religious Prose Writings*. Columbia: University of South Carolina Press, 1986.

Lodge, David. *How Far Can You Go?* London: Secker and Warburg, 1980.

Loesberg, Jonathan. *Aestheticism and Deconstruction: Pater, Derrida, and De Man*. Princeton: Princeton University Press, 1991.

– "Deconstruction, Historicism, and Overdetermination: Dislocations of the Marriage Plots in *Robert Elsmere* and *Dombey and Son*." *Victorian Studies* 33 (1990): 441–64.

Lubbock, Jules. "Walter Pater's *Marius the Epicurean* – The Imaginary Portrait as Cultural History." *Journal of the Warburg and Courtauld Institutes* 46 (1983): 166–90.

McCraw, Harry Wells. "Walter Pater's 'Religious Phase': The Riddle of *Marius the Epicurean*." *The Southern Quarterly* 10 (1972): 245–73.

McMaster, R.D. *Thackeray's Cultural Frame of Reference: Allusion in* The New-comes. Montreal: McGill-Queen's University Press, 1991.

McNees, Eleanor. "Reverse Typology in *Jude the Obscure*." *Christianity and Literature* 39 (1989): 35–49.

Maison, Margaret. *Search Your Soul, Eustace: A Survey of the Religious Novel in the Victorian Age*. London and New York: Sheed and Ward, 1961.

Mare, Margaret and Alicia C. Percival. *Victorian Best-seller: The World of Charlotte M. Yonge*. London: Harrap, 1947. Port Washington, NY: Kennikat, 1970.

Maynard, John. "The Brontës and Religion." In *The Cambridge Companion to the Brontës*, edited by Heather Glen, 192–213.

Milbank, John, Catherine Pickstock, and Graham Ward. "Introduction: Suspending the Material: The Turn of Radical Orthodoxy." In *Radical Orthodoxy: A New Theology*, edited by John Milbank, Catherine Pickstock, and Graham Ward, 1–20. London and New York: Routledge, 1999.

Mill, John Stuart. *On Liberty*. [1859.] Edited by Edward Alexander. Peterborough, ON: Broadview, 1999.

Miller, J. Hillis. *The Disappearance of God: Five Nineteenth-Century Writers*. Cambridge, MA: Harvard University Press, 1963.

– *Fiction and Repetition: Seven English Novels*. Cambridge, MA: Harvard University Press, 1982.

– *Thomas Hardy: Distance and Desire*. Cambridge, MA: Harvard University Press, 1970.

– "Walter Pater: A Partial Portrait." *Daedalus* 105, no. 1 (Winter 1976): 97–113.

Millgate, Michael. *Thomas Hardy: A Biography*. New York: Random House, 1982.

Morris, Pam. "Heroes and Hero-Worship in Charlotte Brontë's *Shirley*." *Nineteenth-Century Literature* 54 (1999): 285–307.

Moynahan, Julian. "*The Mayor of Casterbridge* and the Old Testament's First Book of Samuel: A Study of Some Literary Relationships." *PMLA* 71 (1956): 118–30.

Mozley, Thomas. *Reminiscences Chiefly of Oriel College and the Oxford Movement*. 2 vols. Boston: Houghton Mifflin, 1882.

Mullen, Richard. *Anthony Trollope: A Victorian in His World*. London: Duckworth, 1990.

Mullen, Richard, and James Munson. *The Penguin Companion to Trollope*. London: Penguin, 1996.

Myers, F.W.H. *Wordsworth*. London: Macmillan, 1899.

Nardin, Jane. *Trollope and Moral Philosophy*. Athens: Ohio University Press, 1996.

Neale, John Mason. *Ayton Priory; or, The Restored Monastery*. London: Rivingtons, 1843.

– *The Lewes Riot and Its Consequences: A Letter to the Lord Bishop of Chichester*. London: Joseph Masters, 1857.

Nemesvari, Richard. "Appropriating the Word: *Jude the Obscure* as Subversive Apocrypha." *Victorian Review* 19, no. 2 (Winter 1993): 48–66.

Newman, John Henry. *Apologia Pro Vita Sua: Being a History of His Religious Opinions*. [1864.] Edited by Martin J. Svaglic. Oxford: Clarendon Press, 1967.

– *The Idea of a University*. [1873.] Edited by Frank M. Turner. New Haven and London: Yale University Press, 1996.

– "John Keble." [1846.] In John Henry Newman. *Essays Critical and Historical*. Vol. 2, 421–53. London: Longmans, 1901.

– *Loss and Gain: The Story of a Convert*. [1848.] Edited by Alan G. Hill. Oxford: Oxford University Press, 1986.

– "The Second Spring." In John Henry Newman. *Sermons Preached on Various Occasions* [1857], 163–82. London: Longmans, Green, 1898.

Nussbaum, Martha C. *Love's Knowledge: Essays on Philosophy and Literature*. New York: Oxford University Press, 1990.

Paget, Francis E. *Milford Malvoisin: or, Pews and Pewholders*. London: Burns, 1842.

– *St Antholin's; or, Old Churches and New. A Tale for the Times*. London: Burns, 1841.

Pater, Walter. "Amiel's 'Journal Intime.'" Review of *The Journal Intime of Henri-Frédéric Amiel*. Translated by Mrs Humphry Ward. *The Guardian*, 17 March 1886. In *Essays from "The Guardian,"* 17–37. London: Macmillan, 1901.

– *Letters of Walter Pater*. Edited by Lawrence Evans. Oxford: Clarendon, 1970.

– *Marius the Epicurean: His Sensations and Ideas*. [1885.] Edited by Michael Levey. Harmondsworth: Penguin, 1985.

– *Marius the Epicurean: His Sensations and Ideas*. [1885.] Edited by Gerald Monsman. Kansas City: Valancourt, 2007.

– "Pascal." In Walter Pater. *Miscellaneous Studies: A Series of Essays*. Edited by Charles L. Shadwell, 55–84. London: Macmillan, 1895.

– *The Renaissance: Studies in Art and Poetry*. [1873.] Edited by Adam Phillips. Oxford: Oxford University Press, 1986.

– Review of *Robert Elsmere*. By Mrs Humphry Ward. *The Guardian*, 28 March 1888. In *Essays from "The Guardian,"* 53–70. London: Macmillan, 1901.

Perkin, J. Russell. "Locking George Sand in the Attic: Female Passion and Domestic Realism in the Victorian Novel." *University of Toronto Quarterly* 63 (1994): 408–28.

– *A Reception-History of George Eliot's Fiction*. Ann Arbor: UMI Research Press, 1990.

Peschier, Diana. *Nineteenth-Century Anti-Catholic Discourses: The Case of Charlotte Brontë*. Basingstoke: Palgrave Macmillan, 2005.

Peterson, Linda H. "'The Feelings and Claims of Little People': Heroic Missionary Memoirs, Domestic(ated) Spiritual Autobiography, and *Jane Eyre: An Autobiography*." In Linda H. Peterson. *Traditions of Victorian Women's Autobiography: The Poetics and Politics of Life Writing*, 80–108. Charlottesville and London: University Press of Virginia, 1999.

Peterson, William S. "Gladstone's Review of *Robert Elsmere*: Some Unpublished Correspondence." *Review of English Studies* n.s. 21, no. 84 (1970): 442–61.

– *Victorian Heretic: Mrs Humphry Ward's Robert Elsmere*. Leicester: Leicester University Press, 1976.

Phillips, Marion J. "Charlotte Brontë and the Priesthood of All Believers." *Brontë Society Transactions* 20, no. 3 (1991): 145–55.

Pickstock, Catherine. *After Writing: On the Liturgical Consummation of Philosophy*. Oxford: Blackwell, 1998.

Pope, Alexander. *The Poems of Alexander Pope*. Edited by John Butt. London: Methuen, 1963.

Prawer, S.S. *Israel at Vanity Fair: Jews and Judaism in the Writings of W.M. Thackeray*. Leiden: Brill, 1992.

Prickett, Stephen. "Church and University in the Life of John Keble." In *The English Religious Tradition and the Genius of Anglicanism*, edited by Geoffrey Rowell, 195–210. Wantage: Ikon, 1992.

– *Origins of Narrative: The Romantic Appropriation of the Bible*. Cambridge: Cambridge University Press, 1996.

– *Romanticism and Religion: The Tradition of Wordsworth and Coleridge in the Victorian Church*. Cambridge: Cambridge University Press, 1976.

– "Romantics and Victorians: From Typology to Symbolism." In *Reading the Text: Biblical Criticism and Literary Theory*, edited by Stephen Prickett, 182–224. Oxford: Blackwell, 1991.

– "The Social Conscience of the Oxford Movement: A Reappraisal." In *From Oxford to the People: Reconsidering Newman and the Oxford Movement*, edited by Paul Vaiss, 83–92.

– *Words and The Word: Language, Poetics and Biblical Interpretation*. Cambridge: Cambridge University Press, 1986.

Qualls, Barry V. *The Secular Pilgrims of Victorian Fiction: The Novel as Book of Life*. Cambridge: Cambridge University Press, 1982.

Rahner, Karl, and Herbert Vorgrimler. *Theological Dictionary*. Translated by Richard Strachan. Freiburg: Herder, 1965.

Ray, Gordon N. *Thackeray*. 2 vols. Vol. 1. *The Uses of Adversity 1811–1846*. Oxford: Oxford University Press, 1955. Vol. 2. *The Age of Wisdom 1847–1863*. New York: McGraw-Hill, 1958.

Reed, John Shelton. "'A Female Movement': The Feminization of Nineteenth-Century Anglo-Catholicism." *Anglican and Episcopal History* 57 (1988): 199–238.

"Religious Stories." *Fraser's Magazine for Town and Country* 38 (August 1848): 150–66.

Renan, Ernest. *The Life of Jesus.* [1863.] Introduction by John Haynes Holmes. No translator. New York: Modern Library, [1927] 1955.

Review of *The Rector in Search of a Curate.* N.a. [William Francis Wilkinson.] *Christian Remembrancer* 6 (November 1843): 518–38.

Rhodes, Royal W. *The Lion and the Cross: Early Christianity in Victorian Novels.* Columbus: Ohio State University Press, 1995.

Rigby, Elizabeth. Review of *Vanity Fair.* By William Makepeace Thackeray. *Quarterly Review* (December 1848). In *Thackeray: The Critical Heritage*, edited by Geoffrey Tillotson and Donald Hawes, 77–86.

"Robert Elsmere's Mental Struggles." [Reviews of Mrs Humphry Ward's *Robert Elsmere* by Edward Everett Hale, Marion Harland, Joseph Cook, and Julia Ward Howe, along with a reprint of W.E. Gladstone's review.] *North American Review* 148 (1889): 97–131.

Rogal, Samuel J. "The Methodist Connection in Charlotte Brontë's *Shirley.*" *Victorians Institute Journal* 10 (1981–82): 1–13.

Romanes, Ethel. *Charlotte Mary Yonge: An Appreciation.* London: Mowbray, 1908.

Rowell, Geoffrey. "John Keble: A Speaking Life." In *A Speaking Life: John Keble and the Anglican Tradition of Ministry and Art*, edited by Charles R. Henery, 1–66. Leominster: Gracewing, 1995.

Rowell, Geoffrey, Kenneth Stevenson, and Rowan Williams, eds. *Love's Redeeming Work: The Anglican Quest for Holiness.* Oxford: Oxford University Press, 2001.

Said, Edward W. "Conclusion: Religious Criticism." In Edward W. Said. *The World, the Text, and the Critic*, 290–2. Cambridge, MA: Harvard University Press, 1983.

– *Culture and Imperialism.* New York: Knopf, 1993.

Salusinszky, Imre. Interview with Edward Said. In Imre Salusinszky. *Criticism in Society*, 122–49. New York and London: Methuen, 1987.

Sandbach-Dahlström, Catherine. *Be Good Sweet Maid: Charlotte Yonge's Domestic Fiction: A Study in Dogmatic Purpose and Fictional Form.* Stockholm: Almquist and Wiksell, 1984.

Schiefelbein, Michael E. "A Catholic Baptism for *Villette*'s Lucy Snowe." In Michael E. Schiefelbein. *The Lure of Babylon: Seven Protestant Novelists and Britain's Roman Catholic Revival*, 129–42. Macon, Georgia: Mercer University Press, 2001.

Schleiermacher, Friedrich. *The Christian Faith.* [First German edition 1821–22.]

2 vols. Edited by H.R. Mackintosh and J.S. Stewart. [T and T Clark, 1928.] New York: Harper, 1963.

Schroeder, Horst. "A Quotation in *Dorian Gray.*" *Notes and Queries* 38 (1991): 327–8.

Scott, Nathan A., Jr. "Arnold's Vision of Transcendence – The *Via Poetica.*" *Journal of Religion* 59, no. 3 (1979): 261–84.

– "Pater's Imperative – To Dwell Poetically." *New Literary History* 15 (1983): 93–118.

Sedgwick, Eve Kosofsky. *Between Men: English Literature and Male Homosocial Desire.* New York: Columbia University Press, 1985.

Seiler, R.M., ed. *Walter Pater: The Critical Heritage.* London: Routledge and Kegan Paul, 1980.

Sewell, Elizabeth Missing. *Margaret Percival.* [1847.] New York and London: Garland, 1977.

[Sewell, William]. *Hawkstone: A Tale of and For England in 184-.* [1845.] 2 vols. 3ᵈ ed. London: Murray, 1847.

Shaffer, E.S. *"Kubla Khan" and "The Fall of Jerusalem": The Mythological School in Biblical Criticism and Secular Literature 1770–1880.* Cambridge: Cambridge University Press, 1975.

Shaw, W. David. *Babel and the Ivory Tower: The Scholar in the Age of Science.* Toronto: University of Toronto Press, 2005.

– *The Lucid Veil: Poetic Truth in the Victorian Age.* London: Athlone, 1987.

– *Victorians and Mystery: Crises of Representation.* Ithaca: Cornell University Press, 1990.

Shillingsburg, Peter L. "Reading the Boring Bits: The Crawley Genealogy." *The Thackeray Newsletter* 38 (November 1993): 5–10.

Showalter, Elaine. *A Literature of Their Own: British Women Novelists from Brontë to Lessing.* Princeton, NJ: Princeton University Press, 1977.

Shuter, William F. *Rereading Walter Pater.* Cambridge: Cambridge University Press, 1997.

Simpson, Richard. "George Eliot's Novels." *Home and Foreign Review* 3 (October 1863): 522–49. In *George Eliot: The Critical Heritage,* edited by David Carroll, 221–50. London: Routledge, 1971.

Smith, Margaret, ed. *The Letters of Charlotte Brontë with a Selection of Letters by Family and Friends.* 3 vols. Oxford: Clarendon, 1995–2004.

Spacks, Patricia Meyer. "'A Dull Book Is Easily Renounced.'" *Victorian Literature and Culture* 22 (1994): 287–302.

Springer, Marlene. *Hardy's Use of Allusion.* Lawrence: University Press of Kansas, 1983.

Stanley, Arthur Penrhyn. *The Life and Correspondence of Thomas Arnold, D.D.* [1844.] 13ᵗʰ ed. 2 vols. London: Murray, 1882.

– *Sinai and Palestine in Connection with Their History.* [1856.] 5th ed. London: John Murray, 1858.

Stave, Shirley A. *The Decline of the Goddess: Nature, Culture, and Women in Hardy's Fiction.* Westport, CT: Greenwood, 1995.

Stewart, J.I.M. Introduction. In William Makepeace Thackeray. *Vanity Fair: A Novel without a Hero,* 7–23. Harmondsworth: Penguin, 1968.

Strauss, David Friedrich. *The Life of Jesus Critically Examined.* [1835.] Translated from the 4th German ed. by George Eliot (1846). Edited by Peter C. Hodgson. Philadelphia: Fortress, 1972.

Sturrock, June. *"Heaven and Home": Charlotte M. Yonge's Domestic Fiction and the Victorian Debate Over Women.* Victoria: University of Victoria English Literary Studies, 1995.

Super, R.H. *The Chronicler of Barsetshire: A Life of Anthony Trollope.* Ann Arbor: University of Michigan Press, 1988.

Sutherland, John. Introduction. In William Makepeace Thackeray. *Vanity Fair: A Novel without a Hero,* vii–xxx. Oxford: Oxford University Press, 1983.

– *Mrs Humphry Ward: Eminent Victorian, Pre-eminent Edwardian.* Oxford: Clarendon, 1990.

Tartt, Donna. "The Spirit and Writing in a Secular World." In *The Novel, Spirituality and Modern Culture: Eight Novelists Write about Their Craft and Their Context,* edited by Paul S. Fiddes, 25–40.

Taylor, Richard H. *The Neglected Hardy: Thomas Hardy's Lesser Novels.* New York: St Martin's, 1982.

Tennyson, Alfred. *In Memoriam.* [1850.] Edited by Susan Shatto and Marion Shaw. Oxford: Clarendon, 1982.

Tennyson, G.B. *Victorian Devotional Poetry: The Tractarian Mode.* Cambridge and London: Harvard University Press, 1981.

Thackeray, William Makepeace. *The Book of Snobs.* [1848.] Edited by John Sutherland. New York: St Martin's, 1978.

– *The Letters and Private Papers of William Makepeace Thackeray.* Edited by Gordon N. Ray. 4 vols. Cambridge, MA: Harvard University Press, 1945–46.

– *Vanity Fair: A Novel Without a Hero.* [1847–48.] Edited by Peter L. Shillingsburg. New York: Norton, 1994.

Thomas à Kempis. *The Imitation of Christ.* [c.1426.] Translated by Leo Sherley-Price. Harmondsworth: Penguin, 1952.

Thormählen, Marianne. *The Brontës and Religion.* Cambridge: Cambridge University Press, 1999.

Tillotson, Geoffrey, and Donald Hawes, eds. *Thackeray: The Critical Heritage.* London: Routledge, 1968.

Tillotson, Kathleen. "Charlotte Yonge as a Critic of Literature." In *A Chaplet for Charlotte Yonge,* edited by Georgina Battiscombe and Marghanita Laski, 56–70.

- "*The Heir of Redclyffe*." In Geoffrey and Kathleen Tillotson. *Mid-Victorian Studies*, 49–55. London: Athlone, 1965.
- *Novels of the Eighteen-Forties*. Oxford: Clarendon, 1954.

Tonna, Charlotte Elizabeth. *Conformity: A Tale*. [1841.] Bound with *Falsehood and Truth*. [1841.] New York and London: Garland, 1975.

Towheed, Shafquat. "W.E. Gladstone's Reception of *Robert Elsmere*: A Critical Re-evaluation." *English Literature in Transition* 40 (1997): 389–97.

Tracts for the Times by Members of the University of Oxford. [1833–41.] 6 vols. New York: AMS, 1969.

Trilling, Lionel. "Jane Austen and *Mansfield Park*." *From Blake to Byron*. Vol. 5 of *The Pelican Guide to English Literature*, edited by Boris Ford, 112–29. Harmondsworth: Penguin, 1957.
- *Matthew Arnold*. [New York: Columbia University Press, 1949.] 2^d ed. London: George Allen and Unwin, 1974.

Trollope, Anthony. *An Autobiography*. [1883.] Edited by Michael Sadleir and Frederick Page. Oxford: Oxford University Press, 1980.
- *The Bertrams*. [1859.] Edited by Geoffrey Harvey. Oxford: Oxford University Press, 1991.
- *Clergymen of the Church of England*. [1866.] Leicester: Leicester University Press, 1974.
- "The Clergyman Who Subscribes for Colenso." In Anthony Trollope. *Clergymen of the Church of England*, 119–30.

Vaiss, Paul, ed. *From Oxford to the People: Reconsidering Newman and the Oxford Movement*. Leominster: Gracewing, 1996.

Vicinus, Martha. *Independent Women: Work and Community for Single Women 1850–1920*. Chicago and London: University of Chicago Press, 1985.

Victorian Religion. Editor's Topic. *Victorian Literature and Culture* 31, no. 1 (March 2003).

Vogeler, Martha Salmon. "The Religious Meaning of *Marius the Epicurean*." *Nineteenth-Century Fiction* 19 (1964): 287–99.

[Wace, Henry]. "*Robert Elsmere* and Christianity." Review of *Robert Elsmere*. *The Quarterly Review* 167 (1888): 273–302.

Ward, Mrs Humphry. Introduction. *The Case of Richard Meynell*. In vol. 16 of *The Writings of Mrs Humphry Ward* (16 vols.), vii–xiii. Boston: Houghton Mifflin, 1912.
- Review of *Marius the Epicurean*. By Walter Pater. *Macmillan's Magazine* (May 1885): 132–9. In *Walter Pater: The Critical Heritage*, edited by R.M. Seiler, 127–38.
- *Robert Elsmere*. [1888.] Edited by Rosemary Ashton. Oxford: Oxford University Press, 1987.
- "Sin and Unbelief." 1881. *North American Review* 148 (1889): 161–79. In *North American Review*. New York: AMS, 1968.

– *A Writer's Recollections.* 2 vols. New York and London: Harper, 1918.

Warhol, Robyn R. *Gendered Interventions: Narrative Discourse in the Victorian Novel.* New Brunswick: Rutgers University Press, 1989.

Wells-Cole, Catherine. "Angry Yonge Men: Anger and Masculinity in the Novels of Charlotte M. Yonge." In *Masculinity and Spirituality in Victorian Culture,* edited by Andrew Bradstock et al., 71–84.

Wheatley, Kim. "Death and Domestication in Charlotte M. Yonge's *The Clever Woman of the Family.*" *Studies in English Literature* 36 (1996): 895–915.

Wheeler, Michael. *The Old Enemies: Catholic and Protestant in Nineteenth-Century English Culture.* Cambridge: Cambridge University Press, 2006.

Wilde, Oscar. *The Artist as Critic: Critical Writings of Oscar Wilde.* Edited by Richard Ellmann. [New York: Random House, 1969.] Chicago: University of Chicago Press, 1982.

Willey, Basil. *Nineteenth-Century Studies: Coleridge to Matthew Arnold.* London: Chatto and Windus, 1949.

Williams, Carolyn. *Transfigured World: Walter Pater's Aesthetic Historicism.* Ithaca and London: Cornell University Press, 1989.

Williams, Isaac. *The Autobiography of Isaac Williams, B.D.* London: Longmans, Green, 1892.

Williams, Rowan. *Dostoevsky: Language, Faith, and Fiction.* London: Continuum, 2008.

– *Grace and Necessity: Reflections on Art and Love.* London: Continuum, 2005.

– *Lost Icons: Reflections on Cultural Bereavement.* Harrisburg, PA: Morehouse, 2000.

Williamson, Eugene L., Jr. *The Liberalism of Thomas Arnold: A Study of His Religious and Political Writings.* Alabama: University of Alabama Press, 1964.

Wilson, A.N. *God's Funeral.* New York: Norton, 1999.

Wilson, J. Dover. "Editor's Introduction." In Matthew Arnold. *Culture and Anarchy: An Essay in Political and Social Criticism,* xi–xl. Cambridge: Cambridge University Press, 1932.

Wilt, Judith. "The Romance of Faith: Mary Ward's Robert Elsmere and Richard Meynell." *Literature and Theology* 10 (1996): 33–43.

Wolff, Robert Lee. *Gains and Losses: Novels of Faith and Doubt in Victorian England.* New York and London: Garland, 1977.

Wood, James. *The Broken Estate: Essays on Literature and Belief.* New York: Random House, 1999.

Woodfield, Malcolm. *R.H. Hutton: Critic and Theologian: The Writings of R.H. Hutton on Newman, Arnold, Tennyson, Wordsworth, and George Eliot.* Oxford: Clarendon, 1986.

Wordsworth, William. *Poetical Works*. Edited by Thomas Hutchinson and Ernest de Selincourt. London: Oxford University Press, 1936.

Yonge, Charlotte Mary. *Abbeychurch, or Self Control and Self Conceit*. [1844.] Bound with *The Castle Builders; or, The Deferred Confirmation*. [1854.] New York and London: Garland, 1976.

– *Cameos from English History from Rollo to Edward II*. London: Macmillan, 1868.

– *The Clever Woman of the Family*. [1865.] Edited by Clare A. Simmons. Peterborough: Broadview, 2001.

– *Conversations on the Catechism*. 3 vols. London: Mozley, 1859–1863.

– *The Heir of Redclyffe*. [1853.] 15th ed. London: Macmillan, 1864.

– *The Heir of Redclyffe*. [1853.] Edited and introduced by Barbara Dennis. Oxford: Oxford University Press, 1997.

– *The Heir of Redclyffe*. [1853.] Introduction by Catherine Wells-Cole. Ware, Hertfordshire: Wordsworth, 1998.

– *History of Christian Names*. [1863.] Rev. ed. London: Macmillan, 1884.

– *John Keble's Parishes: A History of Hursley and Otterbourne*. 1898. London: Macmillan, 1899.

– *Musings over the "Christian Year" and "Lyra Innocentium," Together with a Few Gleanings of Recollections of the Rev. John Keble, Gathered by Several Friends*. 2d ed. Oxford and London: James Parker, 1872.

– *Reasons Why I Am a Catholic and Not a Roman Catholic*. London: Wells Gardner, Darton, 1901.

Zemka, Sue. *Victorian Testaments: The Bible, Christology, and Literary Authority in Early-Nineteenth-Century British Culture*. Stanford: Stanford University Press, 1997.

INDEX

Abrams, M.H., 17, 83–4, 174

accommodation, doctrine of, 22, 121–2, 210

Adam, 130, 138, 182

Æschylus, 86

Alexander, Michael Solomon, 114–15

Alexander, Mrs Cecil Frances, "All things bright and beautiful," 51

Allen, Walter: on Charlotte Yonge, 76, 78; *The English Novel*, 3; on *Vanity Fair*, 42

Alter, Robert, 24

Altick, Richard, 9, 235n1

Amiel, Henri-Frédéric, 211

analogy, doctrine of, 14, 71, 85, 101, 174

Anglican church. *See* Church of England

Anglo-Catholicism, 9, 62, 79, 107, 231n17; in Brontë's *Shirley*, 59–60; in the later nineteenth century, 29, 80, 88, 186–7; and Pater, 209, 214. *See also* Oxford Movement

anti-Catholicism, 55, 61, 64, 67–9

anti-Semitism, 53–4, 103–5

Apuleius, Lucius, 214, 216–17

Arnold, Matthew, 7, 26, 94, 110, 117, 121–3, 127–8, 137, 146, 160, 185, 200–22 passim; "Bishop Butler," 94; and the Broad Church, 20–3, 159; *Celtic Literature*, 104; *Culture and Anarchy*, 104–5, 154, 168–70, 191–4; and ethnocentrism, 103–5; "The Function of Criticism," 166, 234n19; *God and the Bible*, 103, 106, 108, 167; *Literature and Dogma*, 34, 43, 52, 105–8, 113, 119–20, 167, 178, 198, 203; "Marcus Aurelius," 215; Oxford Professor of Poetry, 83; "Pagan and Medieval Religious Sentiment," 168–9; poetry of, 15, 99, 122; preface to *Essays in Criticism*, 192; preface to *Last Essays*, 23, 107; as religious Modernist, 22–3, 105, 149, 166–7, 200–3, 207, 222; "Rugby Chapel," 109; *St Paul and Protestantism*, 106, 108, 149; "Stanzas from the Grand Chartreuse," 17, 107, 116, 166; "The Study of Poetry," 10–11, 25, 106–7, 200

Arnold, Thomas (father), 20, 191, 208, 227n27; Broad Church theology of, 21, 105, 117; Charlotte Brontë's view of, 62; doctrine of accommodation, 22, 120–2; doctrine of the Church, 104, 114, 117; and Judaism, 104, 113; in "Rugby Chapel," 109; Thackeray's view of, 32

Arnold, Thomas (son): father of Mary Ward, 7, 160, 207

Athanasian creed, 62

Auerbach, Erich, *Mimesis*, 138

Augustine, St, 42, 214

Austen, Jane, 79, 128, 197; *Mansfield Park*, 76, 142

Bakhtin, Mikhail: on the novel, 3–5, 36; religious beliefs of, 225n3

Marx, Karl, 147
Mary, Blessed Virgin, 72, 90, 141
Mary Magdalen, St, 180
masculinity, 8, 91, 239n3
mass. *See* eucharist
Maurice, F.D., 20, 62
Methodism, 9, 61, 185, 231n21; in *Adam Bede*, 111, 130–1, 143–7, 149
Michaels, Walter Benn, 7
midrash, 13
Mill, John Stuart, 211, 215
Millais, John Everett, *Christ in the House of His Parents*, 138
Miller, J. Hillis, 17, 170, 181–2, 238n6, 240n16
Milton, John, 15, 44, 72; *Samson Agonistes*, 157–8
miracles, 43, 105–7, 113, 131, 160, 169–70, 200–2
Modernism, as movement in the Catholic church, 22, 199–200, 214
Monro, Edward, *Parochial Work*, 66
Moody, Dwight L., 106
More, Hannah, 58
Moses, 49, 70, 109, 145
Murdoch, Iris, 25
Myers, F.W.H.: anecdote about George Eliot, 152–3; *Wordsworth*, 11–12

Neale, J.M.: *Ayton Priory*, 66–7; and sisterhoods, 67
Newman, Francis, 32
Newman, John Henry, 23–4, 191, 208, 214, 234n6; *Apologia*, 6, 13–14, 16, 18, 20–1, 62–3, 129–30, 166, 199, 213, 228n6, 233n4; *Callista*, 214–15, 227n28; conversion, 6, 18–19, 55, 59, 114; George Eliot on, 129–30; *Grammar of Assent*, 16, 211, 213; *Idea of a University*, 4, 95–6, 191–2; on lying beggarwoman and salvation, 52, 116; on Jerusalem bishopric, 234nn15,

16; "John Keble," 19; *Loss and Gain*, 10, 60, 63, 69, 198, 229n3; "The Second Spring," 79; theory of assent, 16, 147, 166, 193, 210–11, 219, 222; Thomas Hardy's view of, 166, 179, 193
Nietzsche, Friedrich, 201, 218
novel of doubt, 9–10, 16, 22–3, 58–9, 70, 73, 201, 239n2
novel of religious controversy, 4–6, 9–10, 197–8; and Brontë's *Shirley*, 55–6, 58–60, 63, 69–70. *See also* early church novel, evangelical novel, novel of doubt, novel of the Oxford Movement
novel of the Oxford Movement, 9–10, 18–19, 154, 241n21; and Brontë's *Shirley*, 59, 63, 66–7, 73–4. *See also* Charlotte Mary Yonge, *The Heir of Redclyffe*
Nussbaum, Martha, 5

ordination, 159, 164, 209
original sin, 53, 90
Oxford Movement, 6, 28, 55, 105, 110, 123, 211; and Brontë's *Shirley*, 59–61, 69–70; and literature, 14, 18–21; and Hardy, 160, 164–5, 171, 186, 192; and Yonge, 75–85, 91, 101–2. *See also* Keble, John Newman, John Henry, novel of the Oxford Movement, Pusey, E.B.

Paget, Francis, 10, 59
Paget, Violet (Vernon Lee), 210
"Papal Aggression," 6, 9, 55
parables, 4, 24, 32, 50; Dives and Lazarus, 47, 49–51, 111, 144; good Samaritan, 142; Pharisee and tax collector, 50; rich man and poor widow, 50
Pater, Walter, 7, 23, 128, 159, 161; letter to Mary Ward, 211; letter to Violet